May happiness come
on secret winds and
surround you
forever in the
ways of beauty.

Copyright © 2016 Cristo Morpho Inc.

Randolph C. Phelps is an agent for this Vermont Non-Profit. All rights reserved. This book or any portion thereof may not be reproduced or used in any manner whatsoever without the express written permission of the publisher except for the use of brief quotations in a book review.

Printed in the United States of America

First Printing, 2016
ISBN-10: 0-9977440-0-6
ISBN-13: 978-0-9977440-0-2
Cristo Morpho

Scripture quotations taken from the *New American Standard Bible*®, Copyright © 1960, 1962, 1963, 1968, 1971, 1972, 1973, 1975, 1977, 1995 by The Lockman Foundation Used by permission. (www.Lockman.org)

Scripture taken from the *Holy Bible, New International Version*®, *NIV*® Copyright © 1973, 1978, 1984, 2011 by Biblica, Inc.® Used by permission. All rights reserved worldwide. New International Version® and NIV® are registered trademarks of Biblica, Inc. Use of either trademark for the offering of goods or services requires the prior written consent of Biblica US, Inc.

Scripture taken from *The Message*. Copyright © 1993, 1994, 1995, 1996, 2000, 2001, 2002. Used by permission of NavPress Publishing Group.

Additional books can be purchased at cristomorpho.com or from Createspace.com eStore ID 6317200

Luella Dunn — Family photo courtesy of Carl Williams.

"Scream for Help" — Self-portrait by Randolph C. Phelps.

The Guru — This is an artist's rendition of Swami Sri Yukteswar. Copyright 2006. Permission granted by www.astrogems.com.

About the Author — Photo taken by Don R. Whipple, Whipple Photography, Newport, VT.

THE COVER IMAGES

Front Cover:
This is a self-portrait taken by Randolph C. Phelps during a forty-day retreat.

Back Cover:
The artist, Luis Royo, is one of the most popular fantasy illustrators in the world. The name of this painting is Coyote Summer. He began his artistic career in the world of painting and comic books in the 70s. In 1983, he began his career as an illustrator, where he achieved his greatest successes, illustrating book covers for the  most prestigious American publishing companies, such as Tor Books, Berkley Books, Avon, Warner Books, Batman Books, and others. He does many cases for films, bands, and video games. Luis Royo established himself internationally as a master of fantasy and science fiction illustration. He has remarkable skill for creating female characters full of sensuality and strength. Rights for permission purchased through Alan Lynch Artists.

To Page

Enjoy!

Randolph C. Phelps

RANDOLPH C. PHELPS

MINUTES
DAYS
YEARS

Finding the Grace of God

Artwork by Kyleigh Phelps kyleighphelps@gmail.com

IN PRAISE OF
TEN MINUTES, TEN DAYS, TEN YEARS

"Your book took me on a ride though different metaphysical planes, past lives, and dimensions."

— *Natalie Nichols*

"Swan Song is a riveting story about a conscious relationship in which the veil of love is torn wide-open."

— *Debbie Bohland*

"Reading your chapters made me weep... They were flowing like honey... I could just picture Jesus talking to you."

— *Nina B, Christian Prophetic Artist*

"Randy walks this Earth with his heart wide open. He deeply touches all those he meets through his gentle kindness, joyful humor and authenticity. On a path deeply guided by service, his devoted connection to Spirit is reflected in the brightness of his eyes. He exudes radiant love and compassion and when you are in Randy's presence, you truly see a reflection of God."

— *Alice Hong, Align Yoga*

AUTHOR'S PREFACE AND ACKNOWLEDGMENTS

I want to tell you a once-in-a-lifetime story. I come to share the nitty-gritty facts of life and love. This memoir, told through my spirit, is as much, maybe more so, about you. I offer my story in large part with the hope that it might guide you on an inner journey of your own. My story is the truth as I see it, carefully written with an awareness of sensitive topics while holding myself to be honest, in a context of believing "the truth will set you free."

I invite readers to set an intention as they read *Ten Minutes, Ten Days, Ten Years*. Toward the end of these chapters, a guided meditation will offer a space in which readers will receive either a word of wisdom, a vision, or the healing they considered while reading my story.

I wrote this book as an enjoyable way to invite people who resonate with my story, to become a part of our sustainable, spiritual community in Costa Rica. Visit our web site to view hundreds of color photos related to the book, Cristo Morpho Volunteer Program, and Cristo Morpho Community in Costa Rica.

www.cristomorpho.com

I would like to acknowledge and thank my mother, who teaches me about kindness and compassion; my father, who taught me about business and matters of the world; my grandmother, who shared with me her passion for Jesus; and Swan Song, who taught me about patience and love.

*I dedicate this book to
all of my spiritual teachers.*

This book contains material with sexual content in the form of pornography and casual relationships. It reveals the underlying issues, causes, and treatments of sexual addiction. I make every effort to present it in a clean and approachable fashion.

TABLE OF CONTENTS

Prologue 1

Part I: The Guru

The Cast 5
 1. Finding The Stone 6
 2. The Lion And The Lamb 19
 3. The Forevermore Factor 29
 4. Sailing 42
 5. Soft Rain 49
 6. Lessons On The Truth 61
 7. Clan Of The Hawk 70
 8. The Call Of The Rhondu 82
 9. An Exercise In Exorcisms 91
 10. Ten Minutes 99

Part II: God's Grace

 11. A Scream For Help 111
 12. Rhythm Of The Breath 120
 13. The Chanupa 128
 14. Death And Desperation 142
 15. The Lighthouse 151
 16. Jesus Calling 159
 17. Fearless Faith 165
 18. Knocking On Heaven's Door 179
 19. The Guide 193
 20. The Forty-day Retreat 204
 21. The Lion's Den 222
 22. The Chains That Bind 231

Part III: Swan Song

The Cast 241
23. My Native Tribe 242
24. Pandora's Box 250
25. My Native Brother 256
26. The Native Medicine 266
27. The Melodrama 277
28. Song Of Solomon 286
29. Available And Unattached 299
30. Swan Song In Costa Rica 307
31. Sacrum Meltdown 315
32. The Buildup To The Showdown 323
33. Sacrum Meltdown II 338
34. Finding A Hero 344
35. Desert Oasis 354
36. The Proposal 362
37. The Aftermath 370
38. Faith, Hope, And Love 378
39. The Final Cut 386
40. The Shaman: Charcoal 395
The Final Guided Meditation 406
Afterward Acknowledgements 408
Just For Laughs 410
Resources 412
Bibliography 414
About The Author 418
Cristo Morpho Community 419

Prologue

Two police cruisers slip silently down the middle of the long dirt driveway toward my family's three-story brick home. Pine trees, 100 feet tall, are staggered along either side of the driveway as if javelins were thrown down from heaven, just missing these intruders. I peer out to see them through a small side window beside our white front door.

I run upstairs, out of breath, and enter my sister's bedroom. Vinyl wallpaper covered with foot-long red roses surrounds me on all sides, but this situation does not smell sweet. Panicked, I open the second story window that faces the river.

In the distance, under a cluster of pine trees, is a granite platform covered with pine needles. A prior owner in the late 1800s built it as his throne. I imagine him sitting like a dignified statue gazing down upon the waterfall while he contemplated life's intricate ways.

If I could jump out far enough, I could grab a branch of the giant pine tree near the house. I squat like a bird on the window ledge, pausing to ask myself, *"Is this the right moment to allow The Guru to have full control of my body?"* It seems like a reasonable solution and an easy way to escape this predicament, but deep down my soul suspects that to surrender itself to another spirit is breaking some sacred spiritual ethic. But then again, why not?

Ten minutes earlier, I was sitting in the lotus position on top of a four-foot-long, gold-framed antique mirror that I had taken down from the bathroom wall and positioned on the edges of the tub. It felt as though The Guru sharing my body for the past ten days was ready to blast out of my third eye. I had positioned the Waterpik shower-massager to direct a strong half-inch beam of water toward my third eye, which I was intently focusing upon. I became distracted by anticipating a jolt as The Guru departed, and I was suddenly overcome by fear. I envisioned a sudden blow of pain that might throw me into the shower wall with tremendous force. I found myself beginning to scream as long and loudly as is humanly possible in one breath. Although this eased my fears of imminent bodily harm, it didn't occur to me that my screaming would raise the concern of my mother, who immediately called the police.

Perching on the windowsill with my heart beating rapidly, I make my plea. "Guru, take over complete control and get me out of this situation!"

What happens next is hard to explain. It's as though I am looking through a periscope. I can't see anything to the left or right unless I turn and face that direction. Jumping to the tree branch seems more challenging now, but begins to look more realistic when it comes into focus through my tunnel vision. I leap from the window ledge and catch hold of the branch.

Life is looking better, I fantasize about taking a nice easy float down to the soft, pine needle-bedding…but before this happens, I hear a *crack!* and a *snap!* My descent suddenly turns into a crash landing. My ankles feel slightly sprained, but they still function. Deciding to run, I discover it's not that easy with tunnel vision. I see a foot here, a branch there…*look out for that tree!* I make a quick left turn. There's a steep, fifty-foot descent to the river. I find myself airborne, somewhere near the granite platform, floating or flying, a big rock heading my way. I feel the impact, hard against my skull. Blood trickles down my cheek. I feel numb, sick, and woozy.

Time passes: ten minutes…ten days…or ten years? As if in a dream, I stand up and wade through the waist-high ferns. I feel like a cornered warrior, forced to retaliate.

I come back to something resembling reality when a tranquilizer is injected into my hip. This wakes me up from one dream and puts me into another. I first notice the smell of hot vinyl seats. Then I realize that I am locked in the back of a police car and have pepper spray in my eyes and a black mesh sack over my head. I feel blood on my face and hands, and my ribs feel cracked or broken. It's painful to breathe. My right shoulder has a bloody scrape where I was dragged on the ground. I feel chains on my lap that lead to a set of handcuffs around my wrists and a pair of ankle cuffs below. I have been captured like a prisoner.

But this is *not* fiction. These events are real. What happened during those ten minutes after I crashed into the rock until I was brought back to reality in the police car? I reveal the unusual events during the ten days preceding this scene, and the amazing spiritual journey that unfolded during the ten years thereafter. ■

Part I
The Guru

"Author W.Y. Evans-Wentz described his impression of Sri Yukteswar in the preface to Yogananda's Autobiography of a Yogi: Sri Yukteswar was of gentle mien and voice, of pleasing presence, and worthy of the veneration, which his followers spontaneously accorded to him. Every person who knew him, whether of his own community or not, held him in the highest esteem. I vividly recall his tall, straight, ascetic figure, garbed in the saffron-colored garb of one who has renounced worldly quests, as he stood at the entrance of the hermitage to give me welcome. His hair was long and somewhat curly, and his face bearded. His body was muscularly firm, but slender and well-formed, and his step energetic." (8)

"Sri Yukteswar's face can be seen on the cover of The Beatles' album Sgt. Pepper's Lonely Hearts Club Band (1967). It appears on the upper left of the crowd behind The Beatles." (Wikipedia)

THE CAST

I have given pseudonyms to the key characters. This allows some discretion, and the fun names reveal a bit about each person's distinguishing trait.

My Dad	*The Lion*
My Mom	*The Lamb*
My Brother	*Gadget*
My Sister	*Priceless*
Grandmother (maternal)	*Lily*
Grandmother (paternal)	*Hosanna*
Grandfather (paternal)	*Buck*
Favorite Barefoot Aunt	*Fuzzy Bear*
Adopted Aunt	*Gigi*
My Ex-wife	*Forevermore*
First Girlfriend	*Sarah Lee*
Rental Tenant	*Lizzy*
Acupuncturist	*Frenzy*
Psychiatrist	*Debbie Goldfinger*
New York Travel Companion	*Cleopatra*
Teacher of Native American Traditions	*My Native Brother*
Martial Arts Instructor	*Mr. R.I.P.* (a.k.a. *Pastor R.I.P.*)
Liberty University Housemate	*Cowboy*
Female Spiritual Friend	*Helen Keller*
Magog Sailing Partner	*Veronica Vogue*
College Girlfriends	*Nani & Glitter*
Hometown Teenage Friends	*Judas Priest & Cheap Trick*

CHAPTER 1

Finding the Stone

THE WORMY APPLE GANG

As a 10 year old, life is a dream. I am a boy. I spend part of the summer at my grandparents' dairy farm in Kirby, Vermont. My siblings, cousins, and I roam carefree. We explore the acres of woods and rolling pastures. My older brother, Gadget, my adopted Aunt, Gigi, and I march single file on the dark, fertile forest soil. Occasionally, the crispy maple leaves *crunch* under our feet. Our uniforms are plain colored shorts, t-shirts, and sneakers. Gigi, who is the same age as my brother and me, is adorned with pink thick-rimmed glasses, and Gadget wears a green felt hat with a full circular brim. It is a bit too large and covers most of his curly blond hair.

We stop to inspect a rotten tree that has fallen. In our imaginary world, the crumbly white bark pieces become chicken. I use my jackknife to cut it into pieces. We all pretend to munch on it.

Gigi, says, "Ummm…yummy chicken!" Suddenly, a stick cracks behind us. We all peer quickly in that direction. We scatter and run over the incline.

I shout playfully, "We are being chased by a wolf!"

Gigi laughs while running and yells, "No, it is a bear!"

Gadget runs by, saying, "It is a mountain lion." We stop to catch our breath beside a brook.

Gigi says, "We are lucky to have escaped."

I ask, "Did you see how big it was?"

She replies, "Yes, kind of. It had dark fur."

I say, "Let's send a message on a boat to warn others." Gigi plucks up a fern. Gadget finds a piece of birch bark. Gigi writes an invisible message on it, speaking aloud as she writes. "We heard a wolf in the woods. It could look like a bear or a mountain lion. Be careful!" I poke a hole in the birch bark and insert the fern to create a sail. As it floats slowly downstream, we watch until it disappears.

We rock-hop up the brook until we meet the trail where the tractor crosses the brook between fields. One pasture is covered with corn about my height. It will grow two or three times as high. Then it will be like one giant corn maze: a great place to play hide-and-seek. But not today.

Today, we follow a cow path that skirts the cornfield. We are heading to our favorite apple tree, which overlooks the surrounding pastures. We climb up and sit on low branches the size of elephants' trunks. From here we can spy the white farmhouse, the old red barn, and the towering silo. The wind gently blows the cotton-candy clouds across the blue summer sky.

There are about forty black and white Holstein cows grazing in the back pasture. Each cow has a numbered tag hanging from a chain around its neck. Late in the afternoon, cows will be herded past us, across the road, and into the barn for milking. I notice that cow number 46 has milk leaking from its teats.

I tell my tree-mates a story: "Grandpa used to milk by hand. Sometimes Mom and her brothers would come up to him with a wide-open mouth, wanting milk. He would squirt milk in their mouths."

They both laugh, and Gadget asks, "Who told you that?"

I reply, "Mom told me."

Gigi says, "They must have gotten milk all over their faces."

I say, "Imagine my Mom and her brothers with milk all over their faces." We all giggle.

We claim our fortress for another timeless day. The proof rests in a half-moon-shaped tree fungus placed on a moss-covered rock. My Aunt Fuzzy Bear carved it with a sharp stone. It tells everybody that we are The Wormy Apple Gang. We have found the best place around.

ABENAKI HISTORY

There's a spot at the top corner of the pasture where we get a spectacular view of the mountains rising from both sides of Lake Willoughby. The locals just call it "The Gap." This 300-foot deep, icy-cold lake is a great place to swim on a hot summer day. Willoughby Lake was made when a glacier plowed through 10,000 years ago. Native Americans, primarily from the Abenaki tribe, have lived in Vermont since then. This lake has been sacred to the Abenaki people for many generations.

According to Vermont Historical Society...

"It was part of the land Ndakinna where the Western Abenakis lived. Their land included what is now Vermont and New Hampshire. It also included parts of Maine, Massachusetts and Quebec, Canada. Historians estimate that 10,000 Abenakis lived in what is now Vermont.

"Abenaki Indians lived on this land. They hunted in the woods and fished in the rivers. The Abenakis grew crops in fields and built wigwams in villages. After the Europeans came, the Abenakis traded with them. The French and English traders wanted furs to sell in Europe. The Abenakis traded these furs for metal tools and cloth. The Europeans also gave the Abenakis new diseases they had never had before. Many Abenakis got sick or died from diseases like small pox.

"Some of the Europeans came to North America

to stay. They started settlements, then towns, and then colonies. The English settlers wanted to own the land where they built their houses and farms. Sometimes the Abenakis and Europeans got along and shared their spaces. Sometimes they fought each other over the land. The Europeans had more guns and more people than the Abenakis. The Abenakis knew the land better than the Europeans.

"The European settlers took most of the land from the Abenakis. Many of the Abenakis moved farther away from the Europeans. Some moved into the forests. Others moved north to the Abenaki villages of Missisquoi and St. Francis. And the Europeans kept coming to what is now Vermont." [1]

But to me, a 10 year old, it looks like someone took a huge ice cream scoop and plopped the chocolate-flavored earth on the west side of the lake to form Mt. Hor. Then they took a few more scoops from deep in the lake and plopped them on the east side to form Mt. Pisgah.

FINDING THE SCRAPING STONE

One Sunday, my mother, The Lamb, joins The Wormy Apple Gang for a picnic at the top corner of the pasture, overlooking The Gap. I am with Gadget, my younger sister, Priceless, Gigi, and my favorite aunt, Fuzzy Bear, who prefers to be barefoot whenever possible.

While exploring a stretch of slate ledges, I find a Native American artifact resting on top of a mound of slate shards. It is shaped similar to an arrowhead but much longer. It's a charcoal black stone that has been chipped a few dozen times along both edges and is about eight inches long and two inches wide.

I treasure it. Years later, I have it examined by an expert from the Fairbanks Museum. He says, "This is not a local stone. Most likely it was traded up the coast from southern states. It was probably used as a scraping tool." I could imagine it being set down many years ago as the Native American owner gathered a variety of slate pieces for weapons or tools. For me to find this rare artifact on our family's farmland makes it even more sacred.

When I am sixteen, The Lamb tells me, "Your grandmother told me years ago that her great grandmother was a full-blooded Indian."

I learn that our family on her side is of Native American descent, most likely from the Abenaki heritage. My maternal grandmother, Lily, was referring to Eunice Jackson. She was a full-blooded Native American. Eunice married Lily's great grandfather, Joshua Dunn, on February 12, 1812, in Jay, Maine. During that time, being of Native American descent was considered a disgrace. It was best kept a secret. Vermont approved a sterilization law on March 31, 1931. It was intended to curtail reproduction for the mentally ill, but often women of Native American descent were targeted and herded into this category. To better ensure their survival, many Abenaki women claimed to be white on their marriage certificates.

Luella Dunn (b. 1844)

In an attempt to find solid evidence that we are Native American, The Lamb contacts one of her cousins, who sends her a photo of Luella Dunn, who is my grandmother's Aunt. Eunice Jackson was her grandmother and my great, great, great grandmother. She certainly appears to be of Native American origin, with her wide face and strong cheekbones.

Finding the scraping tool marks the beginning of a feeling of connection to my Native American heritage. As a child, I often wore leather moccasins and a coonskin cap. I would race through the woods as fast as a deer, pretending to be an Indian. As a teenager, I learned to hunt and track animals. I was always curious about Native American culture. But I did not participate in the Native American traditions, such as the sweat lodge ceremony, until I was in my thirties.

OUR BRICK HOME

I was born and raised in a typical, small Vermont town. There is one gas station that sells used cars, a church with an oversize stained-glass window portraying Jesus, and a one-room schoolhouse with a bell. There is small grocery store that doubles as the post office.

My family three-story home was built in the mid-1850s by a retired colonel. It has a regal quality, and is the only brick construction in this village. A local historian, Mac Ford, said the bricks were hauled by oxen from Boston. There is a stone foundation topped with granite slabs and a double layer of bricks with a one-foot space between the interior and exterior walls. The windowsills and lintels are also granite. Black wooden shutters border each window.

Inside there are nine-foot ceilings and wide, custom-made trim boards. The front stairway leads to the upper hallway, with the railing extending around the opening. Casement windows open onto a small balcony surrounded by a black, ornamental iron railing. Above it, a decorative triangular facade of brick with granite trim rises to meet the gothic-style peaked roof. It is an impressive architectural design adorned with historical significance.

At one time, a trapdoor in the kitchen floor gave access to a completely enclosed crawlspace with a dirt floor. A rug was kept over the trapdoor. Mac Ford believed our home was part of the Underground Railroad: a network of secret routes and safe houses used by slaves to escape to Canada. He thought that a tunnel somewhere in the basement led to the riverbank. As kids we would tap on the walls and search for the tunnel. We never found it.

Down a steep embankment behind our home is the Moose River. We can always hear the water flowing over the rapids. There is a train trestle above them. As a child, I would listen for the train before cautiously stepping across the trestle. There is a ten-inch gap between each timber, and one side extends out three feet. If the train ever comes and I am caught in the middle, then my plan is to crawl out on the extension and hug it. On the other side of the river there are huge foundation stones and the remnants of an old grain mill.

Next door is a dairy farm. They have a red barn the size of an ocean liner. In the spring, the field in front of the barn is filled with yellow dandelions. On a blue sky summer day, the yellow dandelions poke up from the green grass and wave in the wind. With the red barn for a backdrop, it creates a pallet of colors. Farming is like that: a plate full of wholesome living. They raise Jersey cows and sometimes wooly brown and white sheep in a small side shed.

The farmer and his sons chug around on an old John Deere tractor. It is time to hay their pastures. I am not old enough to help yet, but the neighborhood kids that are big enough throw bales of hay onto the open-sided wagon being pulled behind. The hay bales are stacked six layers high and form a pyramid at the top. A rope is carefully tied full length over the top so the tractor can pull the wagon without a spill. Then they go up the front ramp into the big red barn to unload and stack the hay.

One morning at Sunday school, I am asked to memorize Psalm 23, "The Lord is my Shepherd, I shall not want...." At that point in my life, The Lord was not my Shepherd, and I had no need to want. I had everything I needed.

SCHOOL DAYS

I attend a one-room schoolhouse with about twenty neighborhood kids, all of whom are my friends. Our first grade teacher, Miss O, is well liked by all of the students. She drives a white Saab with rusty fenders. She has a big sheepdog with eyes you can't see; they are hidden somewhere, deep under all its hair.

Miss O leaves our school after my first year. After my second year, the new teacher suggests that I skip the third grade because I am excelling in my studies. My parents give their consent, yet I don't recall being part of the decision process.

Vermont consolidated schools in the late seventies. They closed down and sold most of the one-room schoolhouses, including mine. Now I will be riding a bus to a new school, five miles away. On my first day in the fourth grade, I see a few hundred new kids, but only one girl from my old one-room schoolhouse. All my other friends were sent to different schools. Because my birthday is in October and I skipped a grade, I am at least a year younger than the other kids in my class. I feel awkward and begin to search for a way to find the peace and tranquility I once knew.

My grandmother, Hosanna, lives a few blocks away from my new school. Sometimes I walk to her home after school. She had been a school teacher for many years. She encourages me to tell her about my day and listens with interest. In her presence, I feel comfort and love. We play games, and she teaches me how to play cribbage. When I spend the night, she reads aloud about Ethan Allen. As I listen intently, I visualize him swinging a grain sack over his shoulder and holding it in his teeth. She reads to me about the Revolutionary War, when Ethan Allen led the Green Mountain Boys to capture Fort Ticonderoga on Lake Champlain in 1775.

One day after school, I notice two guys from my class standing behind the school. I ask them, "What are you doing?"

One says, "We are waiting to beat up Jimmy."

Jimmy lives down over the bank, on a street parallel to the school. There is a steep trail that he takes as a shortcut. He lives with his mom. She is usually at work, and his dad no longer lives with them. He is poor compared to the other kids. Jimmy is quick to be mouthy and provoke others. He likes to call himself James West, after the television show. In truth, he needs to be as tough as nails, stay alert, and remain cunning to survive. I don't know many other kids without a dad at home. I wonder how hard it is. I like him and certainly do not want to join in beating him up. They have no real reason.

At recess, I play on the red and yellow merry-go-round. The kids push it hard and fast. It makes my whole world spin. Everything has become a blur of whirling colors. It is symbolic of how I feel inside. Academically I am doing well, but socially, it is difficult to connect. I feel like an outsider. Somehow, I lost my inner compass. Life is not making sense like it once did.

MY FIRST GIRLFRIEND: SARAH LEE

In my hometown, I have a girlfriend: Sarah Lee. She lives in a red house next to the church. The kids are asked to help with the candle lighting during the church service. While we do it, I hold her hand. She likes that. We ride bikes with the other kids in town on the grocery store's paved parking lot in the evening, after they close. When Sarah Lee and I stop to talk, we bump our front tires together. At that age, girls begin to mature faster than boys. I know little about how to kiss except what I had learned from watching others. My parents seldom kissed each other on the lips in front of me.

Sarah Lee and I meet at the end of our long driveway. There is a thick rope hanging down from one of the tall pine trees. Sometimes, my friends and I swing on it for hours. One day, Sarah Lee and I go behind some cedar hedges. That is where we have our first kiss. I can smell her cherry Chap-Stick. She keeps applying it to her lips and mine. I guess it's meant to keep our lips from wearing out. We certainly *are* kissing a lot.

One day she says, "Let's French kiss." I don't know what that means.

I innocently say, "I don't know how."

She acts surprised. She says, "You don't know how to French kiss?"

"No," I reply.

She explains, "During the kiss, you touch tongues." So, Sarah Lee teaches me how to French kiss. It feels tingly and warm. After that day, we often French kiss. To signify my devotion, I give Sarah Lee a silver ring that goes around in spirals. It is huge and only fits her thumb, but she is glad to have it.

In the winter, we go sledding in a nearby field. One day, her knee pops out. She tells me it has done that a few times before. I place her on my sled and pull her back home. She is grateful that I rescued her. On Valentine's Day, I want to buy her something special, but all I have is change in a jar. At our home, I find a heart-shaped chocolate box. I go to the little store and buy a bunch of cherry chocolates. They are sold in packs of three, for a quarter. I fill the box with them and wrap it up for her.

In the parking lot, I proudly give her the box of chocolates. She opens it and says, "Chocolates. I love chocolates!" Then she bites into one.

Upset, she says, "Oh no! This one is a cherry chocolate. I don't like cherry chocolates. Are they all cherry chocolates?" I feel foolish for a moment. But being kids, we say what we feel and quickly get over it.

JULIA

Sarah Lee is still my girlfriend in the seventh grade, but we go to different schools. In my class there is a cute girl named Julia. She is silly at times. She will talk into a person's ear when somebody is on the other side. She pretends their head is hollow. Julia has beautiful light brown eyes. We both have a few warts near the ends of our fingers on our right hands. For what it's worth, we have something embarrassing in common. During science class, we are sitting at our desks and our eyes meet from across the room. We hold a spellbound gaze. My heart begins to race. I can't stop looking at her.

She sends a note through a friend telling me that she will be at the winter carnival dance during the weekend. To attend, I will need to climb out of my protective shell. She is worth it. There are already different cliques forming. I feel like I am not part of that crowd. But this could be my chance to break through the social barriers. In a way, I want to be friends with some of them.

The real problem is that I am having my first dilemma with two girls. I consider Sarah Lee my girlfriend, but I have a real crush on Julia. It would be a great time to seek advice. I don't feel comfortable talking to The Lion (my father) about my girlfriend situation. I never recall him discussing things with The Lamb (my mother). He just makes all the major decisions. Usually, he is too busy to be bothered with his kids' minor problems. I decide not to go to the dance. I want to be loyal to Sarah Lee. Afterward, I am shy about it. I never tell Julia the reason why I didn't go to the dance. I assume she was looking for me and felt let down. She must think I am not interested in her. I am crazy about her. I just never had the chance to tell her.

It's not so much about what did happen; it's about what *didn't* happen. I keep my emotions inside. The idea of talking to Sarah Lee about how I feel towards Julia is foreign. Men I have grown up with don't do that. I didn't know how to open up my heart and take the appropriate steps to talk with Julia. I regret it now. If I had gone to the dance, there would have been a decisive moment when I could have shown my courage. It would not have been easy, but I would have asked

Julia to dance. I missed the perfect opportunity. I felt disappointed, but I learned a lesson. The next time I feel a crush on a girl, I will be loyal to my heart. I will not hold back. I will tell her how I feel.

MY MARTIAL ARTS INSTRUCTOR: MR. R.I.P.

In the seventh grade, for no reason, some older bullies threaten me in the bathroom, just as my friends did with James West. They punch me in the gut a few times and demand that I steal them some merchandise from our family business. My response is to attend a martial arts class. The black belt instructor, Mr. R.I.P., introduces a new sense of character and discipline into my life. I start to feel more confident. He is an emotional man from nearby Canada who will burst out singing a phrase from an old rock song, "Jeremiah was a bullfrog..." and then wait for his students to finish the line. He encourages his students to persevere. We race each other across the lawn, do pushups in the brook, and loudly assert a *kiai* as we throw punches by the roadside. The sound echoes back from the green mountains. It reassures each student that he is a worthy opponent for life's battles.

One day, there is a commotion in the back parking lot. Mr. R.I.P. is there in a flash, ready to defend the underdog. He isn't trying to be a hero; it is natural for him to uphold justice. Once, while sparring with him, I get cocky and throw a few fancy kicks. With three solid side kicks, he catapults me across the room. I never knew what hit me. He put me in my place. Over the next ten years, he gains my admiration and becomes a secondary father figure.

HIGH SCHOOL

As a 12 year old, life is a dream. I begin high school. I often hang out with my older brother, Gadget, and friends from our little hometown. I especially admire two of Gadget's older friends: Judas Priest and Cheap Trick. We create our own tribe:

the outsiders. Our weekends are spent in the great outdoors. We like to ride mountain bikes, drive around in jeeps, and go camping in the woods. We fish for trout in the remote ponds and brooks. Most of us can shoot a partridge on the fly.

The townies that live closer to the high school are a different breed. They participate in sports and afterschool extra-curricular activities. They're on the football team, act in plays, or play in the school band. We really are not that different, but we create a barrier based on where we live, what we do, and who we hang out with.

Judas Priest reassures me by saying, "If anybody in high school messes with you, I'll beat 'em up."

Cheap Trick could be a stand-up comedian. He finds a way to make nonsense out of everything. He has given a handful of friends, including me, the ridiculous nickname of Fluffy. He yells it out from afar with much exuberance. I feel safe around Judas Priest and Cheap Trick. Gadget lets me hang out with his gang most of the time. We cruise around in a Chevy Nova with fur on the dash and fuzzy dice hanging from the mirror.

We go to the roller rink on the weekends, the arcade after school, and occasionally to the movies. On Fridays before school, we all go to Anthony's Diner for a logger's breakfast: two eggs made to order; home fries smothered in ketchup; your choice of bacon, ham or sausage; and two eight-inch pancakes with melting scoops of butter floating on a pool of pure Vermont maple syrup. Delicious!

Sometimes in the evenings, we gather in a side room to play pool. Judas Priest rocks out on his drum set with a strobe light and fog machine. I am part of their tribe. They accept me for who I am. But who am I? I have not yet found myself. I have not yet found a passion for anything in particular. At this age, what I really want is to hang out with the rest of the gang. These two older guys are cool! They have their own cars, play jamming rock music, have jobs, and are dating girls. I want to be like them.

CHAPTER 2

The Lion and The Lamb

The Lion attended the same high school twenty-four years ago, that my brother and I now attend. He was a natural leader who commanded respect. He was the football quarterback, on the all-star baseball team, played every instrument in the band, and was president of the student council. As a father, he wants me to be just like him, which is a big order to follow. It makes it difficult to figure out who I am and what I want. I had been taught early on not to express my feelings. I tucked it all inside. When The Lion is at home, I know, as he often says, "Children are to be seen, but not heard."

The Lion insists that Gadget, Priceless, and I take piano lessons. It feels like medieval torture on a sunny afternoon when all the other kids are outside riding their bikes. After a few years, I buy a drum set. The Lion says I can stop the piano lessons if I learn to play the drums. Before I get set up with a superb drum teacher, I learn to play the drums from Judas Priest. He shows me the really important thing: how to twirl the sticks like a rock star.

In line with his vision, The Lion made me play football with a bunch of other boys I didn't know when I was in the fifth grade. Imagine a small boy who knows nothing about football, standing alone on the field holding a pigskin, as eight huge guys wearing pads and helmets charge toward him. The other boys were full of testosterone and aggression, yelling their war cry before coming in for the kill.

In my senior year, with The Lion's urging, I participate in wrestling and track. I am paired up in my weight class with one of the toughest wrestlers in the school. He is a weight lifter and built like a Marine tank. I am like a rag doll, floundering as he tosses me around on the mat. Although I bond with a few friends on the sports teams, after the wrestling season, I feel like a survivor in a P.O.W. camp. I am stronger because I made it out alive.

THE LION

The Lion was born with a broken leg. The accident probably occurred when my pregnant Grandmother, Hosanna, slipped on the front steps of her home during winter. The Lion came into this world in pain. His broken leg was not growing at a normal rate. When he was twelve years old, doctors at the clinic placed staples in his opposite leg to slow down the growth so he would have close to equal length in both legs. He remained in the hospital after the operation for a month due to infection. As a last ditch effort, they used penicillin. If it hadn't worked, they would have had to remove his good leg. There is no question he is a fighter and a survivor.

He was either born with, or acquired, the ability to endlessly taunt his younger brother. As a child, he chased him around with the vacuum cleaner telling him he was going to suck him up inside it. Another time, he dug a hole and claimed it was to bury him. He is commonly sarcastic, frequently spouts off quirky quotes, and will retell a story until my brother and I hold up fingers to indicate how many times we've heard it. It's best that I use some humor when writing about The Lion, as a way to swallow the bitter medicine with a spoonful of honey.

The Lion was driven and became a millionaire by the age of twenty-two. Perhaps the root of his mixed-up priorities is that he became rich at a young age. Money can overinflate a person's pride. The Lion has a meticulous memory for numbers, compulsively counts things, and constantly jingles the coins in his pocket. Being rich and affluent means driving a new Lincoln Continental, owning a colossal home, and having employees, power, and success. His goal is to create an empire. His first priority is to make money; next in line come friends. They keep him well connected. Family often gets worse treatment than friends. But, in reality, family can be trusted more than employees. They are willing to work harder and receive less pay.

There is no question that The Lion provides well for his family financially. Actually, we are envied by other kids and their parents. We have a swimming pool, mini-bikes, snowmobiles, a pool table, modern kitchen appliances, and new clothes every school year. We are showered with gifts for Christmas and on our birthdays. We were each given a safari suit after The Lion returned from a vacation in Florida. We have all the material comforts, but The Lion didn't model the proper moral conduct. What sticks with me is his joking around and saying, "A child is no good until he is old enough to go get me something!"

THE LAMB

I understand why The Lion and The Lamb were drawn together and married. They went to different high schools but were considered the "cream of the crop" in their own ways. The Lamb had wavy, dark brown hair, prominent cheek bones and hazel eyes. She was a beautiful farm girl. She helped raise her five younger siblings and was groomed to be a responsible mother. She was a talented artist who repeatedly won art achievement awards in high school. She was a member of the National Honor Society, which acknowledges students who are exemplary in scholarship, leadership, service, and character. Her beauty is the rare kind that comes from the inside. She is naturally elegant and would complement any man, be he rich or poor, because she is dedicated and completely honest.

THE LION ROAMS

During my teenage years, The Lion comes to visit my brother and me as we are painting the Burklyn Mansion. I am asked to sit with him in his car, and I comply. This is where many of our serious conversations took place. He says, "I will be moving out of the house. I have found a new roommate." I guess it is difficult for him to just come out and say what is really happening. What his statement means is that he has a girlfriend, with three kids, and will soon move in with her. It doesn't work out. Later on, he moves back into our home, I believe primarily to be there for my younger sister, Priceless, until she graduates from high school. She is his adorable daughter. She is that cute little blonde with blue eyes dressed up like a zebra for her dance recital.

My brother, Gadget, at nine years old, knew The Lion had other girlfriends. He was awkwardly trained to practice repeating The Lion's lies in case The Lamb ever inquired. He would say, "I was at the cabin all night. Now you say it."

Back in the brick house, on his way to work in the morning, The Lamb would want some affection, a simple kiss or a hug, when he would leave and return home. As a child, I see his reluctance to giving her a quick peck on the cheek. Somewhere inside, a part of me began to question if The Lion loved me.

When I come back from college, I find The Lamb alone in the kitchen leaning against the counter, crying. She is holding her heart and just can't stop sobbing. The Lion told her he was leaving her again, but this time she knew that he would not return. Priceless graduated from high school on June 6th, and he left on June 9th. I am eighteen but feel like I am eight years old again, completely helpless. I don't know how to comfort my mother. All I can do is be with her.

It's difficult to explain the deeper ramifications of The Lion's leaving on these occasions. In an article entitled *Children*

Deeply Shaped by Divorce, which is provided by Marriage Missions International, the author writes,

> "Most studies show that children of divorce are two to three times more likely to end up with lasting social and emotional problems — things like addiction, mental illness, an arrest record, or a teen pregnancy — but the majority are not scarred in this way.
>
> "But in a first-ever national study of grown children of divorce, which I conducted with professor Norval Glenn at the University of Texas-Austin, these young people told us that, even if they were not forever damaged by their parents' divorce, they were still deeply shaped by it in ways that should make parents think yet again before divorcing.
>
> "It turns out that any kind of divorce, whether or not it's amicable, gives children an entirely new and burdensome job. After a divorce, the parents no longer have to confront their different worlds — their different values, beliefs and lifestyles. In fact, their inability to handle that challenge may have led to the divorce. But the big job of making sense of the parents' two different worlds does not go away once the divorce papers are signed. Instead, this job gets handed to the child alone.
>
> "Many grown children of divorce told us they had to grow up negotiating two wholly separate worlds. They rose to the challenge by becoming a different person with each of their parents. They had a mom-self and a dad-self inside them and pulled out the one they needed, depending on where they were that day. They had to grow up fast and often felt much less emotionally safe than their peers with married parents, even compared with some whose parents were unhappily married." [2]

As a child, divorce was the only reality I knew. I felt hurt, confused, and abandoned, but not as deeply betrayed as The Lamb. I am told he loves me, but as a child one always asks, "Why does our family need to break apart?" As a young man, The Lion set a broader example that marriage is not meant to last forever; it lasts only as long as the man is content.

SEXUAL INTEGRITY

I have begun to scratch the surface in relation to three topics: relationships, my tribe, and my spiritual journey. The fourth topic is more difficult to approach, but necessary: the realm of sexual integrity. I weave these four topics throughout my story. As they evolve, I mature, and vice versa. I feel reluctant to disclose the truth about my previous sexual addiction, but it's as integral to my story as the other three topics I've shared.

I don't realize I have a problem with sexual addiction for many years. By my late 30s, I am in way over my head. I can't look at an attractive woman without creating a sexual fantasy. I have no idea it is a problem until the day someone points at me and says, "There is the beast!" I have since acknowledged my sex-related issues, but continue to feel reluctant about having them exposed in writing. The beast of this addiction is so hideous that I must first wrap it up in chains before it's safe to slowly drag it out into the light.

T.C. Ryan, in an article called *Where Lust Leads*, explains,

> "But the nature of addiction is that the chemicals released in the brain during addictive behavior reinforce the patterns of the addictive cycle. The chemically nurtured, feeling part of the brain is repeatedly strengthened and quickly develops the ability to overrule the reasoning part of the brain. Sexual addiction is

a person's use of sex to alter moods that progresses to the point where they are unable to control their use of sex, suffer consequences, and are behaving contrary to their will and desire. It becomes a substitute for healthy relating; it takes over a person's will, and it's pathological — that is, it's destructive." (3)

I learn about sexual addiction and sexual integrity after years of misusing sex. When writing about my sexual addiction, I feel that I am placing myself on a sacrificial slab. Having experienced what I have to reconcile these issues, I feel this transparency is worthwhile if other men and women can find their own healing or a better understanding about this taboo subject. I also write about it to free myself further from the chains it once had around me.

SEXUAL ADDICTION

I slowly open the door to this dark, basement room with compassion. There are spiral stairs, which lead me down, step-by-step, into becoming trapped by sexually-addictive behaviors. I must face my darker side with compassion. I have made a commitment to move forward and, if it's possible, to never return. Just as there is a spiral staircase leading down into these problems, I now know there is also a step-by-step process for lifting your head up and leaving this place, with self-respect, healthy thoughts, and sexual healing.

The beast is first exposed as sexual addiction when I attend a men's sexual-integrity group at a Christian church associated with Liberty University in Virginia. In these support groups, we often tell the story of our own sexual-addiction history when someone new joins. It captures my attention when a man who has been attending the group for several months says, "I was addicted to heroin, and it was easier to kick that habit than to recover from my sexual addiction."

I usually start my story by saying, "I was spoon-fed porno

at a very young age." Then I tally off the porn magazines, strip clubs, and sexual fantasies. It progressively became worse as I grew from a teenager to a young man. Initially, it is embarrassing to uncover and reveal my hidden, darker side. The other guys' faces hold a sober gaze with an occasional nod. They have heard the same story many times over. It takes a truly deviant confession to phase these guys.

LEARNING TO LUST

As a child, I drew a picture of myself with a briefcase. I said, "When I grow up I want to be a business man, like my dad." I wanted to be like The Lion in every way. I wanted to walk like him, talk like him, and grow up to be him. I looked up to him, as an idol. As a child, I never questioned my father's actions. It is regrettable that when I was at an early age, he displayed an example of how to treat women: without respect.

I don't want to point the finger solely at The Lion because I've been told that my Grandfather, Buck, would occasionally party late into the night with other women while Hosanna was at home with their two boys. This attitude toward women was a generational curse of sorts that was passed down from man to man. Pornography was commonly left on coffee tables at our family's camp, wives were cheated on, and women were thought of as sexual objects, merely for play. These are the men that hand-delivered the beast in a cage to the basement of my psyche and let it go.

I am blessed, for in my life there has always been an opposing force of protection and love to add some balance, usually in the form of a woman. In this case, it's my Grandmother, Hosanna, who is a devout Christian. One day at camp, she grabs up all of the pornographic magazines and sputters in an emotional outburst directed toward Buck and their two adult sons, saying, *"You should all know better!"* The men look at each other with eyebrows lifted and smirk. She looks her husband and sons in the eyes with disgust as she lets out her disapproval with a cry that sounds like a wounded rabbit. She walks briskly with the armful of magazines, which she throws into the flames of the box stove. Over time, the magazines reappear at the camp. When lust is ignited in the heart of a man, it's not easy to extinguish. More often, it burns and spreads to other men like wildfire.

Most of what I learned about sex came from my friends and what I saw in magazines, but one can't learn to care and be intimate with a woman from a Playboy centerfold. Photographs only churn up illusions in the form of lust. Love is really what I want, but I start to believe that sex is the equivalent of love. While at one of our forts, my teenage friends and I decorate a Christmas tree by cutting out two-dozen photos of naked women from an issue of Playboy. As we attach them to the tree, it seems as though we are expressing what we want: to be loved by a beautiful, sexy woman.

THE BIRDS AND THE BEES

Soon after this, while at our hunting camp, The Lion takes my 12-year-old brother, Gadget, on a twenty-minute jeep ride to give him advice about women, condoms, and sex. The Lion's explanation of sex is another fearful moment. I am told to wait at camp, but I sense the importance of this rite of passage. It is happening today. Gadget is having a man-to-man talk in the jeep. When they return, The Lion is on his way towards becoming drunk. His drinking buddy is a large friend who is called Dancing Bear. They debate for a moment whether I am too young to handle a discussion about sex, but after one more drink, The Lion is ready.

He stands up and starts in with a loud, hysterical, frightening laugh. "A woman has two melons...no, two grapefruits..." as he cups his hands on either side of his chest. Neither of the men can contain themselves, and they both let out sinister laughs.

Dancing Bear's laugh is combined with hissing, which

makes it even worse. I am a frightened and confused ten year old boy standing with my back against the door. My shoulders are shrugged forward, and I have limp, claw-like arms held up in front of my chest. I try in vain to protect myself from an invisible opponent. ■

CHAPTER 3

The Forevermore Factor

As a 22 year old, life is a dream. I am a young man in college. I first met Forevermore on the beach at Lake Bomoseen, which is in the western edge of central Vermont. She strikes me right away as a woman with confidence. I need to complete one summer course, trigonometry, at nearby Castleton State College in order to graduate within four years. During the day, I stain a few horse stalls for family friends in this area. Forevermore, by happy chance, lives next door. She comes over to shovel the manure out of the horse stalls. This may not seem romantic, but she is a stunning farm girl, fresh and alive, galloping around on her horse. She is unlike any woman I have known.

We go on walks in the fields together. During the summer nights, I park my 1966 Mustang in her driveway. We sit inside and listen to music and chat. We usually stay up too late, and the next day I fall asleep in my 8 a.m. trigonometry class. Matters are made worse because I don't find the subject interesting and the professor has a boring monotone voice. Forevermore captures my heart. She is intelligent and passionate, simple and carefree. Besides, she is drop-dead gorgeous.

During one of our walks, we come back holding hands. I spontaneously tell her, "I love you." I don't say those words lightly. Her eyes are sparkling. When you are young and in love, every breath tastes like wine.

A few years later, I am attending Saint Michael's College

in Winooski, Vermont for a master's degree in business management. I desire more adventure and want to travel. I plan to go for a semester abroad to study Australian culture at Melbourne University. Forevermore moves to nearby Burlington and rents her own apartment. We have been dating steadily for a few years. I am contemplating proposing to her. Being apart in Australia will give me time to decide. I want to sow some wild oats before settling down.

In Australia, I find an affinity for photography. I enjoy taking photos of our group in nature or interacting with animals. This semester is an expedient learning adventure. Our group of 17 students visits an animal reserve with dingoes and the duckbilled platypus. We go down in a coal mine, watch sheep dogs at work, and attend a concert by the Melbourne Symphony Orchestra in the Sydney Opera House.

On one outing I scale a giant rock the size of a ship, which I later found out was the well-known Cave of Hands. I was skeptical of aboriginal sovereignty at these sacred sites. But a fifth sense told me I was a lawbreaker. I stand halfway up on a twenty-foot ledge that leads to a thin catwalk around the bend. Here I spot and begin to photograph two shaggy big-horned goats. I realize my vulnerability when one raises its head and begins to charge at full speed. I am being chased and soon cling to the edge with a prayer: *Let me live!* I give birth to a new respect for these sacred aboriginal spots with their guardian protectors.

I have some of my photos published in a few magazines and brochures to promote The Experiment in International Living. It's a big boost. It confirms my talent as a photographer and launches my career in photography.

THE MARRIAGE PROPOSAL

Upon my return from a semester abroad in Australia, I am ready to commit to Forevermore. I love her. I need not search anymore. I propose to Forevermore in a hot air balloon over

Lake Seymour during the fall foliage season. I decide to ask her by surprise. We spend the night in a cabin near the hot air balloons launch site. The next morning, under the premise of photographing the hot air balloons, we watch them launch. I take photos of the giant flamethrower filling the floppy fabric, which inflates to become a balloon. It must be held down by sandbags. Somehow, I misplace my lens cap and make a big fuss looking for it. I prearrange to have one balloon for the two of us, but there is another larger balloon that holds eight people launching at the same time.

The woman who will take us up is wearing a leather pilot's jacket. She craftily says, "I am going up all alone." Then she asks, "Would you two like to go up with me?" Of course we accept. I am taking photos of the peak foliage and the other balloon. It is all quite breathtaking.

Once the wind pushes us out over the lake, I look at Forevermore and say, "I have a surprise for you." She jokingly replies, "What! You found your lens cap."

I say, "No, that's not it. I have something for you." I hold out a black velvet box with a diamond ring in it. Then I ask her, "Will you marry me?" She becomes tearful. She looks me in the eyes and says, "Yes! I will."

A few minutes later they yell over from the other balloon, "What did she say?" I am confused at first. Then I figured it out. They all knew I was proposing to her. The pilot and I yell back, "She said yes!"

THE WEDDING CEREMONY

Forevermore and I are married a year later. It is during the peak of the foliage season, under two rows of maple trees in a small picturesque park in Lunenburg, Vermont. Prior to the ceremony, the guests exchange handshakes and hugs, smiles, and small talk.

While I am standing in the paved parking lot, The Lion shares some unwanted advice. He says, "I spoke to my friend, who is Forevermore's neighbor. She said you would be better off marrying her sister." His rude statement takes me off guard. I feel furious inside. How could he say such a thing on my wedding day! I am marrying this woman because I love her, not her sister. I am afraid to express my emotions, otherwise I would ask him to leave my wedding (or punch him in the gut). Instead, I revert to my childhood reaction. I say nothing and do nothing. I pack my feelings somewhere inside.

We chose to have a wedding during fall foliage because it's my favorite season in Vermont. The sun shines on the maple leaves, which turn a vibrant collage of reds, yellows, and oranges. The air is refreshingly crisp and cool. To take a deep breath awakens my soul; it invokes a connection with nature and with the many generations of my ancestors that rest beneath these rolling green hills.

The wedding guests are seated on several rows of dark brown benches borrowed from the church across the street. I stand patiently awaiting my bride. I feel love and support pouring down, like thick honey, from my cherished neighbors, my old school mates, and my uncles and aunts. Of course, my Aunt Fuzzy Bear, Gadget, Priceless, Hosanna, and The Lamb are all present.

The justice of the peace is a woman named Joy. She and her husband, Joe, own one of the last large tracts of farmland in central Vermont. He is one of the old-time Vermont farmers that refuse to stop farming and for whom selling out is not an option. For the last two decades, Forevermore grew up across the road from Joe in an old white house that was built for the farmhand. Joe and Joy treated Forevermore and her sister, Spoony, like they were their grandchildren. They are given full access to roam on the farmland. They gallop across the fields on their horse named Buddy. Her family sketched out a map and made up a label for each knoll, ridge, and brook. This way they could describe in detail the location where they had spotted a deer or a flock of wild turkeys.

Joe walks bowlegged, and his knees cause him great pain after fifty years of farming, but there is always a sparkle in his eyes whenever he sees his girls. Joe is as solid as the land itself. His smile and the look in his eyes are enough to bless our marriage. It need not be spoken aloud. We both feel it. For him, marriage is a deeply-dug well that is meant to be drawn upon forevermore.

Our marriage ceremony is one of those timeless moments. Forevermore wears a custom-made, spandex, knee-length wedding dress. It is fire-engine red to match the leaves and her fiery Italian passion. Her hair is done up exquisitely. The bridesmaids wear casual knee-length dresses of white and yellow. My best man and I have on dapper, black, tailed tuxes. Mine has a fiery red cummerbund that matches the bride's dress.

I can hear the crackling of leaves as the bridesmaids, and then Forevermore, meander in their snazzy high heels down the two rows of maple trees. I am bedazzled and filled with loving thoughts about our future together. Forevermore radiates with sensational beauty and confidence. She comes to stand by my side. We peer into each other's eyes. Our wedding ceremony begins.

The justice of the peace asks, "Is there any reason these two should not be married?"

All of our friends and family are silent. It is a perfectly crisp, sunny day with only one small cloud in the otherwise pristine blue sky. To our surprise, in this moment of quietness, gentle thunder rolls out from behind that one little cloud and for just an instant, a few sprinkles fall from the sky. I stare up in the sky and wonder if God is offering us some sort of ominous warning. We are not sure how to react, so Forevermore and I smile at each other, and then say our vows.

A YEAR-LONG HONEYMOON

We start our life journey together with a year-long honeymoon. We travel out west to live for a few months in Seattle,

Washington, with her sister, Spoony. While in Seattle, Forevermore enrolls in a program for a career as a dog groomer. I am unable to find decent work in Seattle. I become desperate. I am willing to take any job. I water down my resume to get hired in a convenience store.

For a month, I get a gig photographing children and babies in people's homes. It requires a lot of driving and shaking a silly puppet to make them smile. Then I get hired as a guide in Ketchikan, Alaska. By accepting this job, I will be away from Forevermore for a few months. I hop on a ferry with my mountain bike and a backpack. Forevermore will drive our Chevy minivan to Alaska once her dog-grooming training is complete.

As a guide, I use my paddle as a rudder to steer an ocean-going canoe as twenty tourists from the cruise ships paddle around a mountain lake. We pull ashore and I point out the banana slugs and the carnivorous sundew plant. After this job, I am hired to photograph the Native American Tlingit Tribe, which makes totem poles, does intricate bead work, and performs their traditional drumming and dancing. They are content people, and the children are always playing and laughing.

Joyce, who is about thirty, arrives for our photo shoot in her traditional red felt dress, carrying a woven basket. She pauses during our photo shoot to pick and eat a few orange salmon berries. Then we move down beside the sea. She tells me that soon she will be married in a traditional wedding. Her groom will arrive by sea in a canoe.

I make friends among the Tlingits during my two weeks of photographing. I tell some of them that I will make copies of some of the photographs to give them. Later, I am disheartened to find out that the non-native corporation that hired me to take these promotional photographs will not allow the Tlingits to have any of the photos. The corporation owns the legal rights to all of the photos. They tell me they might try to sell them. I am told one such photo showed up on the side of a bus. I apologize to the Tlingit tribe for my false promise. I arrange a photo presentation so they can at least enjoy viewing them. I feel the tension between the Tlingit tribe and the non-native corporation that gained the right to control them, for better or worse, as a profitable business. I am rudely awakened to their current reality. In order for the White man to market them, they had to give up certain rights. It feels like the indigenous people are still getting the short end of the stick.

Once reunited, Forevermore and I travel to explore the interior of Alaska. The last frontier is a wildlife photographer's dream. There are herds of caribou, and the snow-covered caps of Mount Denali in the background are spectacular. While we are there, a large wolf chases a large caribou down the river. He takes it down singlehandedly. As he is feeding, a grizzly bear comes along and wants an easy meal. The grizzly bear chases off the lone wolf and gorges itself. It literally sleeps on the carcass for three days. The wolf came back with two others from the pack. They venture in close to try and grab some meat. The bear swats at one with a huge claw. It runs away yelping like a puppy.

We hike 33 miles along the Chilkoot Trail. The Chilkoot Trail was the most famous route taken by prospectors who made their way to the Klondike Gold Rush. Chilkoot Pass was an aboriginal trail that had been used for years by the First Nations people who lived in this region. The steep mountains and the harsh weather make this trip extremely grueling. We had to traipse through deep snow to get over the pass in the middle of July. During the gold rush era there was a law stating that all who entered Canada had to bring one ton of food and supplies.

Forevermore and I create strong memories while hiking and camping. We are happy tramping around in the rain or snow. In part, being together is what matters the most. After a year, we return back to Vermont. In northern Vermont regions, I give a public photo presentation called "Alaska: Natives, Nature, and Nonsense."

FOR BETTER OR WORSE

Back in Vermont, I begin to work in the family business, and to photograph weddings. We rent a home, and Forevermore opens a dog-grooming salon. She doesn't want to settle down in the vicinity of her new father-in-law, The Lion. She despises how he mistreats women. The Lion is not just my father; he is also my boss. It makes the whole scenario complex and frustrating at times.

Forevermore is a strong advocate for the fair treatment of animals, women's rights, and the environment. She never holds back from speaking her mind. Some people improperly label her as a snob, because she has ravishing beauty and speaks so directly. She is a beautiful and intelligent woman with stunning brown eyes and long dark hair, which I enjoy watching her comb through each evening. Her hair always smells fresh and clean. We lack the skills to communicate effectively when conflicts arise, and we begin to argue over little things that aren't important. I am guilty of not always listening to her. Perhaps, I am caught up in focusing on my own needs.

I continually push myself to live, work, and play hard. My world changes after I herniate a disk in my lower back. The injury limits my ability to sit for long without pain. Our marriage begins to lose the romantic spark. I do not feel like going out to the movies or having dinner with friends. I can no longer share in doing chores like washing the dishes, taking out the trash, or hauling firewood, which was part of my role as a man and her husband.

I can no longer enjoy fun activities like downhill skiing, mountain biking, or hiking, as we once did together. Instead, my daily routine includes physical therapy exercises and a walk each day to keep my body limber and my mind sane.

After months of living with chronic pain, emotional trauma and anger begins to creep in. Often, my back muscles tear for little or no reason. I can open the car door and it drops me to my knees. One afternoon, Forevermore returns from work and I am lying on the carpet watching a movie. She greets me by asking, "How are you feeling?" I explode, "How the hell do you think I'm feeling?" Afterwards, I apologize. She was being kind. I should have shared how I felt.

Just for the record, I was feeling a lot of pain that day. Pain that limits my normal ability makes me feel helpless, and if it is prolonged, it progresses to become hopeless. It can get really frustrating. One morning, my back pulls while I am walking alone on a dirt road. I have to crawl back home on my hands and knees. Underneath, I am asking myself, "Why has this happened to me?"

I follow the example The Lion set for me in terms of how to cope with stress and survive. His methods are to take a pill, have a drink, or take it out on somebody weaker. Unfortunately, some of the bad seeds he planted years ago begin to sprout. For a while, I drink alcohol, but I realize it's only making me depressed.

I begin to watch a few movies each day, rationalizing that watching movies is a healthier way to relieve my stress and pain than drugs or alcohol. Slowly I begin to focus on movies with sexual content. It's not my nature to rent X-rated videos. That would be sinking too low. Yet, I experience an adrenalin rush when I watch R-rated movies, and eventually get hooked on the visual stimulation of the sex and action-packed Hollywood films. There is a melding of the sexy women in the movies within my reality. I start to have sexual fantasies of other women, even when I am with Forevermore. During love-making, I am certain she feels it when I drift away to my fantasy world instead of being in my heart with her, my beautiful wife.

Joe Zychik, the author of *How I Overcame Sexual Addiction and How Anyone Can*, explains,

> *"A person begins addiction by using a substance or activity to escape dealing with the difficulties of life.*

The escape fails because escape never works - and it always worsens life's problems. Then - and this is the big mistake - the person decides to flee further into addiction rather than face the problem." [4]

DIVORCE

My decision to buy a local home in nearby Danville and remain an employee in our family business causes a division between Forevermore and me. Instead of moving into the house I just purchased, she chooses to live nearby with her sister, Spoony, in the house we were all renting together. It's clear in hindsight that we, as a married couple, should have been in agreement about buying a home or any major decision.

Forevermore longs to travel the world. I sense that the physical limitations of my back injury are dampening her freedom. She goes with her sister to spend a month biking in Europe. I go to the local video store and pick out a few more flicks. I naively believed that we would always be happily married. For a variety of reasons, I begin to wonder whether our lives would be better if we were apart.

WHAT DOES THE BIBLE SAY ABOUT AN UNHAPPY MARRIAGE?

"One thing we know for sure: being in an unhappy marriage is not biblical grounds for divorce. In Mark 10:11–12 Jesus said, "A man who divorces his wife so he can marry someone else commits adultery against her. And a woman who divorces her husband so she can marry someone else commits adultery." Based on the Bible, we see that people don't have the right to dissolve an unhappy marriage. God intended that marriage be for a lifetime.

"Ephesians 5 presents marriage as a picture of

the relationship God has with us. This is one reason why God has such an interest in keeping marriages intact. He is the One who established the concept of "until death do us part." He established this for our own good. Failed marriages and broken homes are devastating to the husband and wife, not to mention the children involved. Financial ruin is only one of the unhappy results of divorce. The family unit is the basic building block of any society, and rampant divorce has a tragic impact on all of the culture.

"*This is not to say that God wants to force us to remain forever in an unhappy marriage. He doesn't ask us to just grit our teeth and suffer through it. When God approaches marital problems, He does so from the perspective of how to fix them, not how to dissolve the marriage. For example, the Lord speaks of demonic impact in marriages (1 Corinthians 7:5). He states that the couple should be active in the sexual relationship so that Satan cannot tempt them. He encourages husbands to treat their wives with understanding so their prayers will not be hindered (1 Peter 3:7). From these passages we can see that marriage is a spiritual battlefield. It takes work to fight for the relationship, not to fight in the relationship.*

"*God encourages us toward reconciliation. Matthew 18:15–16 demands open, honest communication that deals with hurts and frustrations caused by sin. It even encourages us to get help to resolve problems. God also calls us to find our joy in Him (Philippians 4). Joy is a superior experience to happiness. Happiness is temporal and temporary, but joy rises above all circumstances and lasts for eternity. Joy is something you can have regardless of conditions. In all of God's guidelines for experiencing joy, none of them require a spouse to cooperate. A spouse does not control our capacity to have joy or peace. James 1:3–4 tells us that deep, abiding joy comes as we persevere through trials, with God's help, and as our faith matures and strengthens. Mere happiness tends to be fleeting and depends upon temporal factors like circumstances or other people. Joy, on the other hand, is true contentment that comes from internal factors like our faith in the Lord. True joy is everlasting and not dependent upon circumstances."* [5]

THE FOREVERMORE FACTOR

During this stage of my life, I did not seek the Bible for guidance. I ask Forevermore, "Do you want a divorce?"

She says, "Yes!" without any hesitation.

There is never any further discussion. In her mind, after she signs the divorce papers, we are all over. Before I know it, she is with another man, one that is galloping beside her on horseback, even before I drag myself alone into court to make our divorce legal.

When it sinks into my heart that we are actually divorced, I am devastated, teetering on the verge of a breakdown. Our marriage lasted four years, but it continues in my mind for the next decade. My heart has a tender spot where all our memories are engraved.

Perhaps it's understandable why I now become sad during the autumn. I call it "The Forevermore Factor." When I see all the beauty in the vibrant red, orange, and yellow leaves, it only reminds me of our beautiful wedding day. Now I feel all alone and depressed. All my pain is buried under the layers of colorful leaves. Now I am glad to watch them drop to the ground. Each winter the snow temporarily covers my dream of being happily married and living together with her.

I remove all of Forevermore's photos and all the items that remind me of her from my home. As a wedding gift, The Lamb and Fuzzy Bear sewed us a handmade queen-size quilt. It has an intricate design with a mesmerizing storm-at-sea pattern, consisting of shades of dark and light blues interspersed with white. When seen from different angles, this combination of triangles, squares, and diamonds gives the effect of the motion of multiple waves converging during a chaotic storm at sea. We cherished it, but there are too many emotions wrapped inside it to consider sleeping under it without her. Yet there is so much love and beauty embedded in that quilt that I cannot bring myself to part with it. Our marriage began as beautiful, then it ironically became the storm at sea. Now, the confusion, the helplessness, the loss, the anger, the loneliness, and the fear of that storm rage on inside. ■

CHAPTER 4

Sailing

As a 31 year old, life is a dream. I am a supervisor overseeing and purchasing items for a trendy department in several stores that our family business operates with success. A few years after my divorce, I impulsively purchase a 24-foot McGregor sailboat. It's a way to conjure up fun and put adventure back into my life. There is an overnight cabin, and it can sleep four people. It's great for a weekend on northern Vermont's lakes. I sail with friends and family, primarily on Lake Memphremagog.

My friend, Cleopatra, and I often go sailing on long weekends. When there is not enough wind to sail, we chill out in the sun, read, or dive off the side for a swim. My favorite time to be on the sailboat is during sunset. We often have a barbeque dinner as the lake becomes still. At night, we lie out flat on the deck and look up at the stars. One day we dock to explore Province Island, which divides the international border. On this foreign soil, we spot dozens of pheasants, and there are even wild boars. We thought we had found Fantasy Island.

With some hesitation, I accept an invitation by Cleopatra to move in with her. She is from a Jewish family, born and raised in Queens, New York. She fell in love with Vermont and moved here after she saw fresh snow sparkling in a field like diamonds rolling in the sun. Cleopatra is part of the generation that went to Woodstock and never really came back home. We have jubilant experiences together; going out dancing with her undoubtedly means staying until the club closes down for the night.

I become certified for bareboat chartering at the School of International Sailing, located on Mallets Bay on the northern part of Lake Champlain. I consider purchasing a larger sailboat to explore islands in the Caribbean. Cleopatra, another female friend, and I charter Ragamuffin, a fifty-foot sailboat, with a captain and his wife, to sail for a week around the British Virgin Islands. My two sail mates spend the bulk of their time sunbathing as I rig the sails. I decide that being a captain of a sailboat in the Caribbean is not for me. Yet it is nice to kick off our shoes to watch the porpoises and turtles and whales that swim alongside our sailboat.

SALINE ISLAND

We travel to various Caribbean Islands, including Aruba, with long sandy beaches, and Bonaire, renowned for its snorkeling in the coral. Cleopatra considers these her tropical vacations, but I am searching for a place to establish a spiritual retreat center. On our last two trips, we fly into Grenada, then hop on a ferry which brings us to Carriacou Island. I am negotiating to lease 52 acres, called Saline Island. Nine siblings inherited this island from their father, George John, who purchased it decades ago. It's a secluded paradise with sandy, white beaches surrounded by lush mangrove forests and swaying coconut trees. There are towering black volcanic caps where wild goats roam, a salt pond where they harvest salt, and a beautiful cove for snorkeling with the angel, zebra, and trumpet fish among the coral reef.

It's my dream to start a spiritual retreat center in the Caribbean, perhaps on this island. We meet at their cottage on the island, and I present a business plan. We plan to meet again in Grenada to negotiate a price for leasing the island. We have both consulted with our lawyers, and I have high hopes that our next meeting will conclude our negotiations.

Outside, it's the height of Carnival celebrations. Carnival is a festive occasion; the streets are filled with people in glittery costumes, elaborately painted faces, and parties that go on for days. Island music blares through refrigerator-size speakers or dark-skinned men pound on homemade oil-pan drums late into the night.

Amidst the chaos of this celebration, the siblings can't come to an agreement among themselves about what they want to do with their island. A few local siblings want to continue to use the camp as a place to spear fish, relax, and drink beer. We then receive word that their lawyer has been hit by a car. He has suffered a broken leg and must go to the hospital, so they will not be attending our negotiations. It's not going to happen. We end our negotiations. I return to Vermont rather disappointed.

AN INTIMACY AND ATTACHMENT DISORDER

Cleopatra desires to be in a long-term relationship with a man. I am not in love with her. I introduce her as my friend, not my girlfriend, which makes her mad, but it better represents my feelings. After living with Cleopatra for a few years, I begin to search for other women to date. Now with hindsight, I should have moved out. After Cleopatra discovered my quest, she gave me the boot, without any hesitation.

Single again, I realize I never processed my divorce with Forevermore. Cleopatra was a pleasant distraction, but I need to face and feel the pain. In an attempt to erase all the beautiful and painful memories, I cut out all but one of her photos from our wedding album. The one I left is a dark silhouette of our bodies in an embrace in a hallway. Now she is more like a shadow or a ghost. I have been repressing my feelings surrounding my divorce, and they built up like a dam that is ready to overflow. When the dam finally breaks, it takes down the walls. I am filled with a torrent of anxiety and depression.

It hurts my heart to let go of Forevermore. I have spells

of what is called *saudade*, which is a Portuguese word that means: feelings of intense longing for a person you once loved. At times, it is an obsession. After our divorce, I idolize our perfect moments for the next decade. I wipe the slate clean of all our petty arguments and any harsh feelings.

Now, I just feel lonely. Being legally divorced does not feel any different from being married. There were moments when I desired a divorce, but underneath, what I really wanted was to find a way to stay connected. Unbeknownst to myself, our relationship needed deep emotional intimacy to survive. This meant expressing my emotions and *really* feeling empathy for hers.

Sexual addiction, to a large degree, is an intimacy and attachment disorder. I had not yet learned how to be emotionally intimate. I rarely communicate my emotions effectively and I block off the circuits that feel empathy and compassion for others. I found it impossible to detach because "letting go" meant I was losing whatever little scraps of love, (which were merely an illusion) I had left. Somehow, I came to falsely believe that I would feel less pain if I held on tightly.

FRENZY, THE ACUPUNCTURIST

To cope with my depression and anxiety attacks, I receive regular acupuncture sessions from a woman named Frenzy. She has it together. She has wild, straggly, blond hair. I find out later, when she means business, she conveys it in a frenzy of swearing. She's a flower child from the sixties who lived in various spiritual communities.

Frenzy's office has an Oriental charm, with bamboo decorations and the smell of burning mugwort and simmering tea. It's difficult to gauge how much the acupuncture improves my depression, but I do feel slightly better for a few days after each treatment. Frenzy genuinely cares for my situation.

She lends me a book called *Acu-Yoga* by Michael Reed Gach. She says, "Start each day with ten deep breaths." This simple breathing exercise allows me to become grounded, stay calm, and start each day on a positive note. I begin to practice yoga a few hours each day. After I practice yoga, my feeling of depression is replaced with a sense of peace. For the first time, I start to turn within myself and face my pain.

VERONICA VOGUE: CROSSING THE BORDER

One afternoon, I am at Lake Memphremagog tending to my sailboat. I meet a slightly older woman named Veronica Vogue, who has journeyed down on the ferry from Magog, Canada. I invite her to go sailing. She joyfully accepts. Being the captain of my own sailboat carries certain responsibilities and rewards. At this point, I am seeking a romantic interlude. Let's put it bluntly: I am craving sex, which in my confused mind is the equivalent to being loved.

It's a gorgeous afternoon for sailing. We have a little wine and cheese, and it's fun to be out on the water. At one point, she leans her back against me in the sailboat. Her touch is flirtatiously appealing.

I drive her back up to Magog in my S.U.V. At the Canadian border crossing, they ask, "What is the purpose of your trip?"

I answer, "Strictly pleasure."

We have dinner together in the quaint city of Magog, overlooking the water. Veronica, like most Canadians, dresses in a vogue fashion, with a blouse made of netted material. We have a stimulating conversation. She is foreign and somewhat bored with her life, but she seems rather exotic and alluring to me. Veronica is taking a getaway from her husband. She smokes a cigarette while telling me that her marriage is shaky, but she does not want to share the details. This time is reserved for her to get away from him.

We walk along a paved path by the beach. I am giving her my full attention, and she is responding. We have a long hug near the water.

She says, "It's time for me to return to my hotel room."

She is hinting that it's time for me to go.

I say, "I don't want to leave. Can I spend the night with you?" She pauses to check in with herself.

She asks, "What is it that you want?"

I say, "Sex would be nice."

She takes a few deep breaths, contemplating all the implications.

Her response comes with a slight tag of reluctance. "Sex is what you want? Here is my hotel key. I will get another one at the front desk. Meet me in room number 44 in ten minutes."

I go to my S.U.V and get my shaving kit. Anticipating a lascivious sexual affair, I pull out a condom and place it in my pocket.

Her hotel is right by the water. I walk down the wide, red-carpeted hallways past rows of white doors with gold numbers until I reach room number 44. I knock on the door. She comes out of the bathroom. While standing, we embrace and kiss. She has just been smoking a cigarette. It's true, to kiss a smoker is like licking an ashtray, but what comes to my mind is even worse. It's one of The Lion's comments about anything of disgust: "It's like kissing your sister on the lips."

I barely make it through her kiss without gagging.

Veronica says, "My husband must never know about this."

I agree not to tell him. She picks up the phone and calls down to reception. A few minutes later, a bellboy arrives at the door holding out a small silver tray with a condom on it. She pays him, along with a three-dollar tip. Obviously, we are both anticipating the need for a condom.

This is all building up to a crescendo. I am preparing for the big performance. We have most of the essential ingredients, but one is lacking: love. We roll on the sheets, moan and groan, and claw to take each other's clothes off. Underneath her clothes, she has on sexy, black, thong underwear and a lacy bra. There is a problem. I have a desire for sex, but one essential body part is not cooperating. I try to find ways to stall. It's starting to get embarrassing. I have never had this sort of dysfunction with a woman.

I dare not repeat her exact words. Let's just say at this moment, Veronica Vogue tells me exactly what she wants, and she is *extremely* clear about when she wants it — *right now!* Well, it's not going to happen that way. How am I going to explain this to Mrs. Veronica Vogue?

It turns out there will be *no* big performance tonight. By now, it's no big secret. She deals with it gracefully enough. As we lie in bed, she smokes another cigarette.

We say goodbye and I drive across the border, back to where I belong. I did not love this woman. I did not even enjoy kissing her. My body let me know it. My heart did not want to lend itself to a married woman, regardless of how sensual and exotic she appeared. My mind and its lusty thoughts had a plan, but thankfully my heart trumped over my body. If I can stop judging my body's performance, then I can listen to what it really needs. Sex with Mrs. Veronica Vogue is not what my body needs.

> *"The one who commits adultery with a woman is lacking sense; he who would destroy himself does it, wounds and disgrace he will find, and his reproach will not be blotted out. For jealousy enrages a man, and he will not spare in the day of vengeance. He will not accept any ransom, nor will he be satisfied though you give many gifts."*
>
> (Proverbs 6:32-35 NASB)

CHAPTER 5

Soft Rain

Imagine a series of soft rain showers, and each time it rains, a few pieces of a puzzle fall to the earth. I innocently pick them up as I find them. I don't think it odd to find a puzzle piece or two; somebody might have dropped them. I gather the random pieces in a wooden box. As time goes by, I fit some of the pieces together. I believe that I am starting to figure out my puzzling life.

I have been praying ardently for a yoga teacher or guru to enter my life. In my prayers, I request… *the wisdom to help others, regardless of how much suffering I must endure.* God hears my persistent prayers, and they manifest, but certainly not as I expected….

September fourteenth starts like any other normal day. I wake up and splash water on my face. I cook some home fries and scrambled eggs for breakfast. I sit down to eat, as usual, on my porch. My cat, Safire, nuzzles my leg. Then it begins to rain softly. I notice a few puzzle pieces on the ground by my doorstep. How bizarre! It is like they fell from the sky.

DOWSING

After my endeavors for a retreat on Saline Island failed, I set a new course. I become a dowsing fanatic. It's relatively easy to do, with the National Dowsing Headquarters located in my hometown of Danville, Vermont. At first, I am simply curious. I am my own teacher. I dowse to find out about dowsing. Soon, I discover a way to immerse myself by escaping into an exciting and unknown spiritual world that is providing me with answers normally hidden from view.

Dowsing is an ancient form of divination used to seek information. It utilizes handheld tools such as L-rods, pendulums, and even the body rocking forward and backward to provide answers in a kinesthetic way with either a yes or no, numbers, or by pin-pointing a location. Dowsing is most commonly known in association with searching for underground water, but it can also find ley lines and be used to gauge energy levels. Dowsing can be applied to search for artifacts, missing persons, substances, and entities.

Perhaps I am not properly educated or protected for dealing with the spirits I am calling forth. Initially, I start by dowsing for water and energy lines and then dowse rocks, plants, and animals. I set up energy grids around my home with rocks I haul from a nearby brook. Dowsing is generally related to forms of earth energy, which leads me to my favorite topic: healing. I begin to use dowsing to find ways to heal my family, my friends, and myself.

Dowsing begins to encompass all facets of my life. Dowsing guides me about what to eat, whom to meet, and where to go. I am having fun! But sometimes, when I am not specific about a question, or when I am tired, my answers come in riddles. I begin to wonder what spirits guide dowsing and if those spirits are always looking out for my best interests. I convince myself that little harm can come from two L-shaped metal rods as a gauge for a spirit to answer yes or no.

> *"Let no one be found among you who sacrifices their son or daughter in the fire, who practices divination or sorcery, interprets omens, engages in witchcraft, or casts spells, or who is a medium or spiritist or who consults the dead. Anyone who does these things is detestable to the Lord; because of these same detest-*

able practices the Lord your God will drive out those nations before you."

(Deuteronomy 18:10-12 NIV)

It turns out that today is anything but normal. Through dowsing, I am sent a code of ethics concerning communication with spirits, which I write down in my laptop. In addition, I am given a warning that I should not share this code of ethics or I will pay a hefty price. I promise to never reveal it or allow anybody access to it. Dowsing informs me that I will receive the final instruction after I sit in lotus position for fifteen minutes. This is not an easy task. After my back injury, I have had extremely tight thighs and hip muscles. I could probably get into lotus position for a few minutes, but fifteen minutes would be excruciatingly painful.

THE FINAL INSTRUCTION

I take a deep breath and sit down in lotus posture, determined to meditate for fifteen minutes. I want to receive that final instruction. I have experienced a lot of physical pain; when it will not go away, it engulfs my whole world. Pain is like an annoying, drunken friend. I can tolerate it, but I wish it would just go somewhere else. Over time I have learned to adapt and accept pain as my reality. The pain is easier to handle when I have the ability to stop it. I am curious about that final instruction, so I don't. While in the posture, I rub my palms together rapidly until they are burning hot. I take a few deep breaths and blow into my hands. Next, I do a series of short breaths through my nose, called "the breath of fire." Now my mind is clear. I focus on my third eye.

After I complete fifteen minutes in lotus posture, I lie flat on my back to relax. Suddenly, my legs start to tremble in short rapid movements. It works its way up through my legs, up my back, down my arms, and across my face. It feels like something is trying to crawl inside my body. My legs twist tightly around each other like a pretzel. With my legs still squeezing tightly, I go up in a shoulder stand. My breath is shallow. While inverted, I perform the breath of fire in short bursts to contract my abdomen. Suddenly, a swirling smoke enters my heart. I feel movement under my skin near my heart. It's like space is shifting and adjusting. It's not uncomfortable. I don't feel afraid. Next, there is a mild tingling as my spirit and that of another merge to share the same space.

As the author, I feel inclined to place a disclaimer at this point. If any reader is foolish enough to try these same silly steps, I need to warn you about one tiny side effect: your nervous system gets fried!

What just unfolded feels natural, yet I know it's an uncommon occurrence. I admit, I am not sure how it all fully transpired. Let me just say, I am not alone anymore. I am fully awake and aware of experiencing some new sensations. There are no instruction manuals about this sort of thing. This is how I can best describe it: a doorway to my spiritual perception opens up. I am suspended in time and space somewhere in the universe. For a lack of words, I will call it the cosmic consciousness. There is not just one spirit, but simultaneously many spirits coexist in this space.

When you open the door to a house and walk inside, light and air also come through that doorway. They are not invited. They are not good or bad. They just always enter when the door is open. It felt that same way with the spirits. I am not afraid. Once the door leading to the cosmic consciousness is open, it does not just slam shut. It remains open a while. In a way, the whole universe is in there. Either I enter it or it enters me. Then we merge together. Maybe this universe was inside of me all along. I just never knew how to access it.

Regardless, there is one spirit present that predominates. It seemed to have the power to enter my body. This spirit will hereafter be called "The Guru." The Guru opened the doorway. According to the Bible, a spirit, be it good or evil, must be invited in order to enter a body. I took that step, somewhat unintentionally. I also believe my actions, the proper breathing technique, and the yoga postures were essential.

SWAMI SRI YUKTESWAR

I lie flat on my back and stretch my arms up above my head. I let out a 300-year-old yawn. Then I sit up and watch a car pass by on the road. The Guru looks through my eyes at the car. In my mind, The Guru says, "That is a car!" Perhaps his way of adjusting is to focus on the first moving object that comes into view.

A deep, gentle voice whispers, "I am Swami Sri Yukteswar." The Guru's voice is distinct, and his thoughts are separate from mine. It's clear that we are sharing the same body. We are sharing the same senses, and mine feel slightly enhanced. He is aware of my emotions and my thoughts. We communicate in my mind, but it sounds like we are speaking, as in a regular conversation. Our conversations have no limits or boundaries. He responds to my questions in a polite manner with the utmost patience.

This guru has composure. I acknowledge that I have merged with somebody who has great power and understanding. My posture changes. I hold myself more like a king, with my sternum and side body lifted up. My head faces forward, no longer looking down. When I assume this subtle shift in posture, I feel his inner peace and confidence surface.

The Guru explains he is from a lineage called Kriya yoga. He has entered 30 bodies prior to mine. He is able to retain the knowledge from each mind. He learned the technique of how to enter a body through Kriya yoga, as instructed by his guru, Lahiri Mahasaya. I have a copy of *The Autobiography of a Yogi*, by his disciple, Paramahansa Yogananda, and begin to read the parts about Swami Sri Yukteswar. Overall, there is a sense of timelessness. There is no urgency. I don't rush. I am living in the present moment.

I did pray for a guru. Somebody upstairs was listening. Perhaps next time I need to be more specific and pray, "I want a guru to enter my life — *not* my body." Anyhow, I am thankful and feel our student and teacher connection is based on a mutual desire, even though I can't fully grasp all that is unfolding. Yoga philosophy says that gurus and disciples come together when the time is right. Swami Sri Yukteswar explains that he is a guru of wisdom, which was part of my prayer request. Perhaps we are destined to be together.

THE FIRST FEW DAYS WITH THE GURU

The Guru and I go through some cosmetic changes. We no longer wear any metal because it affects the energy flow. I rip the zippers and metal buttons off a few pairs of loose-fitting pants. The texture of the clothing against my skin becomes important. I only sleep a few hours each night. My typical meal is simple grains with a steamed green vegetable and a piece of fruit for dessert or a snack. I drink a few quarts of mega-green spirulina the first few days. Then I call the local health food store and order a case of it. My sense is that this assists in the transformation on a cellular level; plus it boosts my energy.

I ask The Guru to talk about the past bodies he has entered. He is reluctant, but makes a few remarks. He has entered the bodies of both men and women in various parts of the world. Once, he entered the body of a doctor, which I conclude was a positive experience. He prefers to speak of his life as a guru in India and speaks fondly about his disciple, Paramahansa Yogananda. He tells me about taking long walks with him along the river, the fragrance of the blooming trees, and the smells of spring in India. These are the memories that he cherishes. Being raised in a home next to a river, I can relate to the tranquil sound of the flowing water.

During the first night, The Guru guides my hands to do

manipulations on my body while I am in a semi-sleeping state. The Guru is definitely in charge here and takes over to use my hands to self-massage or press key trigger points. I hold stretches in strange positions, which bring relief to the muscles in my legs, back, neck, and shoulders. They have been tense for years. The Guru has a heightened sense of body awareness, superior to my comprehension. After the first night, I am given step-by-step instructions to learn the most important stretches to benefit my body.

The Guru sternly says, "You need to pay attention." It normally takes a few repetitions for me to retain a new routine.

I am shown a wonderful stretch where I grab my left toe and pull it behind my head. The Guru is a patient teacher and extends compassion for the condition of my aching body.

For ten years, I failed to acknowledge my limits or listen to my body's warning signs, like mild pain. Eventually, it became a habit to push myself without taking breaks or stopping, even when my body needed to relax. I sense The Guru did not know how tight or restricted different muscles and body parts were until he got inside. Even a guru can't choose a body and take it for a test run. He must work with the body he has chosen. He explains that it is not an easy process to enter a body; my understanding is that the soft spot on the top of a baby's head, known as the fontanel, is the portal where a spirit enters. I assume many factors must line up and that one gets chosen partially by destiny or grace of the Guru.

Leaving a body is a different story. He says, "It's painless to leave a body after it dies."

I hope there are other options!

During the day we practice focusing on an object for ten minutes. The real transformations will take place in my mind. I am instructed to find a small object with a glimmer, then stare at that spot. It is best if I don't blink…just focus. I make a joke during this exercise. The Guru sternly brings me back to focus on the object. During this practice, he is serious. If my gaze is broken, then my attention is lacking. He tells me that communication can occur simply through thoughts between a disciple and their guru, but the disciple must develop the ability to focus.

During this time, I notice that I can locate select people, objects, and driving directions through what I call my spiritual radar. A few days after The Guru enters the scene, my laptop is stolen from my home. I left it on the desk in my house, open to the page with the code of ethics concerning communicating with spirits, that I promised to never leave accessible. (Oops!) I assume the thief is a drug addict friend of my lower level tenant, Lizzy. I don't try to find the laptop or the thief. What I really need is to find a coworker who has a backup for an important work project that was on the stolen laptop.

My coworker is not at his home, so I drive away from his house and start to think about him. About a half-mile away, I pull over. I walk across the road, jump over a guard rail, trudge through some tall grass, and cross over a small brook. It opens up into a field where there are two high school soccer games in progress. Somehow, I know this is where he will be. I walk straight up to him.

TRACING MY NATIVE HERITAGE

I sit late one afternoon on a grassy hill to meditate. I go deep inside to hear the birds and feel the wind. The sun begins to set as I stare up toward the pink, wispy clouds. I see a wild vision in the clouds. It starts with four Indian chiefs looking down upon the earth. Then I see a pregnant woman with braided hair, reclining on her back with a look of discontent on her face. She leans forward slightly, and a fountain of debris is released from deep within her belly. Afterwards, she leans back, now with a relaxed, contented look. She is Mother Earth spitting up the pollution, the poison in society, and the wrongs done to this planet. The Native Americans and indigenous cultures around the world have generally been ransacked and left displaced. But they know how to live in harmony with nature. They know that their actions affect the next seven generations. Perhaps we can humble ourselves enough to learn from them.

This brings us back to the Native scraping tool I found at my uncle's farm when I was ten years old. I use dowsing to register the aura or energy field around it. An average person will register an aura at 10-20 feet. The flatter top and bottom edge of the scraping tool emits an aura 550 feet, the rear extends 450 feet. The sharpened side edges register 798 feet, and the spear point registers out a whopping 1600 feet. Dowsing informs me that it originated in Mississippi with one tribe, passed hands to another tribe, then was in Abenaki hands for 38 years. Each tribe blessed the stone in their own way. I can feel it emanating a healing power when I hold it.

Early one morning, I take the Native scraping tool and begin a ceremony. I am in bed in my underwear under the blankets. I firmly press the sharp point to trace a line starting on the inside of my right instep, up across my hip, along my shoulder, and down my right arm to my wrist. I pause at major points in my hip, shoulder, and wrist. Some sort of healing is starting to be activated by the Native scraping tool. I sense it would be better if I am lying flat on the earth.

There is dew on the grass and it's about forty degrees. The sun is starting to rise. I lie down, shivering, and retrace the lines over the same points. My mind focuses intently on the Native scraping tool and the connection it has with the ancient people that first carved it. The Guru and I are heading into uncharted spiritual territory. The Guru is keenly interested in revealing any knowledge from the Native scraping tools prior ancestral owners. My sense is that being of Abenaki descent provided the key to access this gateway.

I feel like the lines that I trace on my body with the stone have opened a portal door. I am in a dream state. I watch my Native lineage, tracing back through my Native ancestors, generation by generation. It's being stacked up in a pyramid of blue, glowing human silhouettes. Suddenly, it stops like a spinning slot machine. I am at a point in time when a primitive ancestor is massively upset. Tears begin to flow from my own eyes. I can feel our connection through my flesh and my spirit. My ancient ancestor is horrendously angry because some of our ancestors lost "The Gift." It's one of the most treasured gifts in the ancient culture: the ability to communicate with animals.

Then we begin to merge. I temporarily embody this ancient being. Next, I jump up and stand with my legs spread wide. I hold the rock with both hands over my head and yell out in his ancient language. It has not been spoken for dozens of generations. My voice echoes off the surrounding green mountains. In my vision, I see the energy from the Native scraping tool shoot upward in a blue, laser light beam that radiates up and circles the earth. I sense that we are attempting to communicate the ancient wisdom from his extinct culture to our modern generation.

In my underwear, I walk through the woods to a pond behind my home. I am still embodying the spirit of my ancient ancestor. I begin to speak in chatters and grunts, beckoning the wild animals to come closer. There is no response. I have never heard these noises coming from my lips before. I call out in hawk squawks, deer grunts, coyote yelps, fox barks, and rabbit squeaks. Sometimes, it's a high-pitched sound made by sucking my breath in. Animals like to gather near the pond. I realize that if the trust between animals and humans has dissolved, it will take days or weeks of living in the woods with the wild animals to reestablish our friendship.

I walk back down by my house. I go to a wire-mesh fenced in area where I am raising ten white turkeys. I've been struggling to find enough fresh green grass for the turkeys. I rip down the wire enclosure and let them all run free. In a high-pitched language, I tell them to stay away from the road and that there are foxes and coyotes around. I let them know they can go up to the pond for water if they want, but I will place food and water inside their shelter. I speak loudly into the woods and inform the coyotes and foxes that the turkeys are loose. They may take one or two, but we need to share and live in harmony. The turkeys stay near the barn and live much happier, healthier lives.

SPEAKING IN NATIVE TONGUES

After I experience the merging in spirit with this ancient Native ancestor, I gain the knowledge to speak different Native American languages. I examine a chart of all the Native American tribes in North America and identify fifty languages that I can speak. The Guru is most interested in this phenomenon. Even today, if I speak out to pray in what one might call "tongues," it comes out in a Native language. It is a gift. It's a hard one for most Christians to understand. I use these Native languages to pray or sing when guided. There is a feeling of gratitude in the air when I sing a song or pray in a language that has not been spoken for eons. Native American ancestors smile down when they hear a language that they cherished and once spoke being rekindled.

Do I know for certain that I am speaking fluent Native American languages and not a bunch of gibberish? No, but what is more important to me is that when I pray or sing in these languages, it's from my heart. I don't always feel comfortable singing them around strangers. When anyone speaks in a foreign language, they get some funny looks. On rare occasions, I command unwanted spirits to leave a body or request healing by utilizing the Native American languages and songs. I don't understand these mysteries well enough to explain it, but these Native languages are filled with power. Those who are the recipients of my prayers or songs feel positive shifts, in the form of healing.

The primal feeling that I experienced with that ancient

spirit can be felt by all people. It doesn't really matter if your ancestors are Native American or not. We all have the ability to connect with nature: the earth, the trees, the water, the stars, the animals, and ourselves. There is no clutter attached to this feeling. It will remain eternally pure and accessible for all people.

CHAPTER 6

Lessons on the Truth

My life has been intense since The Guru entered it. Changes continue to take place in my body, emotions, and mind. Sometimes, different spirits that I know are not The Guru communicate with me. On these occasions, I start to learn how to discern between different spirits.

For a spell, I begin having delusions in all five senses. It happens one by one. My hunch is that The Guru has control over my senses. He starts to alter my sense perception. One morning, the scrambled eggs at The Lamb's house have that pungent smell of rotten eggs and they taste like chalk. I spit them out and gather all the eggs cartons from the fridge and hide them in the woodshed. I look at a picture of my sister's family on the mantel. Half have red eyes. I am sure the devil is living in that half and the rest are angels. I begin to question all that I know, because I no longer know what is real. My senses are all screwy. Some of my friends and family are starting to think I have lost my mind.

The Lamb probably thought she would find some relief when I say, "I am going to tell you why I am being so weird."

I tell her with all sincerity, "Extraterrestrial beings have come to take over the earth. They have chosen me as an initial test dummy. I can feel where they inserted a computer chip in my skull. It gives them the power to control my actions." I can feel where the chips were inserted, so it must be real. When I talk to my mother in this way, she is filled with concern.

She begins to think, *Ahhhh, my poor son really has lost all his marbles.*

Perhaps, I am a puppet and The Guru is playing games by pulling strings to control my senses. If that is not the case, there is a chemical imbalance in my mind. Regardless, I learn from these experiences that I cannot always trust my own senses. It's contrary to what I normally accept as the truth. I am experiencing some exceptions to the rules. If I am battling some unknown spirit, I can't always believe what I see, smell, feel, taste, or touch. The delusions in my five senses bring my awareness to a new level. I need to operate from a deeper place where the truth resides.

LUSTY THOUGHTS

The Guru states he is not without flaws. Each person has issues. They either work through them in their past lives or they come up again. The Guru tactfully explains that he has a problem with lustful thoughts. He tells me, "Now it's our problem. You need to get it under control." Great! I have a lusty guru. Maybe this is The Guru's way of saying I need to face my own lusty thoughts. If somebody tells me not to think about sex, then it instantly causes a sexual image to pop into my head. Remember, I have had a circus of pornographic fantasies floating in front of my eyes since I was eight.

The Guru commands, "Stop thinking of sexual fantasies!" It makes me anxious and fills me with fear. I try to focus on something else and clear my mind. But then another sexual fantasy pops in. We try a few different strategies with no success.

The Guru says, "I am open to your suggestions."

My suggestion is sprinting down the road. Often hard physical exercise distracts my mind.

He says, "If you think a sexual thought, you will be struck dead, so you had better run fast."

The Guru has a sense of humor.

Luckily, it's not an instant death, but when I have lusty

thoughts, I feel my stomach acid gnawing at my insides. This gives more relevance to the notion that if I am not able to focus on something other than a sexual fantasy, The Guru could leave my body and then I really will drop dead. I decide that I better run fast...more fear...lustier thoughts...*don't do it again*...more anxiety...and more fear...and more sexual fantasies. Oh no! Pain in the stomach! *I will die soon...better run faster...am I scared? Yes! I am scared! I can't run any faster and I am out of breath!*

What I am attempting to do, without success, is repress my thoughts. Joe Zychik, in his book *The Most Personal Addiction: How I Overcame Sexual Addiction and How Anyone Can*, explains his revelation regarding repression,

> *"I knew I had discovered something so important, it could change my life and the lives of millions of addicted people. But getting that message out took another 25 years. So let me share with you what I have observed since 1975 about repression and how addiction is successfully overcome.*
>
> *"I define repression as: an attempt to consistently exclude from consciousness a thought or feeling you decide is threatening. If you conclude that a thought or feeling is not good for you, that it is bad, that it is a threat, your first reaction will be an attempt to consistently keep it out of your conscious mind. The attempt to continuously keep it out is repression. Repression occurs two ways: 1. You consciously try to drive the desire out of your mind, and/or 2. Your subconscious automatically keeps it out. The most common form of repression is subconscious.*
>
> *"The symptom of subconscious repression is: At the beginning of the attempt to stop, the desire seems to have gone away or lost most of its power. If you ever attempted to overcome addiction and failed, you*

probably went through a phase in which you truly felt like the addictive desire had left you or had lost most of its power. Although you sincerely believed you had triumphed over your addiction, what you were experiencing was subconscious repression.

"To protect itself from distortion, the mind sends out pain signals when it encounters repression. The pain of repression can be greater than the pain of acting addictively. To relieve the pain of repression, you return to the addiction.

"A client of Joe Zychik exclaims, 'You mean I don't have to push the thoughts out of my mind?' I told him, 'Your attempt to push them out makes it impossible for you to face them. The mind needs to experience its own emotions so that they can be coped with.' He dropped his Twelve Step meeting and his conventional, licensed therapist. I taught him how to experience an addictive desire fully and completely. Then I taught him how to choose whether or not to act on it. Every step of the way he told me, 'This is the exact opposite of everything I was told.'" (6)

THE TRUTH

One of Swami Sri Yukteswar's biggest lessons is to understand what is meant by "truth." It really has an impact. The truth has many faces and is relative to the circumstances. What I have been told or tell myself and believe for years does not make it true. In the past, I chose to live an illusion because I did not want to accept the truth about some aspects of myself. If I can let go of the security of my past mixed-up beliefs, I can dare to doubt everything. Now, I can start fresh. Slowly, I investigate each situation, question my own knowledge, discover from the facts, not preconceived notions. When I hit a wall, I rely on God's wisdom or "my heart" to discern the deeper mysteries. God wants me to know the truth.

When the truth is told, it resounds with divine purity.

One day, The Guru says, "You cannot accept anything I say as true." Just my luck. I get a lusty guru that lies…or maybe not. Now it's up to me to figure out what is true and what is not! After I think about it, I realize this teaching about the truth is an incredibly real gift.

> *"You are of your father the devil, and you want to do the desires of your father. He was a murderer from the beginning, and does not stand in the truth because there is no truth in him. Whenever he speaks a lie, he speaks from his own nature, for he is a liar and the father of lies."*
>
> (John 8:44 NASB)

The devil always uses lies to deceive. I cannot assume people are always telling me the truth. People lie all the time, but the worst offense is the lies we tell ourselves. The truth can be laced with lies. And if you know something is a lie, then the truth can be deduced from it. Actually, the truth may change over time. What is true for me may not be true for you. Why would I expect The Guru to be an exception?

MY PARENTS TELL LIES

During my teen years, The Lion made a promise that if I could go through high school without drinking alcohol, he would buy me a car. It was an incentive that worked. I took his promise seriously. After graduation, I passed by a black 1937 Pontiac with suicide doors parked at a garage in Plainfield, Vermont. On a cardboard sign in the window, it was marked $800. I told The Lion, "I have found the car I want." He said, "I don't believe you made it through high school without drinking."

In his way, he taught me that I should never trust anybody, not even my own parents, especially if it had to do with money. I put up a fuss. He couldn't prove I was drinking and reluctantly agreed to fork over half the money.

My brother, Gadget, is a natural mechanic, inventor, and collector. When he was nine years old, he made a cart with wooden wheels, a car steering wheel, a back bed for hauling, and a brake handle. Gadget got a worse deal; The Lion never offered him a car. He bought his first car and had a few Volkswagen Beetles that he was fixing up in the yard. The Lion said to him, "If you don't remove those pieces of crap out of the yard within one week, they will all be hauled to the junkyard."

When my sister, Priceless, graduated, there was no deal to be met. As a teenager, she had her own private phone line in her bedroom, and a pony. He surprised her by secretly purchasing her a gift: a 1977 240D Mercedes Benz. It was parked on the lawn, all washed and waxed, with a big pink ribbon on top.

It's up to me to figure out with The Lion and The Guru what is the truth in each situation. But I sense that when the Guru says, "You can't accept anything I say as true," that it comes from a place of caring about me. When The Lion makes a promise or says he wants to help me out as an adult regarding money, it can come from a place of taking care of himself first.

It's not always convenient for The Lion to honor his word. I notice that his story is sometimes altered or parts are left out depending upon the receiver. One of the quotes he repeats is, "What you perceive is what you believe." Sometimes, he persuades others to perceive what *he* wants them to believe. In this case, the truth is twisted, it somehow became insignificant to him.

Truth is defined in Merriam Webster dictionary as "sincerity in action, character, and utterance".

At the other extreme lives The Lamb. I know many sons believe that their mom is a saint, but after The Lamb sewed over two dozen quilts to donate to AIDS babies, I seriously wondered about her.

One day while driving along, I asked her, "Have you ever lied?"

She said, "Yes, I lied once."

I said, "As a teenager I lied to you many times. There must have been times you told me little lies?"

She replied, "No, I only lied once in my life."

I said, "Okay, tell me about it."

She was slightly embarrassed, but shared her story, "When I was a girl on the farm, your grandfather would often punish my older brother for little or no reason. He was searching for him with the belt and he asked me if I knew where my brother was. I knew where he was hiding, but I said, 'no'."

I said, "Mom, that does not even count as a lie."

There are times when a lie resounds with truth because it comes from a place of love. In her case, telling the truth would not have protected her brother. The Lamb lives in that place of love. Even when she told what she considered to be a lie, it resounded with the truth.

While in this spiritually-altered state, I am flying high. It's all one big adventure. I am living, at times in a delusional state, with moments of fear or ecstatic bliss. The Guru goes along for the ride and sometimes encourages me to go further into these wild illusions until they explode into nothingness. Once I understand the truth, it seems ridiculous. It's usually all in my mind. That's how I make progress. If The Guru were to point out my flaws, it would be less effective. Until the truth reveals itself, I am haunted by these dragon-size shadows on the wall that turn out to be tiny moths innocently flying around a candle flame. Fear is the reality that we are fed, create, or cling to when unable to discern the truth. Ignorance is a veil. The role of a guru is to guide the student to lift the veil for themselves.

The Holy Scriptures are meant to guide us toward that truth. The spiritual teachers who wrote them had a strong connection to God. They listened to His soft voice. It's natural when one understands the truth to want to share it with others. But Jesus took it beyond the bounds, when He said,

> "I am the way and the truth and the life. No one comes to the Father except through me."
>
> (John 14:6 NIV)

Jesus is in union with God. He did not just come to convey the truth. Jesus *is* the truth and the life. This is mind-boggling! These are qualities that we normally associate with God. Jesus is distinct from God. But He offers a way to get to God. That's probably worth checking out.

One day, The Guru says rather nonchalantly, "You are going to read 32 spiritual books. The Holy Bible will be the first one."

THE TRUTH IS IN YOUR HEART

The truth cannot be debated if it comes from that sacred place inside your heart. When we come to this conclusion on our own, it's more powerful and meaningful; plus we retain it. Let's wander off the track and do a short exercise to try it!

Sit comfortably, close your eyes, and enter the space in your heart. Just be there for five deep breaths. Really relax your legs and arms, shoulders, and jaw muscles. Breathe in love with a soft smile on your face. When you exhale, breathe out any tension. Now, bring to mind a person or animal that you love dearly. See their face and feel your love for them. Be with them for a few moments and enjoy it. Nice!

Now imagine that a spiritual teacher comes along and taps you on the shoulder.

She says, "You do *not* really love this person or animal."

Do you believe this spiritual teacher? Is there any doubt in your heart about your love? If you have any doubt, return to your heart to find the truth. Once you feel and know the truth from your heart, then speak your response back to this spiritual teacher out loud. Explain to the spiritual teacher how you know the truth about your love for this person or animal. Can you feel how powerful it is to own an undisputable truth from your heart? ■

CHAPTER 7

Clan of the Hawk

I am at a convenience store reading a historical paper about an Abenaki exhibit in Newport, Vermont. This article, like other occurrences, seems planted, waiting for me to come along during this preordained moment. I call and make arrangements with Bea Nelson to have her examine my Native scraping tool, and to visit the Abenaki exhibit.

I am wearing black sport pants cut off jagged under the knee when I removed the zippers, leather moccasins, and a Mexican wool blanket. It's fashioned into a poncho with a huge Aztec head on the center of the back. I carry a rabbit-fur pouch with the Native scraping tool in it. I am later told that during this altered state, I have pinpoint black pupils that indent my eyes further into my high cheek bones. I walk with confidence and often stare off with a profound look when I converse with my guru.

The Lamb has an interest in our family genealogy. She joins me during my visit to Bea Nelson, who enthusiastically shows us the local Abenaki arrowheads and tools found along the shores of Lake Memphremagog. I have a sense of urgency and ask her targeted questions about the local artifacts. I say, "There is nothing remotely similar to my Native scraping tool."

We go to a table displaying a map. Bea says, "Show me on the map where your Native artifact was found. If you want, it can be established as a sacred Native American site."

She mentions the local Abenaki tribe called Clan of the Hawk and suggests that I go meet Chief Spirit Water. Her proposal sets off an alarm. We must go visit him... today! Time becomes tediously slow as Bea continues to ask questions and search the map. I become impatient and insist that we must leave. I rudely clap my hands loudly. I say, "I must leave now." Bea is taken aback by the loud clapping. I apologize and we depart to visit Chief Spirit Water.

SHAKING UP CHIEF SPIRIT WATER

We arrive at Evansville Trading Post, which Chief Spirit Water owns and operates. It's a central gathering point in town for groceries, gifts, hunting and fishing supplies, and everything you could imagine to sustain a Vermont village during the harsh winters. I ask my mother to wait as I inquire inside for the whereabouts of Chief Spirit Water. I am told he will return in one hour, so I walk down the road across a bridge and sit beside the road to meditate and gather my thoughts. A neighbor drives into his yard in an old pickup truck, eyeballing me. A huge maple tree has recently been struck by lightning and has fallen on his lawn. The sound of chimes ring out gently in the flow of the wind. The man walks gingerly by the stacks of canning jars on his front porch.

I call out, "That tree being hit is a sign that change will come."

He says, "Something is in the air."

I sit on a rock in the sun and speak with my guru, reciting the facts that I will relay. Chief Spirit Water returns. I meet him in the gravel parking lot.

I introduce myself by saying, "I am a yogic monk from the Kriya order with a message of great importance."

Chief Spirit Water is a grandfather of sorts, gentle and calm. He has white hair down around his shoulders, covering the back of his head. His round eyes sparkle and smile in the corners. He tells me that he is on a tight schedule today.

I explain, "We need you to be the father of a new nation for a new order."

I am not getting through to him. I explain the situation in Abenaki. He attempts to walk away.

He says, "I want no part as a father of a new nation."

I grab him by the shoulders to force him to stop so he will listen. He brushes me off, slightly shaken and visibly upset as he continues to walk away. I know grabbing him was rude, probably an insult, especially when he is the chief. After the incident, I feel sorry that I used force to get his attention.

CEREMONIAL GATHERING GROUND

The Lamb and I stop at the Clan of the Hawk's ceremonial gathering ground as part of our Native heritage exploration. The grounds are peaceful and surrounded by tall pine trees. We walk around in the sunny, golden fields of grass. I am in a dreamy state, viewing my surroundings as if the village were in a glass snow globe. There is a Christian church with a small steeple, which strikes me initially as being out of place on these Native grounds. Inside there are wooden benches. On the wall there is a poster showing the territories where all the Native American tribes lived in North America. There are books on the table explaining tracking and wilderness survival skills. This must be the place where the younger ones gather to learn from Chief Spirit Water and the other elders.

Next to the church there is a small, barn-board building; a hand-painted sign proclaims it to be the Native American Museum. There is no lock on the door. I enter to find rows of glass cases filled with bones and arrowheads. There are dozens of stuffed animals and birds, and furs limply hanging off the benches, from the ceiling, and in any open space remaining. The museum feels like it's cage-cleaning day at the zoo and all the animals are squeezed into one tiny room and forgotten.

Beside the museum is a small rustic cabin, with an old wooden chair shedding red paint resting alone on the porch.

The door is wide open, revealing a small wood stove with a scorched cooking pot perched on top. Behind the two buildings weaves a wide stream surrounded and filled with boulders of assorted sizes and colors. I notice gray clay seeping down from the far side of the stream bank into the water. Willoughby Brook flows through these sacred grounds, like a gigantic, glittering snake that slides back and forth from the deeper cold waters of Lake Willoughby. The whole place makes me feel like I am being welcomed back home after a long journey. I feel the warmth, like slipping my hands back into woolen mittens on a frigid winter day.

In the center of the horseshoe of buildings, there is a fire pit encircled by a wooden fence. A few car seats and wooden benches are scattered randomly around the outside of the fence, facing toward the circle. There is a small tin roof over one area, which must be where a small group gathers to play drums and chant Native songs. I imagine a few men from the Clan of the Hawk tribe, decked out in their traditional leather with fringes and feathers, dancing around the fire during their powwow. But times have changed; maybe nowadays most of the men wear blue jeans and t-shirts.

There is a labyrinth made out of pointed stones in a far field with tall, uncut grass clumps poking up close to the rocks. I walk over to the labyrinth with The Lamb. I brought a small drum and begin to play a steady beat as The Lamb enters the maze. I strike the drum to the beat of her slow, mindful steps. I sing a song in Abenaki. It is a beautiful language. I sing about the connection between Mother Earth and the sun. The Lamb usually has a natural smile on her face, but I notice her smile expresses additional pleasure because today she is embracing her heritage. When she reaches the center, I stop playing the drum and send her loving thoughts.

STONE TREE, MAKER OF THE MEDICINE WHEELS

A tall man in denim overall jeans walks toward us. He has

long, stringy hair and a week-old scruff that has not yet grown in enough to hide his rock-solid chin, jaw, and cheekbones. His facial structure, by no coincidence, resembles the rocks in the labyrinth. He is Stone Tree, maker of medicine wheels and divine dowser of the rock nation. He introduces himself and escorts us over to the other side of the field to show us two medicine wheels that he has formed. These are fairly small medicine wheels, each eight feet in diameter. He explains that some rocks are buried under the ground. Then a pattern of rocks is overlaid, and the pointed rocks sticking up around the outside are set in place last.

He says, "It creatz good medicine."

I tell him briefly of the vision of the new order. He stops to roll a cigarette and starts to rock back and forth. He gives a confirming nod of agreement about what is to come. I learn that Stone Tree communicates with each rock to receive specific instructions through body dowsing before finding its new home. Many rocks came from the river over a mile away. He will stop his old beat-up pickup truck whenever a rock calls out, regardless of its size. Then he will find a way to pry, push, carry, or pull each rock onto his rusty truck bed in order to bring it back to his gathering spot under the pine trees.

Stone Tree walks us by Willoughby Brook and talks about the spirits he has seen rushing by.

With a slow drawl in his voice and wide eyes, he says, "Some of themz spiritz are the size of buffalos, with wings."

He insists that I meet the Clan Mother. We walk toward the pine trees. When I get my first glimpse of his Smithsonian-size collection of rocks stacked along the road edge and under the pine trees, I am flabbergasted. There are hundreds and hundreds of rocks. They are everywhere. One black, prickly stone is the shape of a whale fin; another looks like the mouth of an alligator; and a row of long, black stalactites sits on a mound of pine needles. A crystal temple sits on a clump of moss. I am told that fairies frolic around this stone.

He has also seen them gathering the crystal dust to spread about the forest.

The rocks are eerie projections of Native spirit animals. Each called out to him through its prehistoric fossilized stone shield. Every rock holds a tale, and Stone Tree is the curator of this mammoth-size exhibit. It becomes clear that Stone Tree is capable of telling his rock tales as long as somebody is willing to stay and listen. There is no official closing hour. Besides, some stones, such as the panoptic panther and the planetary asteroids, are more active during the night.

CLAN MOTHER, LARGER THAN LIFE

The outer walls of Clan Mother and Stone Tree's home are made from blue tarps laced together with yellow rope. It extends out and is tied around several living pine trees. Clan Mother swings open a blue tarp that forms the door of their home. She has the exuberance of the opening act on stage at the county fair. She is 300 pounds and larger than life, with uncombed, jet-black hair and tobacco-stained teeth. She has tree-trunk-size legs that she quickly explains are radiating with pain.

The sun strikes Clan Mother's clear eyes. The Guru, Swami Sri Yukteswar, instantly recognizes Clan Mother. She is his favorite revered disciple: Paramahansa Yogananda. Our gaze becomes that of two long-lost lovers being reunited. I sit cross-legged on the ground and she in a chair. We face each other. I hold her hands. Tears of joy stream from her eyes.

Clan Mother chokes back the tears to say, "I knew you were coming to visit me. I have been waiting for you. I saw it in my dreams."

We speak for a few minutes and then settle side-by-side into a silent, meditative, heavenly state. When at last I arise to depart, Stone Tree hands me a gift. It's a large bowling-ball-size, white rock. It captures the shape and grandness of Clan Mother.

I depart, saying, "I will be back tomorrow."

MAKING THE MEDICINE WHEEL

I return the next day by myself. Stone Tree and I search to find a location to make a new medicine wheel. Its purpose will be to connect the ancient indigenous ways with the modern-day generation. Once in the woods, Stone Tree shows me a spot where he has marked out a thirty-foot medicine wheel using yellow corn kernels. The lines make a pentagram star. The corn pieces intersect and cross each other, forming various-sized triangles. We agree this will be the perfect location for our new medicine wheel.

We draw a circle in the center the size of a manhole and extend the five-arms of the star around it. Then four lines extend out from the end of each of the five star points. We move slowly and remain completely silent. He painstakingly dowses each location and locates the right stone from his collection. It is placed on the ground to mark its ordained destination. Each stone is partially buried according to his precise calibrations. He is like an architect following the blueprint for laying the foundation of a skyscraper.

I see through my spiritual eye a snake, as thick as a fifty-five-gallon drum and as long as a New York City block, slithering toward us. Covering its body are red, black, and yellow interwoven triangles. During my time spent in the outback of Australia, I was told the dreamtime stories about this snake.

The Rainbow Serpent Story

"Far off in Dreamtime, there were only people, no animals or birds, no trees or bushes, no hills or mountains.

"The country was flat. Goorialla, the great Rainbow Serpent, stirred and set off to look for his own tribe. He travelled across Australia from South to North. He reached Cape York where he stopped and

made a big red mountain called Naralullgan. He listened to the wind and heard only voices speaking strange languages.

"This is not my country, the people here speak a different tongue. I must look for my own people. Goorialla left Naralullgan and his huge body made a deep gorge where he came down. He travelled North for many days and his tracks made the creeks and rivers as he journeyed North. Goorialla made two more mountains, one of the Naradunga was long made of granite, the other had sharp peaks and five caves and was called, Minalinha. One day Goorialla heard singing and said, "Those are my people, they are holding a big Bora." At the meeting place of the two rivers, Goorialla found his own people singing and dancing. He watched for a long time, then he came out and was welcomed by his people. He showed the men how to dress properly and taught them to dance. A big storm was gathering, so all the people built humpies for shelter.

"Two young men, the bil-bil or Rainbow Lorikeet brothers came looking for shelter but no one had any room. They asked their grandmother, the Star Woman but she had too many dogs and couldn't help them. the Bil-bil brothers went to Goorialla who was snoring in his humpy but he had no room. The rain got heavier and the boys went back to Goorialla and called out that the rain was heavy. Goorialla said, "All right come in now." The Bil-bil bothers ran into Goorialla's mouth and he swallowed them. Then he began to worry about what the people would say when they found the boys missing. He decided to travel North to Bora-bunaru, the only great natural mountain in the land. Next morning the people found that the boys were gone and saw the tracks of Goorialla and knew that he had swallowed them.

"You may never see these lakes or mountains, but

after the rain you will see his spirit in the sky, which is the rainbow. This is the reason why he is called Goori-alla the Rainbow Serpent." (7)

The pictures they drew and carved resembled the design on the snake that is slithering around our medicine wheel. I don't feel threatened, but I would not be surprised if this dreamtime snake gobbled down another man. The snake winds its way up to the medicine wheel and silently slides down the center hole, going down, down, down toward the core of the earth.

THE NATIVE SCRAPING TOOL CEREMONY WITH CLAN MOTHER

Clan Mother invites me inside her earthen home. Behind the blue-tarp walls, there are two bedrooms. Hanging from the walls are furs and woven baskets. The floor of their upper level is dirt. I am led down steps to another level, which is dug into the earth. It all resembles an archeological dig site. On the lower level, there is a wood-burning stove with a few chairs around it. She pours herself some coffee and makes me a cup of tea. We sit down near the wood stove. I give her a copy of *The Autobiography of a Yogi*. I explain, "Reading this book may explain more about the supernatural connection we both feel."

The Guru and disciple both feel an incredibly strong bond of devotion, trust, and respect, far beyond what is normally felt between a father and son or a wife and husband.

I suggest that perhaps Clan Mother can experience some form of healing with the Native scraping tool. She is in favor of anything that could ease the pain in her legs. Her prophetic dream about my arrival adds a certain level of anticipation. We choose a location near a small sweat lodge site by the edge of Willoughby Brook. I carry over a thin futon for her to lie upon. Prior to starting our ceremony, she swallows a good-sized portion of spirulina powder mixed with juice. She happened to have some in her earth home.

The brook is immensely peaceful. I explain how I traced the Native scraping tool up the sides of my body. We take a knife and slit her sweatpants so the rock can trace a line up her legs. I begin chanting in an ancient tongue. In this Native language, I ask Mother Earth to come down and bless our ceremony. I sense that Clan Mother needs to touch the earth; she agrees. I pull her off the futon to rest on the nurturing soil of the earth. I use the point of the healing stone to trace the lines, starting on the inside of her right instep, up across her hip, along her shoulder, and down her right arm to her wrist. I continue to chant by her side for the next ten minutes.

I wonder what she is experiencing.

She is silent and staring wide-eyed up into the sky like she is caught up in a trance. I am waiting for an ancient relative from another generation to pour into her soul.

I ask in a calm voice, "What is happening, Clan Mother?"

Her eyes open as wide as quarters and she replies loudly, "The leaves and the trees above me are moving and alive!"

She raises her arms up toward the sky and vigorously wiggles her fingers. This is not quite what I expected! Of course, her experience is valid, just different from mine. Later on, she mentions that her legs feel slightly better. She is grateful for the ceremony.

LITTLE FOX AND MOON SHADOW

I go over by the church and sit to meditate. I sense that Chief Spirit Water will arrive soon. I want to apologize for shaking him. A dog comes running up to me with the skull of a fox in its mouth. I think it peculiar, but it's the beginning of my learning how the Native spirit can speak through animals or their bones. The skull is an introduction to the arrival of Little Fox.

Little Fox has white hair in a ponytail sticking out from under his rimmed cap and wears mirror shades. His clean-shaven jaw stands out. His female companion, Moon Shadow, is thin, with a dark complexion. She wears a large sun hat.

They arrive on foot and both are casually dressed in jeans. My first thought is that they wear these clothes to allow themselves to fit into a crowd unnoticed. Perhaps they are a cosmic couple from another spiritual realm, visiting in disguise. Chief Spirit Water's pickup truck comes rumbling down the dirt road. He has come to join us.

I introduce myself to the group as a yogic monk from the Kriya order. I keep composure and utmost respect. I apologize for grabbing Chief Spirit Water. After a few minutes of conversation, Chief Spirit Water gets back in his pickup truck and heads back to the Trading Post.

Little Fox asks The Guru, "Who is your guru?"

I say, "It's Lahiri Mahasaya."

Little Fox pours out his heart to explain how one should react if given a message from the Spirit. He says, "You hint and let facts unfold through others and yourself. It's not the way to go around forcing things to happen. Grabbing the chief was wrong, and it's better to let things take their natural course." He continues to explain, "There are many spirits in all of us."

He begins to talk in a Native American language. To stress his point, he takes off his mirror glasses and stares me straight in the eyes. I stare back and realize that he is Lahiri Mahasaya, the guru of my guru. I immediately give a deep-kneeling bow in the dirt. He keeps on talking, even though I am bowing at his feet, like it's nothing unusual. The features, the look, the eyes, the wisdom, the walk, all seem familiar.

Lahiri Mahasaya had some remarkable metaphysical powers. In the book, *The Autobiography of a Yogi*, Paramahansa Yogananda wrote the story told to him by Kali Kumar Roy:

> "It appears that the master had an aversion to being photographed. Over his protest, a group picture was once taken of him and a cluster of devotees, including Kali Kumar Roy. It was an amazed photographer who discovered that the plate which had clear

images of all the disciples, revealed nothing more than a blank space in the center where he had reasonably expected to find the outlines of Lahiri Mahasaya. The phenomenon was widely discussed.

"A certain student and expert photographer, Ganga Dhar Babu, boasted that the fugitive figure would not escape him. The next morning, as the guru sat in lotus posture on a wooden bench with a screen behind him, Ganga Dhar Babu arrived with his equipment. Taking every precaution for success, he greedily exposed twelve plates. On each one he soon found the imprint of the wooden bench and screen, but once again the master's form was missing.

"With tears and shattered pride, Ganga Dhar Babu sought out his guru. It was many hours before Lahiri Mahasaya broke his silence with a pregnant comment:

'I am Spirit. Can your camera reflect the omnipresent Invisible?'

'I see it cannot! But, Holy Sir, I lovingly desire a picture of the bodily temple where alone, to my narrow vision, that Spirit appears fully to dwell.'

'Come, then, tomorrow morning. I will pose for you.'

"Again the photographer focused his camera. This time the sacred figure, not cloaked with mysterious imperceptibility, was sharp on the plate." [8]

After they walk away, I sit and meditate. For The Guru and me to find his favorite disciple, Paramahansa Yogananda, and now his past guru, Lahiri Mahasaya, is a bit uncanny. If the yogis in the Kriya lineage have superhuman powers, like entering my body and not appearing on film, perhaps they can also send dreams, words, or thoughts to another person's mind. I pause to consider it all. I believe through God and the grace of The Guru, anything is possible. ■

CHAPTER 8

The Call of the Rhondu

I drive back to my home. I have a talk with my guru about the evil that surrounds us.

I ask, "Is one person or place more evil than another?"

I let my imagination roam and figure certain roads to my house are safer than others. Some roads suddenly become evil and should be avoided. I recently met a neighbor, who is a well-known international dowser, and he told me he was going to the dragon gathering weekend. I don't know what happens at a dragon gathering, but I surmise that he and his dragon followers are evil. Now, he is clearing ground to build a structure up the road from my home. I decide I better avoid him. But he knows I am here. My guru is getting concerned — very concerned.

I say to The Guru, "We must keep an eye out because if evil forces know I am in this stumbling new form, then I can easily be eliminated. I am like a fawn lost in the woods."

I peer out my window into the darkness. It's 2:30 am. That is when I hear the most blood-curdling wild call of evil I have ever heard. It's coming from down in the woods across from the road in front of my property. I visualize a shaggy, dark, moose-shaped figure with razor-sharp teeth. I name it the Rhondu. It no doubt has the intention to smell me out, grab me, and devour me. Fear starts racing through every cell in my body. My heart is pumping fast. I decide it's time to get away fast. I run toward the door and grab the Native scraping tool on the way. I jump in my old Ford Taurus. It feels risky to drive down my driveway past where I heard the deathly call of the Rhondu. I take the corner out of my driveway and punch the gas pedal to the floor. I hit speeds of 60 mph on the dirt road. Dust is flying up when I skid around the corners. The Guru leaves my body and floats above to check on the status.

He says, "The chase is on!"

I feel my life is at stake. It's exhilarating! I know if the Rhondu or any evil spirits catch me, it's all over. I imagine they will hit me with a blunt force that will splatter my body like a fly on a wall. I am giving it my best damned effort to elude them.

The Guru asks, "Do you know any friends along the way where we can stop and hide?"

I reply, "It's too late. They are not nearby."

We pull on to I-91 north and floor it. The Guru periodically leaves to check the status from above. At those times, I am alone in my body. If I yell he comes back, but it takes a moment. I realize I miss him when he is gone.

Just for fun, I yell out his name, "Guru, where are you!"

He replies, "What is it?"

I say, "Oh nothing."

He says, "Stop playing games; we are being chased by evil spirits."

The Clan of the Hawk is my chosen destination for safety. A few miles before the exit, I feel the spirits are fast closing in.

My guru calmly says, "This will be the end. There is no way you can escape now."

I am preparing for the blow of an evil spirit. Suddenly, a thought surfaces about the Native scraping tool. If I throw it out the window, it may distract the evil spirits, or maybe it's what they are after. I wait for a mile marker so I can return to find it. Then I toss it out the window.

The Guru exclaims excitedly, "They are looking at it!"

I start off the Orleans exit going fifty mph and lose control of the car. I spin around and skid off backwards, sliding on the grass. No real damage is sustained, but the car is definitely not moving.

The Guru yells, "You better get your ass out and run!"

I run a mile toward downtown Orleans village. There is pain in my shins and no air left to breathe. I am sweating profusely. I have a flashback to the time we ran sprints to remove lustful thoughts. But this feels more like a marathon. When you think your life is about to end, you push past the pain. Once, I feel a bad spirit thrust near. It's a miracle I am still alive.

I run past a convenience store. It's 3:30 am. I am eight miles away from Clan of the Hawk. I decide to knock on a neighbor's home and ask for a ride. After a few minutes, a man, half asleep, opens the door in his underwear.

I explain, "My car has been wrecked. I need to be part of a ceremony that starts at 5:30 am at the Clan of the Hawk. It's extremely important that I get there. Can you bring me?"

Half asleep he responds, "Ahhhh ohhhh yeahhh, sure."

I wait in his shed. He gets dressed.

The Guru tells me, "You are safe."

It's working out. We make small talk on the way. I am never as happy as when we drive through the gate into the Clan of the Hawk.

OPENING THE MEDICINE WHEEL PORTALS

I immediately go to Stone Tree at his earth-chamber home. While he is getting up, I bathe in the brook. The bright orange sun starts to rise. I pause to meditate, and sense that the giant, dreamtime snake is nearby. I gingerly commence looking around for it. Sitting on a stump in front of the new medicine wheel, I begin to drum and chant. Then a notion comes over me. I must get up high above the medicine wheel to activate it. I start to climb up a sixty-foot pine tree, until I am very near to the top. I can look over and see the church steeple. There is only another eight feet of tree above me. While swaying in the wind, The Guru questions my sanity. I am getting annoyed with him, mostly due to my lack of sleep.

I start to yell out and then chant in an ancient language for ten minutes. The medicine wheel activates. It spreads a message through a beam of bright blue light. I sense that medicine wheels are portals that were used to communicate between former tribes. The message I deliver from the ancient people explains how we can all live in harmony with the animals, the trees, the plants, and the sea creatures and treat this earth as a sacred home. We all need to share this planet.

My message explains how we can live simply and be sustainable. It means growing our own food and using what the natural environment provides for power sources, utilizing the sun, water, and wind. It calls for making relationships our primary focus and being an active participant in community. Last of all, we need to live from the heart and let love guide our actions.

As I come down from the treetop, The Guru is moaning about how dangerous that was. If I had fallen from that height, it probably would have killed me. I ignore his nagging.

I ask Stone Tree, "Did you feel the activation of the medicine wheel and the transmitting of a message?"

He closes his eyes for a moment.

He says, "Somethin' happen, thingz are feelin' different."

LIZZY AND THE BIRTHDAY PARTY

Leaving Clan of the Hawk, I flag down a car on the road. I offer them $60 to drive me back to my hometown. This leaves me short of cash, but I still go to buy some organic veggies and a few more bottles of spirulina at the health food store. It turns into a small fiasco because I don't have enough to pay for it, so I call The Lamb. She comes and writes out a check. Then she drives me back to my home.

During the afternoon, there is a big birthday party for my neighbor Lizzy's two-year-old daughter in my yard. She sent me a cute homemade invitation, but I forgot it was happening today. Lizzy lives in my lower duplex apartment and started following the Grateful Dead when she was twelve. We have become friends. She is street smart, but not always truthful. She's very likable and an expert at finagling people to get what she wants.

Lizzy is in a recovery program for heroin addicts. She is being paid a weekly stipend and must get a drug test regularly. At first, I was surprised to find out that the program pays her even if she drinks alcohol, smoke cigarettes, or does what are considered lesser drugs, like marijuana. I come to realize that heroin is a deadly drug. The first step is to get free from it. Nothing else really matters if you can't do that. She and a group of her teenage friends all got hooked. It started when a drug dealer came into the small town of Hardwick and offered them some milder drugs before stepping them up to something they thought would be even better. Now, she counts off her friends who have died from an overdose.

I can see that Lizzy genuinely wants to improve her life. She is struggling to gain back the custody of her daughter. I admire that. I want to support her recovery. Plus, she is rather smooth and cool in her own way. The real challenge has been when her old heroin-addicted party friends stop by. They can show up at any hour, but it's usually in the middle of the night. Most heroin addicts will do or say whatever it takes to get their next fix.

Regardless, Lizzy has made a big deal about promising her daughter a pony to ride on her birthday. She hires a local guy, who delivers a pony in a truck. Her daughter and the other young kids ride it around the yard. They are having a blast with the pony.

I am shocked to find out that Lizzy is now attending a local Christian church. I guess it's her way of finding new friends and living a cleaner lifestyle. Today, she has invited her whole new church family to be a part of her daughter's birthday celebration. I am hanging out with Lizzy and her church friends on the lawn, eating a burger from the grill. I know a few of her church friends, but frankly I don't have a clue what it means to live as a Christian.

I want to liven up the party, so I point two 200-watt speakers from my house towards the party and blast my stereo. I play a few songs like "Light My Fire" and "Riders on the Storm" by Jim Morrison and the Doors. My choice of music is not well received.

To my surprise, Lizzy is attending a Christian church established by Mr. R.I.P. He was a monumental figure in my life as my martial arts instructor. It's hard to fathom him as a pastor. Meeting a few Christians is one thing, but when somebody I greatly respect like Mr. R.I.P. decides to follow Jesus, it makes me wonder, "Why did he turn to Jesus?"

I am told by a friend from my martial arts class who is at the party, that he was suicidal and had been hospitalized at a facility in Pennsylvania. They shared what sounded like a rumor about his having an affair with one of his younger female martial arts students. I don't want to spread a rumor or speculate in my book, but this is rather juicy stuff.

TESTIMONY FROM PASTOR R.I.P.

I really want to know what radical change led Mr. R.I.P, martial arts instructor, to become Pastor R.I.P.? I asked Pastor R.I.P. to write about what happened. I want it to be in his own words to set the record straight. It's in his heart (and mine) to share it with you:

"I Will Restore..."

"How did I ever get here?" That is exactly the question I had to ask myself when I spent 17 days in a hospital in the hills just north of Pittsburgh, Pennsylvania. I was there locked in a ward with over 20 other people who were there for life controlling issues. For some it was addiction to things such as drugs, alcohol, pornography, or work; for others like myself, the issues were of a different sort. They had to do with the sense of hopelessness, depression, and dealing with wanting to end it all with no other options in sight.

Here I was at 33 years old in a New Life Clinic being treated for near suicidal depression; but why? I was at the top of my game, at least in some people's eyes. I had a successful career in sales, I was married to a brilliant, hardworking, and beautiful woman, and I was the instructor of a successful martial arts school with over 100 students. I seemed to be so alive and motivated, yet inside my heart and soul I was suffering from a terminal condition that resulted from years of struggling with abandonment issues, sexual immorality, and alcohol and drug usage, fueled by a passion for winning and success.

After over a decade of teaching taekwondo, becoming a national-level competitor and coach and international level referee, I had built my own empire and was what most people would call a self-made man. As I continued to train young athletes and help them become national champions, taekwondo became my life's passion, and I began to spend more and more time at the gym and less time tending with my own wife and her son.

When I was 32 years old, I really lost my moral bearings and began to have an eye for one of my younger students, who was a national champion and had dreams of being in the Olympics. I began to personally train her and cultivate our relationship, which I wanted to see evolve into something other than an instructor and student one. After pursuing this young woman, she eventually rejected my affections and stopped coming to train. When she did, she told her parents and my wife, and reality hit the fan.

For several months, the shame and guilt of what I had allowed myself to become began to follow me around like a very dark cloud. The cloud became thicker and blacker, and I began to drink more heavily and found myself wanting to smoke more and more dope, to numb the pain. The emotional erosion took its toll. I had messed up my own life and that of others so badly. As a result, I spent several months preparing to take my own life. I had written farewell letters to my wife, my parents, and others, and was making definite plans to exit my miserable life. Things spiraled downward so fast and hard that my wife arranged an intervention with one of my best friends, who was able to remove me peacefully from our home.

After spending a few days with him and his wife, my wife arranged a one-way trip to Pennsylvania for me to get some counseling. When I checked myself into that hospital and began to undergo the barrage of questions and tests, it all seemed like a foggy, bad dream. I was asked to write at least three pages of an autobiography of my life as part of the intake procedure. As I did, I found myself recognizing the reality of my abandonment issues, the insecurity of being a fatherless child, grown into adulthood. The years of looking for love in all the wrong places, and the substance abuse all seemed to hit home. There I was, locked up and away from my friends and family, with a bunch of people who were as out of control as I was.

In the days that followed, I found myself surrounded by Christian people who were able to look beyond my sin and dysfunctionality and extend the love of Christ in ways I had never experienced. There were daily Bible studies and quiet times, role playing encounters, and one-on-one counseling. The interaction with loving, mature believers began to penetrate my martial arts and self-made man armor plating. The program used a Christian twelve-step program that involved surrendering your life to Jesus Christ… which sounded okay, but I had no idea what that meant; I was about to learn!

One day I met with my case worker, who said I needed to talk to the chaplain, a pastor who was on duty. That day the Spirit of God tore the scales off my eyes and the light of the gospel came blazing into my heart and life. Pastor James led me in a simple sinner's prayer, and I threw myself at the foot of the cross where the love, grace, and mercy of God overtook my life.

For the first time in my life, on that special day, May 13, 1993, I heard the voice of God. "It's going to be alright," was all I can remember, and at that lowest point of my life, that was all I needed to hear. Little did I know that my precious wife had also been born again some three months earlier and had been praying for me. That is how this process began, and now I have been ministering for seventeen years.

I am reminded of a couple of key scripture verses that have impacted my life. The first is found in Joel 2: 25-27, which begins with these words; "So I will restore the years…" Yes, we can stand and testify that our God is indeed a restoring God. He has restored our marriage, our relationship, our family, our love for one another, our minds, and our lives.

CHAPTER 9

An Exercise in Exorcisms

I leave the Birthday party and go to visit my friend, Cleopatra. I am exhausted after my wild ride in the middle of the night and from sharing my body with a guru for the last five days. It's pretty obvious to her by my new clothes, bizarre actions, and the way I introduce myself as a yogic monk, that I am not the same old guy. Cleopatra is concerned and frightened, and does not know what to do. She rushes to find Helen Keller.

HELEN KELLER TO THE RESCUE

There are other people who are concerned, but only one person is able to grasp the situation and take action. This is my friend, Helen Keller. She is a tall redhead with thick bones and green eyes, somewhat resembling a Celtic witch. She has the ability to retain plant knowledge, which probably comes in handy when she brews up herbal potions in her pot.

I call her Helen Keller because she can be overwhelmed by stimulation though her sight and hearing. She compensates with a powerful sense of touch and feeling. She feels her way through life, trusting her intuition in both the physical world and in the spiritual realm. She has an eccentric connection with animals. Her method of coping with any situation is divergent from the norm. She finds out the facts and assesses the situation. She will turn to others when she does not know the answers. She is more concerned about the quality of the outcome than how long it takes to get it done. She is persistent in finding a solution to fit the circumstance in front of her. She is a woodworker who specializes in repairing antique furniture. In her trade, she faces unique problems and must figure out the logical steps to restore wood back to its original weathered and aged appearance.

Helen is eating in the church with her boyfriend, Moon Dog. They are at an appreciation lunch for those who had booths during a craft fair at the local Fairbank's Museum. She had an exhibit showing how to cane antique chairs. Cleopatra bustles up to their table. She says, "You need to come quick. Something has happened to Randy." She looks unusually concerned. They both leave the remainder of their meal to follow her outside. She fills them in with what little she knows.

I meet up with Helen Keller on Main Street. She can tell right away that something strange has happened to me. I walk more upright and rigid. I tell her, "There is a guru in my body. I want to tell you about it."

Helen can sense something foreign in my energy field. It's the presence of what I call "The Guru." She says, "I need to go pick up my stuff at the museum. Can you stop by my house later?"

"Sure, I can stop by in about an hour," I reply

While I am walking through a parking lot in town closer to Helen's home, I pass by my acupuncturist, Frenzy.

She takes a glance in my eyes and says, "You have an entity living in you. This is serious. We need to get it out!"

She schedules an acupuncture appointment on the spot for later that afternoon.

I sit down with Helen Keller at her home. We have a cup of tea. I describe what has happened during the last five days. She notes that my pupils are pinpoints and my behavior is anything but normal.

She says, "Spirits can raise havoc!"

After she starts to get a better sense of what is happening, she insists that I take some precautionary measures.

She says, "I don't want you to stay alone in your home. You need to be under the surveillance of a family member at all times."

Helen's next step is to call upon a dowser experienced with spiritual interventions to perform an exorcism. The guy she calls is named John Wayne. She surmises that the spirit entered into me through dowsing, so it can depart in the same manner.

I am sitting at Helen's house on the porch while she is on the phone

The Guru asks, "Do you want me out of your body?"

I realize I am tired, but the truth and wisdom that has been revealed to me in the last five days is earth-shattering.

I ask Helen, "Would you like to have The Guru in your body?"

She replies, "No way!"

At times I feel overwhelmed, but I don't want this grand adventure to end.

After taking some time to decide, I tell The Guru, "No, I want you to stay in my body."

Cleopatra's son stops by. He is learning Japanese. I am in the shower when he passes on his way down the stairs to leave. To his surprise, I yell out, "Sayonara," which means goodbye in Japanese.

Meanwhile, I have forgotten all about my appointment with Frenzy. I speak to her on the phone that evening. She is outraged, but I apologize and reschedule another appointment with her for the next day. I say, "I will be there this time."

NO BIG DEAL

In my quest to find out more about what it really means to have a guru in my body, I visit a local yoga teacher to discuss the situation. I want to get his opinion. He has an upstairs office next to his studio. I say to him, "A guru has entered my body. I have some questions. I thought you could help."

He says, "I cannot speak to you right now. It's time for my personal yoga practice. I will be done in an hour."

I hang outside in the lobby. He goes in a side room and shuts the door. Clearly, he does not want to be disturbed. There is a poster on the wall showing 100 different yoga poses. Some of these postures are highly advanced. While waiting, I do the most advanced poses, many of them for the first time in my life. When he returns, we speak for a few minutes. He concludes by saying, "Come back to one of my regular scheduled hatha classes." It seems a guru living in my body is no big deal to him.

I return home to grab some clothes and get my cat; I plan to leave her with Helen. Oh damn, I completely forget about appointment number two with Frenzy. I call her. She is normally calm and polite mannered in her office, but now she is yelling out a storm of profanities, "You need to set your intention and get this f...ing entity out of your body!"

Frenzy is serious. Her plan is to utilize acupuncture to perform an exorcism to energetically blast The Guru out of me.

She says, "This cannot wait until Monday. This entity is working to make you avoid the appointments. I will make a special appointment for you on Sunday morning at ten."

I tell her, "I am taking it seriously. I will be there."

I GOT A MESSAGE FOR YOU

At Helen's advice, I go to our family brick home to stay with The Lamb. Don't ask me why, but I do 258 long, deep bows. Perhaps these bows were a way to repent for the three phone calls I was about to make. I leave a message each time, which I assume shook up the intended receivers. I reach out from an emotional place to express some rather hostile feelings in a provocative way.

The first call is to The Lion.

In a gristly warrior voice, I leave a message saying, "YOU

ARE GOING DOWN! YOU ARE GOING DOWN! YOU ARE GOING DOWN!"

When he hears the message, he is terrified. He imagines I am physically coming after him. He knows I have studied martial arts for ten years. He thinks his life is threatened. He starts toting a loaded pistol on his hip in case I show up. I guess somewhere inside I feel angry about the damage he has inflicted.

When I said, "You are going down," I was speaking prophetically or symbolically. I didn't mean it as a physical threat. For him, "going down" means losing what is most precious to him: money and his powerful status as a business owner. A few years later, his empire crumbles. He sells off 14 retail stores, four apartment blocks, and a several rental homes.

The second call is to an old girlfriend I call Sex Kitten. We were dating for about a year. During our time together, lust reached a new level. I was not comfortable with everything we did, but I went along. I did not want to upset her. I lacked the assertion to say, "Okay, let's stop doing this!"

I call her and let her know, "THERE IS A SPIRIT OF LUST IN YOU!"

The third phone call is to a female yoga teacher whom I met a day after The Guru entered my body. When I attended her yoga class, I felt that she was another past student of Swami Sri Yukteswar. After class, I invited her to come visit me at my home. When she arrived, I told her she was a student of mine in a past life. She was open to the possibility. We talked about yoga, and she gave me a CD with beautiful Himalayan music. The Guru likes it more than I do.

I attempt to call her and leave several phone messages. I feel she can somehow help with my precarious situation. Her husband does not appreciate some guy calling himself her guru leaving weird messages. She never returns the calls.

STRUCK WITH A PASSION FOR JESUS

I don't know why, but that night I am struck with a passion for Jesus. Perhaps The Guru knew that I needed Him. I am sleeping in my sister's bedroom, the one with the vinyl wallpaper covered with red roses a foot in length. In a storybook fashion, I get down on my knees and pray with tear-filled eyes. I make a simple and personal request. I ask Jesus to enter my life. I do not know much about Jesus, but I begin to seek him.

That evening at 10:30 p.m., I call Pastor R.I.P.

I ask, "Can I attend your church on Sunday and get baptized?"

He says, "I am glad you want more of Jesus. You are welcome to attend the Sunday morning service. It starts at ten."

Pastor R.I.P. assembles a husky team of deacons ready to give me what they think I need. You can probably guess what they want to do…. Yes! It's another exorcism! This one is planned to take place in front of the altar, directly after the regular church service.

Now I have three different healers all ready and eager to perform an exorcism to remove The Guru, which I do *not* even want gone. It's crazy! A guru is a teacher and an instrument of God. They seek to serve others in a compassionate, loving manner. When one finds such a source, it's like a cool pool in the desert. A guru can perform miracles on God's behalf; often their actions make no sense, but they get great results. A devotee will trust and follow the advice of their guru, even when it's not obviously logical. Clearly, a guru can be in the flesh or in the spirit.

My appointment with the acupuncturist is the same time as the church service. Frenzy is going to be more peeved than ever before! I put on a blue pinstriped suit and go to church. I think I am going to be baptized. I had not attended our small hometown church except for Easter or Christmas for the past twenty years. Since then there has been a Jesus culture revolution. I sit in the front row next to Pastor R.I.P. I notice that after he gave up teaching and practicing martial arts, he gained a little weight around the waist.

There is rock-style praise and worship band. Everybody is standing up and clapping hands to the beat. I have a Bible and start slapping it hard with one hand to the rhythm. Yeah! Then, I look around and realize nobody else is beating up their Bible. Oops!

After the sermon, Pastor R.I.P. calls people to come up to the front altar for prayers. I am excited! Soon I will be baptized. It's my turn. Four large deacons gather around me. The pastor places olive oil on my forehead.

I say, "Hey! Where is the water?"

Pastor R.I.P. starts praying, "Remove this evil spirit…"

Then they all start speaking and praying in tongues.

I am thinking, "What is going on?"

The Guru is sitting back, smiling at it all. The pastor must want me to fall over backward because he keeps pushing my forehead straight back. I can only bend backward so far. The husky deacons catch my body and lower me to the floor.

Then Pastor R.I.P. crouches down beside me to whisper loudly, "What is the name of the evil spirit living in you?"

I never considered The Guru to be an evil spirit. I assume the pastor wants some form of the devil to be in me.

I say, "Beezelbub."

I am trying to say the name "Beelzebub," but it came out wrong.

He says, "AHHHHH. The God of Bees, now bees be gone!"

The Guru says, "Looks like I am not going anywhere."

Eventually, they finish praying and let me up. I am given a few hugs and they proclaim this day as my spiritual birth. The Guru thinks it was all great fun. It was an exorcism by surprise attack. I didn't have much choice once they surrounded me. Their exorcism may have removed a few dark entities, but it surely didn't remove The Guru.

MY NEW BIBLE

On the positive side, I am given a NKJV Bible with the words of Jesus highlighted in red. On the negative side, I have a very upset acupuncturist. I go home with a desire to read the Bible from cover to cover.

The Lamb is hosting a family reunion at her house. I don't want to make a scene. I grab my new Bible, a backpack, and a fleece and head out the door. I walk to visit a friend but nobody is at home. They have an assortment of fresh garden produce lying out on towels. I take a few veggies to eat: a clove of garlic, a pepper, a cucumber, and a tomato. I find a quiet spot in an abandoned camp in a back field and settle in to start reading.

During the sermon, Pastor R.I.P. had said, "The Word is alive."

I begin to read and look at the Bible with fresh eyes. Could it reveal some answers to questions relevant to my life? I feel guidance is present in the Word, but it also resides in the spaces of silence between the words. Well, it says on the seventh day God rested, so after I finish reading Genesis, I lie down and take a nap; then I return home at dusk.

The Guru has been in my body for ten days. I wake up early and go for a jog. Yes! I am able to run again. I can't believe it. I am amazingly grateful. I jog out to a spot on a dirt road where I used to practice martial arts before my back injury. I believe that the prayers at the church took hold during the night. My back really feels better today. I watch the beams of sunlight shining through the clouds. It's like I can peek up into heaven or somebody is watching down. Could it be God's grace? I feel all fresh and alive again.

CHAPTER 10

Ten Minutes

Two police cruisers slip silently down the middle of the long dirt driveway toward my family's three-story brick home. Pine trees, 100-feet tall, are staggered along either side of the driveway as if javelins were thrown down from heaven, just missing these intruders. I peer out to see them through a small side window beside our white front door.

I run upstairs, out of breath, and enter my sister's bedroom. Vinyl wallpaper covered with foot-long red roses surrounds me on all sides, but this situation does not smell sweet. Panicked, I open the second story window that faces the river.

In the distance, under a cluster of pine trees, is a granite platform covered with pine needles. A prior owner in the late 1800s built it for his throne. I imagine him sitting like a dignified statue gazing down upon the waterfall while he contemplated life's intricate ways.

If I could jump out far enough, I could grab a branch of the giant pine tree near the house. I squat like a bird on the window ledge, pausing to ask myself, *"Is this the right moment to allow The Guru to have full control of my body?"* It seems like a reasonable solution and an easy way to escape this predicament, but deep down my soul suspects that to surrender itself to another spirit is breaking some sacred spiritual ethic. But then again, why not?

Ten minutes earlier, I was sitting in the lotus position on top of a four-foot-long, gold-framed antique mirror that I had taken down from the bathroom wall and positioned on the edges of the tub. It felt as though The Guru sharing my body for the past ten days was ready to blast out of my third eye. I had positioned the Waterpik shower-massager to direct a strong half-inch beam of water toward my third eye, which I was intently focusing upon. I became distracted by anticipating a jolt as The Guru departed, and I was suddenly overcome by fear. I envisioned a sudden blow of pain that might throw me into the shower wall with tremendous force. I found myself beginning to scream as long and loudly as is humanly possible in one breath. Although this eased my fears of imminent bodily harm, it didn't occur to me that my screaming would raise the concern of my mother, who immediately called the police.

Perching on the windowsill with my heart beating rapidly, I make my plea. "Guru, take over complete control and get me out of this situation!"

What happens next is hard to explain. It's as though I am looking through a periscope. I can't see anything to the left or right unless I turn and face that direction. Jumping to the tree branch seems more challenging now, but begins to look more realistic when it comes into focus through my tunnel vision. I leap from the window ledge and catch hold of the branch.

Life is looking better, I fantasize about taking a nice easy float down to the soft, pine-needle bedding...but before this happens, I hear a *crack!* and a *snap!* My descent suddenly turns into a crash landing. My ankles feel slightly sprained, but they still function. Deciding to run, I discover it's not that easy with tunnel vision. I see a foot here, a branch there...*look out for that tree!* I make a quick left turn. There's a steep, fifty-foot descent to the river. I find myself airborne, somewhere near the granite platform, floating or flying, a big rock heading my way. I feel the impact, hard against my skull. Blood trickles down my cheek. I feel numb, sick, and woozy.

Time passes: ten minutes...ten days...or ten years? As if in a dream, I stand up and wade through the waist-high ferns. I feel like a cornered warrior, forced to retaliate.

I come back to something resembling reality when a tranquilizer is injected into my hip. This wakes me up from one dream and puts me into another. I first notice the smell of hot vinyl seats. Then I realize that I am locked in the back of a police car and have pepper spray in my eyes and a black mesh sack over my head. I feel blood on my face and hands, and my ribs feel cracked or broken. It's painful to breathe. My right shoulder has a bloody scrape where I was dragged on the ground. I feel chains on my lap that lead to a set of handcuffs around my wrists and a pair of ankle cuffs below. I have been captured like a prisoner.

I have no memory of what happened after the impact. It's all a mystery. My memory completely blocked out what happened for about ten minutes. Perhaps it was due to the impact or it was so traumatic that my mind chose to erase it. I was told I put up a fight and went down hard. The Lamb is not willing to share the details of what actually happened. Her only comment is, "That day was a Mother's worst nightmare!"

GOD'S GRACE IN THE HOSPITAL

A medical unit arrives and the police explain the situation to them. The ambulance crew is reluctant to transport me to the hospital. They feel I could be dangerous. The police are being cautious, with just cause, after my difficult apprehension. They know I am in some sort of altered state, but it's not drugs, as they presume. It's an urgent situation because I have some life threatening injuries. Finally, one police officer volunteers to deliver me to the hospital in his police cruiser. I awake in the local hospital, handcuffed to a metal bed. The Lion and The Lamb stay by my side for most of the night. I am told that one police officer kept me under surveillance, for security reasons, all night long.

The next day, Gadget and Priceless come to visit me. Soon afterwards, I am transferred to a larger hospital in Burlington,

Vt. The doctors make a puncture to insert a hose to drain the fluid in my lung, and the damaged ribs heal rather rapidly. I receive reconstructive surgery to install three titanium plates with screws to repair the fractured bones under my left eye. To complete the operation, they lift up the whole left side of my face and reattach it under the gums in my mouth and under my left eyelid. I have an excellent surgeon. There are no noticeable scars. I can feel the screw heads under my skin if I rub them. On occasion, I feel slight numbness from nerve damage on the left side of my nose to the corner of my lip.

I barely feel any physical pain or discomfort throughout the whole recovery process. I am kept under surveillance in a level-two psychiatric ward for the next 25 days. It is designated for those with minor mental disturbances. It all went smoothly. I know without any doubt that God's grace was present before, during, and after the injury to my head.

Since The Guru entered my body, I am speaking Spanish and German better than I could before. Perhaps my memory is better able to recall foreign words that I had learned, or maybe with the acquisition of The Guru I have tapped into a universal language bank. The hospital performs various tests, including having me speak in German to a person who is fluent. Their conclusion is that I am not fully fluent but know some words. This is pretty remarkable because I never had any exposure to the German language. A physiatrist diagnoses me as having bipolar disorder. This means I have oscillating moods of depression and mania.

They say I have a classic case of bipolar disorder. They even ask me to tell a group of visiting medical students about my experience. They don't believe a guru entered my body or that there were any spiritual forces implicated. Basically, their theory is that the chemicals in my mind malfunctioned to create the whole scenario. Their medical explanation is that I had a 10-day manic episode. I was elated during the ten days, but their methods don't test spiritual components. The bipolar-disorder theory lacks an explanation of how I acquired a whole array of new spiritual gifts. I believe it was a spiritual intervention by The Guru, Swami Sri Yukteswar. I don't doubt he has the capability to enter a body. I have more reasons to believe it was him than to believe it was not him, but I can't say that I am absolutely positive.

SCORES OF VISITORS

All this commotion happens in a small Vermont town. People here don't like to go to the hospital unless it's something serious. I can imagine the word traveled fast, with something as bizarre as me jumping out of a second-story window to elude four police officers. I have scores of family and old friends that call or visit me in the hospital. When people call or come to visit, it shows that they care. It's a small part of their day, but a big deal for me when I am alone in the hospital.

The Lion visits me, and this action alone shows he is concerned about my welfare.

He asks, "Is there is anything you want?"

I say, "I would like a gold cross. Not the chain, I have one. Just the cross."

During his next visit, he brings me a gold cross. I am thankful and wear it for years. The Lion gives me the cross along with his remark, "The price paid for this cross was way too much!"

He is trying to tell me this gift was too expensive. But I can sense that he feels glad I am still alive. I know it's not what he meant, but in his words there is another kind of truth, if you relate it to Jesus.

Pastor R.I.P. and his pastor, The Bishop, come to share a word of wisdom and pray with me. Pastor R.I.P. says, "There are 31 days in the month and 31 Proverbs. Read one a day. Proverbs will allow you to understand man and the world better; Psalms will allow you to understand and be closer to God." I take his advice to heart.

I find inspiration from reading the Bible. I make a collage out of magazine clippings in the art room. It shows God and all of creation. It symbolizes how the Bible has taken a more significant role in my life.

INTERGALACTIC DETECTIVE

After the whole Guru incident, I feel like I had been asleep in a time capsule for 25 years. It's more than a mere "What happened?". I go through a process of trying to unravel what happened during those ten days and the ten minutes after the impact. Some reference points and knowledge of the facts shared by my family and friends have been revealing and reassuring, but the momentary lapse of memory after the impact remains.

Questions come up after ten days of being in an altered spiritual state. Did The Guru really enter my body? Why did dowsing give me that final instruction? Did I make a big mistake by asking The Guru to take over my spirit? Why did I get tunnel vision after I asked The Guru to take over my spirit? If I was under the safeguard of The Guru, why did I receive such a life-threatening impact? Did all these events happen for a reason? It brings up more questions than answers.

Sometimes it's better to have somebody from outside of the box look in at the situation. In order to make sense of this incident, let's broaden our perspective and investigate what happened in a fun and different way. I am going to call upon a fictional character, Miss Clarity I.D. She is an intergalactic detective who has a reputation for solving tough spiritual mysteries throughout the Universe.

I find Miss Clarity at an intergalactic lounge called Saturn's Turn. I spot her peering nonchalantly out toward Saturn's rings. She is wearing a tight red dress that looks like it's made of petroleum jelly. Miss Clarity is not from planet earth. She is similar in size to a human, but her body is much longer with greenish-amber scales like a snake. Her huge eyes are green and yellow like other reptiles. She uncoils, after being comfortably spiraled up on a black furry loveseat in the sun. Her forked tongue extends to take a sip of a blue frosty cocktail from a tall glass. She motions to me by patting her long tail on the seat next to her. I walk over and introduce myself before sitting down. She hisses loudly and the bartender sends over an orange terra ductile with a cherry. It arrives on some sort of neon floating Frisbee, which zips back once I snag the drink. It's quite tasty.

I start the conversation, "I would like you to investigate an incident on planet Earth. It's a lush planet bustling with various life forms."

She responds with a smile, "I know plenty about it, silly earthling. I was not hatched last week. What can I do for you?"

I ask, "What do you know about a guru being able to enter a human body?"

She replies, "They are an advanced life form, disciplined yoga practitioners, originally from India. Some of these master teachers were or are enlightened beings. They are capable of transferring their conscious energy or spirit while alive, or after death, to inhabit the physical body of other humans."

I explain, "I had what I believe is a guru living in my body. I was warned in the initial communication with spirits through dowsing not to allow any spirit to take control of my spirit. It seemed like good advice, but I did not follow it."

Clarity casually retorts, "Typical human; most earthlings don't follow my advice either. I bet it became crowded in there?"

I continue, "Yes it did. After ten days I asked The Guru to take over my spirit."

She draws out an electronic cigarette that was tucked in her belt and takes a few puffs, "What sort of physical changes took place?"

I reply, "I instantly had tunnel vision. Maybe I was given

worthy and warranted advice through the dowsing."

She interjects, "Let me point out, I have not yet established whether we can trust this dowsing spirit's advice. What else did you notice?"

I say, "It seems that The Guru could control my senses. At one point, I experienced delusions in each of my five senses, but that was before I asked The Guru to take over my spirit."

She says, "If The Guru had the capability to enter your body and could control your senses, it's reasonable to expect he could be capable of taking over your spirit upon request. If, in fact, he took over your spirit I would expect you perceived some changes."

I nod and reply, "If there were spiritual shifts, they were very subtle. But my vision was like peeking through an empty toilet paper roll."

Clarity says, "It's most probable that shifts would occur spiritually, but it's very serious to surrender your spirit to another."

She takes a breath and sighs, "It seems that the natural instinct of humans is to keep control of their own body and spirit. I find it interesting that you asked The Guru to take over your spirit."

I explain, "I was under a bit of stress that day. Four police officers were chasing me around the house. I trusted The Guru and felt he was better suited to handle the situation."

Clarity's eyebrows lift and she interjects, "It's impossible for me to determine if your request was for the better or worse."

I say rather shyly, "Well, sixty seconds after my request to The Guru, I experienced what most humans consider a severe traumatic injury to my head that could have easily caused my death."

Clarity says, "Oh my! I am assuming that you did not die. That injury seems like an important detail."

I chuckle and say, "Yes it is. Anyhow, I am wondering if

The Guru is still in my body."

She responds, "Well, you need to figure that out for yourself. Were there any changes that you noticed after the impact?"

I pause to think and then reply, "Other than getting all bloody and having a sick, numb, woozy feeling. I can't recall much of what happened after the impact."

Clarity says, "Really! On my planet we call it a "mind warp." Did your tunnel vision ever cease and come back to normal?"

I say, "Well yes! It came back just after the impact. I never thought about it, but I never had the tunnel vision again."

She asks, "Could it be possible that The Guru left your body and spirit at the time of the impact?"

I answer, "Anything is possible. I could not always believe The Guru, but he said 'It's painless to leave a body after it dies.'"

Clarity's eyes light up, "There are few human beings in this universe that don't lie. But you can always trust a unicorn. Perhaps, once you were unconscious, The Guru departed your body?"

I say, "Yes, that makes sense. I never considered it. I seldom heard The Guru's voice after the impact."

Clarity scans over some information from a computerized hand-held device before she continues, "I find that a guru, by the definition found in earth's history, can work in one's life in ways I don't understand. It's possible that The Guru guided your body to receive a blow to the head in the most compassionate way known to him. It allowed The Guru to depart and you, silly human, to continue on your journey slightly altered."

I say excitedly, "You mean The Guru could have planned my injury as a way for him to leave my body; for the proper conditions, I had to be momentarily unconscious. It's better than the second alternative, which is to be dead. If what you say is true, it's incredible!"

Clarity replies, "If that is the case, then The Guru really cared about your well-being. You did say you trusted him. From my observations, you silly humans are rather stubborn when it comes to changing behaviors. My hunch is that he came to assist you."

I respond, "What you're saying is I needed a big God slap to wake me up and to change my ways?"

Clarity, in a dignified manner, says, "Yes, that is one way to say it. Do you have any more questions?"

I reply, "No more questions. Thanks for the clarity, Clarity."

She lets out a hissy guffaw and says, "Very amusing! Call on me when you need clarity. Our case is complete. You will get my bill electronically in three minutes."

We say goodbye. Once I stand up, she coils back into a spiral on the black furry loveseat. I stare out for a moment at Saturn's rings, until my bill arrives. Saturn's rings really are magnificent.

Perhaps a better approach is to examine my spiritual transformation over the next ten years. There is no doubt, I have been touched by God's grace, and it left me with an insatiable hunger to know and understand God, the Truth, and Love.

"As the deer pants for streams of water, so my soul pants for God."

(Psalm 42:1 NIV) ∎

Part II
God's Grace

This is a self-portrait that I entitle "A Scream for Help." I had no intention of killing myself. As a photographer, I aim to take pictures with impact. It was, in part, an assignment from my psychiatrist and also my way of expressing how I was disgusted with the western medical system.

CHAPTER 11

A Scream for Help

After my release from a level-two psychiatric ward at the hospital, the typical western medicine prescription and diagnosis occurs. I am disheartened to hear the medical doctors say that I need to take prescription medication for the rest of my life to keep bipolar disorder under control. The doctors, or the medical system, consider my body, mind, emotions, and spirit to be disconnected. They want each sector to be individually diagnosed and medicated. It feels distant from the true wholeness and harmony known as healing.

If I listen and comply with all of the doctors' advice for medications and accept that I have all the diseases on their extended lists, then I am already doomed. It feels like my doctors are collaborating like a terrorist network to take another patient hostage in the system. Some doctors have laid claims on my body, but the psychiatrists are holding out for my mind. It probably brings a higher price. As part of my ransom, they are requesting that I hand over my sanity. No deal!

In the end, the terms of the negotiations for my release from the hospital include that I must agree to take prescribed medications and continue to have appointments with a local psychiatrist. I am not keen on taking the prescribed medications, but I do it for several months to appease the doctors. I am discharged to the care of a local psychiatrist named Debbie Goldfinger.

She seems to be the first professional who shows genuine

kindness. She really cares about my situation. She tells me to call her during the middle of the night, if necessary. She is empathetic about my not wanting to take prescribed medications. We find some holistic alternatives. During a normal session, I share what is going on, and Debbie suggests ways I can be more social or express my feelings. I admit my attitude needs some adjusting.

During one session, she is attempting to find a new way to get me to express what I feel. She asks, "Can you find an artistic way to express yourself?"

I am fervid about photography, so I take a self-portrait with my mouth wide open in a scream. I am holding two pistols. One is a 38 special and the other a 9 millimeter. They are each held up and pointed at either side of my forehead. I enlarge it along with a few other photos to 8x10s and bring them to my next session. Debbie looks at each photo and finds a way to compliment how I am expressing myself. It feels like we are playing a game. When she comes to the photo with the pistols pointed at my forehead, her eyes open wide and she gasps. She attempts to hide the fact that she is shocked.

She exclaims, "Oh my! It looks like you are expressing some anger here."

I respond, "Yes! This is my self-portrait. I call it 'A Scream for Help.'"

Once the full impact of this demented photo strikes home, her energy shifts. She keeps staring at the photo. Her face becomes puckered and wrinkled. I assume the worst possible nightmare for a psychotherapist is to have a client commit suicide.

She asks in a concerned tone, "Those guns are not really loaded?"

I reply, "I wouldn't kill myself. I am expressing my frustration with the medical system."

She suggests, "I am making a request. Can you keep your guns with a family member for the next several months?"

I reply, "Sure, I can do that."

NEGATIVE THOUGHTS

An unhealthy process starts when I and others began to constantly focus on my pains and wounds. When a friend says, "How is your back today? I hear you are in pain."

I say, "Yes, my back hurts today."

In my mind, like a skipping record, I repeat, "I am never going to heal. I am always going to be in pain. I am not going to be able to work. I am not going to be able to have any fun."

My emotional sick-boy stew is simmering with anxiety, depression, mania, irritability, mental fatigue, unwarranted fears, panic disorders, suppressed anger, grief, loneliness, and trust issues. It's no surprise that once insomnia visits, my soul seeks to numb out or escape through television, alcohol, drugs, sex, and the occasional thought of suicide. All that matters when I feel as sick as a leper rolling in the agony of my pain, is to find a way out. The last thing my soul wants to do is a make friends with my pain, feel it in my heart, and have some quality time together. There is one person who has been treating me worse than anybody else: myself. *Boy, I am pathetic, somebody please stop this jerk!*

Well, maybe it took a guru to open my eyes. It is hard to change long-existing habitual patterns. They feel normal. My positive and negative thoughts are powerful. My negative thoughts have the ability to attract more illness. They actually reinforce my illness and give my cells permission to become as I believe. This is not the path to healing; it's the path toward prolonged suffering.

Thankfully, after The Guru, my attitude begins to change. With the assistance of a steady yoga practice and the Bible, I began to develop the power to control and purify my thoughts. Until my thoughts become more purified, it's best to avoid the environments, behaviors, and people that stimulated those negative thoughts. One of the root causes of my chronic conditions was stress. Because I was not adequately prepared or permitted to express my feelings in a healthy way, I stored pain in my body.

The greatest disharmony for me as a child included the fear of men, being socially challenged at school, and my parent's divorce. As an adult, I had a high level of stress at work, especially with The Lion being my boss. Of course finances were a concern, but I was able to cope with it all until after the emotional turmoil from my divorce. That was the big one!

INTERNAL RHYTHM

The love I felt from my wife brought me peace and harmony. Once it was gone, I lost my internal rhythm. According to Hazrat Inayat Khan,

> *"When a child's rhythm and tone are disordered, the healing that a mother can give, often unconsciously, the physicians cannot give in a thousand years. The song she sings, however insignificant, comes from the profound depths of her being and brings with it the healing power. It cures the child in a moment. The caressing, the patting of the mother does more good to the child than any medicine when its rhythm is disturbed and its tone is not good. The mother, even without knowing it distinctly, feels like patting the child when it is out of rhythm, singing to the child when it is out of tune."* [9]

My divorce disrupted my natural rhythm. My loss of love eventually even affected my breathing pattern. I believe the implications of divorce in this regard can be more severe for a man than a woman. A man will calibrate his rhythm to that of his wife. In this manner, she replaces his mother. A woman has her rhythm intact naturally with her monthly menstruation. It connects her to the cycles of the moon and the earth. Of course, men can find ways to connect to the earth and the moon, but it feels natural to make that connection through a woman.

It was natural for me to seek a relationship with another woman soon after my divorce; perhaps it was to keep my internal rhythm in synchronicity. I spent much of my time with Cleopatra. I give her credit, for she knew how to rebuild my self-esteem. It did not take much, but a few well-placed words of encouragement made a world of difference.

HOSPITAL VOLUNTEER

As a 33 year old, life is a dream. I am eager to serve. A few months after I return to my home, at the suggestion of my psychiatrist, Debbie Goldfinger, I volunteer at a local hospital. I make beds, file charts, deliver urine samples, and read poetry to the patients. My tasks are simple and humble. I observe the nurses, who show incredible compassion for their patients. They exhibit kindness, often more from how they say it than from the words. When a nurse says, "How are you feeling today, Martha?" her tone gives Martha permission to express her feelings and be heard.

On occasion, a patient will die and the nurses on the floor become very quiet. They have to cope with death regularly. Often they come to know a patient as a friend. I don't know what they are feeling inside; sometimes I notice a tear flowing down a cheek. The nurses compassionately express their emotions among themselves. I suspect that some detach from feeling the pain, but the real heroes in the group embrace life and accept death. One's individual form of faith is personal. I once heard a nurse standing in the corridor whisper prayers softly. Her eyes were gently closed. I am not sure she noticed me. This type of heartfelt prayer must have the power to heal and comfort both the giver and the receiver.

SUNDO WITH HYUNMOON KIM

I start off my yoga career with a Korean style of healing and meditation called SunDo. A Korean Master named Hyunmoon Kim established a retreat center near my home in Barnet, Vermont. I am told that this ancient practice was handed down from hermits who lived in the Korean mountains. Because of the direct lineage, the practice has retained much of its original form.

During the 90-minute practice, there are few verbal instructions given. It starts with a series of warm-up exercises and ends with a cool-down. The heart of the practice is holding postures with breathing exercises designed to strengthen and balance internal energy and sooth the internal organs. After each set of postures is done one hundred times, the student can advance to the next level of postures. During the breathing meditation, there is a recording of a traditional Korean chant. I can't understand a word, but it is rather peaceful. Different breathing patterns are learned at different levels and the chant helps guide one to know when to change postures or how long to inhale and exhale.

Students do their set of postures during the forty-minute meditation portion of the class. Over time, the student naturally becomes aware of his or her body, mind, and spirit transforming through the SunDo practice. There is profound beauty when one discovers for themselves a relevant truth in their own practice. It can never be taken away or disputed. These gems cannot be handed out; they crystallize.

Master Hyunmoon Kim is a large, strong, dark-skinned Korean man who speaks with the gentle voice of a monk. He says, "One must practice each day to be effective, like a baker makes bread each day. Better yet, practice in a group and it will lead to more energy, like many sticks on a fire."

I attend the local SunDo classes and practice regularly in my home for the next four years. After a few years of practice, I have a desire to teach, so I attend a retreat with Master Kim in Barnet. During the retreat, he explains, "One must give full concentration during meditation, remain like a statue during a posture, if you want to get in touch with the universe inside."

It's difficult to get the new breathing pattern correct along with the inward spiral visualization within the lower abdomen. His instructions are just not sinking in. I can't get it. I am feeling frustrated. Instead of pushing it any further, Master Kim takes me aside and shows me how to do a full, deep, traditional bow. I start standing with my hands in prayer. Next, I bow down on my knees with my palms flat on the ground. Then I touch my forehead down and push myself back upright with my palms. He does it beside me until I learn it. A deep bow is a humble act; the fact that he takes the time to show me how to do it properly shows he cares.

> *Fun bowing exercise: In order to feel the humbleness of a deep bow by yourself, do several of them. If you want to try it with a friend, then face each other. One person can remain standing as the other bows to them three times. Take turns. For some, it can be harder to receive a bow than to give one.*

KRIYA YOGA

As part of my quest to find out the truth about The Guru, I attend a Kriya yoga class. Swami Sri Yukteswar, the one I call The Guru, lived from May 10, 1855 – May 9, 1936. I desire to find the purest source of his teachings. One of his students, Hari Harinanada, established a Kriya yoga center in New York City. I am disappointed to find out that he recently left his body. But he appointed a young man from India, who is in his late 20s, Super Star Ananda, as his successor. He is renowned for having a brilliant mind and can recapitulate the yogic scriptures by memory. I want to attend a class taught by Super Star Ananda.

I am told that in order to attend any Kriya class, I must take initiation into Kriya yoga, otherwise they will not reveal the teachings. It seems like placing the horse before the cart, but being the only way, I concede. They ask me to bring flowers and a piece of fruit as an offering for the initiation ceremony.

On the appointed day, I take a train to New York City. I stop to purchase a few yellow roses and a coconut before I arrive.

There are a dozen other people who are initiating. In the front of the yoga studio, there is an altar with photos of their Kriya lineage: Hari Harananda, Swami Sri Yukteswar, Lahiri Mahasaya, and Babaji. I feel a strong presence from a large photo of Swami Sri Yukteswar. At times, it feels like he is staring at me. It's a strange feeling, but I feel more comfort than not from his photo. The legend is that Kriya yoga came from Babaji, who lives eternally as a young man in the Himalayan Mountains.

One by one, we go to decorate the altar with our offerings of flowers and fruits. It is a beautiful, colorful display. Super Star Ananda is standing by the altar, waiting to initiate us. He holds his hands on the top of our heads and sometimes touches our spine to transmit the energy from the Kriya lineage.

I feel a slight tingling, but nothing dramatic happens. Afterwards, all the new initiates and a few dozen regular students join in a Kriya yoga practice instructed by Super Star Ananda. It is a nice practice, and during the meditation portion, there is a vibrant, pulsating, blue light in my third eye. When I focus on the light, it becomes brighter and forms the circular shape of the sun. I wonder if this is the tunnel of light that guides people to heaven after they die. It feels like I could dive into it. I dare not, for I might not be able to get back.

After the meditation portion, Super Star Ananda says, "Now lie down on your back and relax."

I ask him, "How do I relax?"

He replies, "You just relax."

His response did not answer my question. I feel that his

tone implies that I should know how to relax. I need a more detailed instruction. I really don't know how to relax.

During the lunch break, I chat with other classmates at a street-side cafe about our initiation and our first Kriya yoga class. We stride back through the bustling city traffic wearing sunglasses. The midday sun makes the pavement sizzling hot, yet we are all cool. We just got initiated! Now, we are part of the Kriya yoga lineage, whatever that means.

In the afternoon, we rejoin the others to listen to a discourse by Super Star Ananda about the philosophy of Kriya yoga. I purchased two small bottles of orange juice with the intention of offering one to Super Star Ananda as a refreshment. During a pause in the program, while we are assembling, I lift up one bottle of orange juice and ask Super Star Ananda, "Would you like an orange juice?"

He snaps back, "No! I am the juice."

It brought some laughter, but his joke points out his greatness. Master Hyunmoon Kim is the only other yoga master I have known. He is a humble man. When asked a question, he would pause, listen deeply, and reply with compassion. Super Star Ananda may have had great Kriya powers, but during our day-long encounter, he didn't show me any kindness. ∎

CHAPTER 12

Rhythm of the Breath

YOGA MEANS UNION

At this point, I start to live a nomadic lifestyle. I volunteer in the summer and autumn at various spiritual retreat communities. During the winters, I explore the Caribbean islands and continue my search for a location to start a spiritual community. I am blessed to have the freedom to live this lifestyle.

I am drawn to retreat communities that offer yoga. I know it keeps me sane by allowing my body and mind to relax. Yoga is a healthy way to escape my pain, anxiety, and depression. It's not so much an escape as an entrance to a more peaceful world. I start to get to know myself again, as a friend, and begin to like who I am. Buried under the pain lives that child who enjoyed swinging on rope, eating ice cream, and lying in the grass, lazily gazing up at the puffy clouds. Yoga allows the innocent child within to come out to play again.

The nature of the principal of yoga is unity. We are all on our own journey, but connected. We are here to learn, to be open, and to accept ourselves and others. When my practice is to love myself, then it's not difficult to love and accept others. I become more aware of my connection with other people through the practice of yoga. The people I meet through yoga are a fun, caring, and loving bunch. People attend yoga classes for various reasons, but it seems we all enjoy being together. It feels like we are all one big family.

Yoga is a healthy lifestyle that will forever be part of my spiritual path. It started off as a personal commitment to a daily practice. Over the years, the daily discipline of a yoga practice transformed me. It opened my heart, kept me present, and melted away the stress. Now I consider yoga any action that I do with loving kindness. On the path of yoga there is a huge invisible finger that points towards God. I am told that He lives somewhere on a puffy white cloud in heaven. In the beginning, I don't know how to reach God. He is so far away. Eventually, I figure out that the finger is actually pointing at my own heart. This is where God lives!

GOD REALLY EXISTS

While in Vermont one winter, I press in closer to find God. For thirty days, I do a disciplined routine of prayer, meditation, and silence, and I read the Bible daily. I want to know that God really exists. I read a passage about Isaiah calling out to the Lord.

> *"Then you will call, and the Lord will answer; you will cry for help, and he will say: Here am I."*
> *(Isaiah 58:9 NIV)*

That is exactly what I do on the last day. I jump up and down and throw a little temper tantrum like a child.

I yell out, "God, show me yourself!"

I don't stop; I just keep crying out. "I want to see you, GOD! I am not going to let up until you pay attention!"

Surely God will notice my tears during a childish fit. I want God to appear in whatever form He chooses. It could be a vision, an angel visitation, or a bright light. I lie down on my back and close my eyes. At that moment, I receive a vision that I shall never forget.

In it, a ghostly blue spirit rises up out of my body at my

waist and peers back at me. It's like I am at a mirror-smooth lake and I am looking up at a reflection of myself from in the water. I see God for the first time. He is a reflection of myself staring back into my own eyes. I feel like an innocent child.

I say, "This is God? It's me!"

I feel like somebody just swung open the gate and let my spirit out of prison. It's mind blowing. I no longer doubt that God's light and love live in me. It does not answer all my questions about God…many will remain a mystery…but if God is in me, then God is in you, and God is in everybody.

THE LOVE BLAST

The first yoga community I visit is at the Himalayan Institute of Yoga Science in Honesdale, Pennsylvania, in the winter of 2003. I attend a month-long self-transformation program. I chop a lot of vegetables, learn how to prepare and cook healthier food, and participate in daily yoga classes.

There is one teacher named Julia who studied with the late founder, Swami Rama. After the end of one of her yoga classes, I sit cross-legged in a row with the other students. She peacefully faces us in silence. She gathers love in her heart with her hands held in a prayer position. Then she sends a burst of love to our hearts. It physically travels like a beam of light. It blows me away. I don't physically move, but I feel reverberations that shake my soul.

Julia teaches restorative yoga. After the love blast, I schedule a private session. After listening to my issues, she places me in a supported child's pose. Bolsters support my chest and my face is turned to the side. All my muscles relax.

Julia says, "Be still in this posture for five minutes." I am always active. I think to myself, *Five minutes is a long time to be still.* During those long five minutes, I feel held and nurtured. I feel my breath returning to find its natural rhythm. I am relaxing, no longer trying to do anything. I am healing!

The Rhythm of the Breath

Forget for the moment all that is in your mind.
Feel the contact with your body and the solid dark earth,
heavy and grounding. Notice your breath.
Feel the rhythm of the earth around you:
the movement of the wind, the seasons,
birth and death, naturally.
The mesmerizing flames from a fire.
A wolf trotting in the woods.
The waves hugging the beach and crawling back,
again and again, powerful with rhythm.
Feel your breath.
Imagine you inhale a flowing stream –
vibrant, filling every cell with vital energy.
The stream flows into a serene pond,
with the calmness of a devoted mother
nurturing a newborn child in her arms.
The pond gently leaves by way of another stream.
The exhale begins –
The rhythm, the cycle is unbroken.
It begins again. Feel the connection, the gentle flow.
In your heart, your essence, your soul.
The heartbeat of the solid dark earth.
And realize…. You are…
The breath of the Earth.

During one of my walks, there is a foot of fresh snow in the field. The wind is blowing and tossing around mini whirling gusts of powder. I run to the top of a knoll and hold my hands up. I cry out to the Creator of this universe. For the first time, I am ready to surrender. I want God's presence in my life. I don't know exactly what it means. It feels different. I let go of a part inside that is no longer serving me. It fills with a desire to know and serve a divine, loving God. When I open up my heart, a light shines into the dark caverns of my soul.

SETTING THE ROOM ON FIRE

I ask for a private meeting with the new spiritual head, Pandit Rajmani Tigunait. Swami Rama requested that after his death, Pandit Rajmani take over, with one stipulation: he must remain silent for two years and observe the retreat community before making any changes. I respect the wise request. It impresses me that Pandit Rajmani could be silent for two years. I am eager to share with him my guru experience. I want to know his opinion.

I auspiciously find the one book Swami Sri Yukteswar wrote in their bookstore. It's called *The Holy Science*. The theme of his book is to examine the underlying unifying philosophies of Hinduism and Christianity by comparing *The Yoga Sutras* to the *Holy Bible*. I am intrigued and spurred on, after finding the book, to know more about him. At this point, I am not sure if The Guru is still in me. I am still trying to figure out what happened.

I meet with Pandit Rajmani in his office. After some casual conversation, I begin to explain how Swami Sri Yukteswar entered my body. All of a sudden, he jumps up out of his seat and bolts out the door like I just set the room on fire. He has a look of cautious perplexity on his face. No answers about The Guru are coming from him.

THE SACRED SILENCE

I continue my search for a yogi who will have the knowledge to answer my questions. A friend tells me there is one enlightened yogi in the United States named Baba Hari Dass. He was the inspiration for a retreat called Mount Madonna Center. He came to regularly teach and serve in this community, whose interests are unified by the common practice of yoga. It is located on 355 acres of mountain-top redwood forest and grassland overlooking Monterey Bay, between Santa Cruz and Monterey, in northern California.

He took a vow of continued silence in 1952 and lives the highly disciplined and austere life of a yogic monk. He does not encourage people to live as he does, but guides each to live their own life by doing what is best for them in their given situation.

I fly out for a weekend retreat that he is teaching called Disciplines of Peace. He is a kind, gentle, and peaceful man. I can feel the room light up when he enters. He writes on an erasable board and takes the time to answer individual questions, often with humor. I am able to meet with him privately to ask my personal questions. I ask him about being silent and share that I feel my spiritual path could include more silent time.

He writes on paper, "It's good to keep silence some times. Every part of the human body needs rest. Silence can be given to the mind, if one does not contact people."

I tell him I have a burning desire to establish a spiritual retreat. I have been searching for a location in the Caribbean islands during the past few winters.

He writes, "It's a good aim, but first, prepare yourself to take such a big responsibility."

I explain, "I am concerned about my health and have some physical limitations."

He writes, "Yes, your health is your first duty."

I have written down what I identify as my major issues and hand it to him. It explains how I have muscle tension, back issues, and difficulty expressing myself.

I explain, "I was devastated after my divorce and since then have spells of anxiety and depression."

I mention a few things about my parents' character; The Lamb, who acts saintly, and The Lion, who is a controlling businessman with random acts of ruthlessness or generosity.

He writes, "Your physical problems you partly inherited from your parents and the way you grew up. You can't go back, so you need to find ways of freeing your mind and body completely from the old conditioning."

I show him a list of my weekly routine, and he puts check marks next to the items he feels are most beneficial. My routine includes silence, yoga, concentration exercises, selfless service, aerobic activity, and a healthy diet. He suggests that I do regular meditation and Pranayama (breathing exercises) to release the old mental conditioning.

In regards to being silent, he says, "Talk only when necessary."

I ask him "What can I do to better understand God?"

He answers, "Purify your mind. Identify your ego attachments and desires honestly."

I save the big guru question for last, just in case he might try to rush away. I rapidly say, "I believe a guru entered my body. I don't know if The Guru is still in me. I don't understand what really happened. During the experience I gave up control of my spirit. Shortly thereafter, I received a fractured skull, which required reconstructive surgery that included three titanium plates screwed into my forehead. Afterwards, I began a feverous search for God and the truth."

He pauses and then writes slowly, "If you feel The Guru entered inside your body, then trust that guru. If it's only your imagination, then it will fall away."

Afterwards, I return to Mount Madonna a few different times for one-week and two-week segments of a 1000-hour yoga therapy course. Babi Hari Dass becomes a predominant spiritual influence during this time. We write letters back and forth. His humble honesty in the letters often touches my heart.

Once, after answering my questions he writes, "I have written so much today that my fingers hurt. I am unable to write anymore."

Whenever I visit Mount Madonna, I join Baba Hari Dass in the weekly Satsang. During this time, those in attendance can ask him questions. Both times I return to Mount Madonna I become involved in a relationship with a woman in the yoga therapy program, either sexually or romantically. I write a note for Baba Hari Dass for advice around my behavior.

He says, "Get professional treatment."

It is good advice, but I have too much pride to admit that my sexual behavior could be out of control. In my mixed up mind, I say to myself, *I am not that kind of man. I let go of some unwanted habits like drinking alcohol, and sex is how I choose to fill in the gap. Sex is a healthy and natural alternative.* Eventually, I start to realize the importance of time to build an intimate friendship before it becomes a relationship. These sexual encounters or romantic flings that start fast, end suddenly. ■

CHAPTER 13

The Chanupa

I have learned more from the sacred ceremonial pipe, commonly called the *chanupa*, than from any human teacher. I am emotional and in tears as I reminisce. Just before participating in my first sweat lodge ceremony, I have a vision: a chanting medicine man with a long eagle-feather headdress dances and twirls around in circles. He turns into a whirlwind of animal spirits, and a red-tailed hawk soars out of him and flies up into the sky. The hawk's flight turns into an arrow that strikes the side of a buffalo. Next, I see the Native American people giving thanks for the buffalo. They show their respect by utilizing all the meat, bones, and hides.

A woman dressed in white buckskins, whom I later find out is known as the White Buffalo Calf Woman, appears beside the buffalo. She walks towards me and says, "You need to learn how to use the chanupa so your prayers will be heard." Then she turns into a white buffalo, a swan, and a woman again before disappearing. I wonder if the vision is real or created by my imagination.

The White Buffalo Calf Woman brought the first chanupa to the Lakota Nation. She explained the symbolic meaning and showed them how to use the chanupa to pray. It is a fascinating story. I enjoy the version told by John Fire Lame Deer that appears in *American Indian Myths and Legends*, by Erdoes and Alfonso Ortiz.

Soon after, I have an encounter with a real wild swan. It

is an unnatural and remarkable experience. I am walking by a river when I spot two wild swans. I slowly go to the waters edge. One swan swims boldly toward me and looks me in the eye. I am actually able to touch its tail feathers, and the White Buffalo Calf Woman lets me know through our encounter that she is not just a fabrication of my mind. She is as real as the wild swan.

Her message is that there is a connection between what I experience in the Spirit World and what happens in the physical world. Both worlds are real. They each have a purpose, and I interact with them differently. Prayer is how I cross the bridge and communicate with the spiritual realm. In return, the Spirit World communicates with me through visions, dreams, responses to my prayers, or through signs in the physical realm.

MY FIRST CHANUPA

Today, there is a thunderstorm in the air and it's raining lightly. It's the perfect time to place the bowl and stem of my first chanupa together. I am standing on a sacred mound of moss in the woods overlooking a stone wall near my tent site in upstate New York. On a nearby tree, there is a big gnarly knot forming a silhouetted Native profile that seems to guard this spot. Hanging six feet high in a nearby oak tree is a deer skull that I found on a mountain top. In the distance, watching my every move through the branches, is a three-foot grey stone statue of an Indian holding a bow and arrow.

When I first begin to get signs to make a chanupa, I ask a friend I call My Native Brother if he will teach me how to make one. After praying about it, he agrees to show me.

My Native Brother shares his knowledge about how to make a chanupa using the traditional ways.

He says, "Make the bowl and the stem by hand, without any power tools. This way your energy will be in it." He explains how to burn a hole through the stem using a red-hot metal rod that has been set in the coals of a fire. He teaches me how to honor the directions, smudge, and handle the chanupa.

Smudging with sage is a powerful purifying technique from the Native American tradition. Smudging calls on the spirits of sacred plants to drive away negative energies, and allows me to better center myself. Smudging can be done with tobacco, sweet grass, sage, or cedar. I burn sage in a turtle shell and use a red-tailed hawk feather to fan it.

My Native Brother explains, "A pipe carrier uses his left hand to hold the bowl and his right hand to hold the stem."

He looks me in the eye and says, "You need to move slowly when you carry or handle the chanupa. It's a sacred item and an extension of your heart. The chanupa will teach, if you listen."

After I located what I felt was the perfect piece of cherry wood, I began to make the stem. It was a lot of work to do it all by hand. When I made it, the burning rod was not long enough to reach through the 14" piece of wood, so I entered from both ends and the holes met haphazardly in the middle. The hole was off center, and the interior burn ended up in the shape of a lightning bolt. For me, this was a sign that lightning energy is in this chanupa. It must enjoy being in thunderstorms. When making a Native American handcrafted item, it's acceptable and expected that there will be one flaw. It lets us know we are not perfect.

After I finished the stem, I decided it was easier to purchase a bowl online, so I ordered a red-pipestone bowl made by the 4th-generation pipe maker, Alan Monroe. From my limited knowledge, it's a good-quality traditional pipe.

I imagine that the first time I insert the stem into the bowl will be dramatic. There will be thunder clapping and lightning in the sky! I am ready. There is excitement in my blood. My Native Brother taught me to move slowly during these sacred moments, so I do. First I smudge myself with sage, and then the bowl and stem. I lift the two pieces up to the level of my chest.

It begins to rain a little harder. In my egocentric mind, I am about to become a sacred pipe carrier. I wait for the thunder. KABOOM! I can feel the power. Now is the moment! I insert the stem into the bowl for the first time and...and... and.... it breaks the bowl in half! *What!* The bowl breaks in half. *Ohhhh no!* This is not what I expected. I feel humble and small. Why did this happen?

I sit down to contemplate and look at the two pieces of the bowl. Buying a pipestone bowl seemed a lot easier than carving a stone myself, but now it rests in my hands, broken in half.

I wait in silence and check deep within myself. Then it comes: I need to make the bowl with my own two hands. Yes! There are no shortcuts, no quick and easy ways on this Native American path called the Red Road. I hold the two pieces. At least now, I can better understand how to make a bowl because I can see both the inside and outside. Today is not all in vain. My pipe is speaking to me and *now* I am starting to listen — really listen.

MAKING MY PERSONAL PIPE

My heart merges with the stone and wood as I place my time and energy into making a chanupa. The pipestone I choose for my pipe is black. It comes from Kanori, Canada. I figure my Abenaki ancestors were located closer to this black pipestone than the red pipestone commonly used from Minnesota. The bowl represents the feminine qualities, and the stem represents the masculine aspects. When both pieces are fitted together, it's like a man and woman coming together for a wedding ceremony. Something magical happens; the bride tends to glow. The power of a male stem is dormant until coupled inside the female bowl. Once the two pieces are united, it's activated. Alone, each piece, as a man or woman, has a purpose, but once together their purpose is no longer just about the individual. It's about becoming a team to serve each other, their family, and the larger community. With the chanupa, I pray for myself, but usually it's for family, friends, or a cause larger than myself. I pray for the tree nations in the rainforests that are being burned, the four-legged animals like the polar bears that are being affected by global warming, and all the creatures in the sea nation affected by pollution like the dolphins, sea horses, and whales.

THE AMERICAN BALD EAGLE

Just as a man and a woman have different needs, the feminine bowl and the masculine stem call for different types of energy. I am currently a volunteer at a rapture center, so I place the bowl in the cage with two American bald eagles for a week before I begin to work on it. The pipe will absorb the energy from living and non-living matter in its surrounding environment, just like us. During our conception and as a youth, we are more susceptible to being molded by our environmental influences. I assume that the bowl, before being conceived, is similar. It's calling out for exactly what it needs. I am listening.

Let's tune in to why this pipe bowl desires American bald eagle energy. Let's consider the symbolic meaning and qualities represented by the American bald eagle. The bald eagle is the emblem of the United States of America. They are the only eagles found exclusively on the North American continent, so they are true Native Americans. Bald eagles typically mate for life, except in the event of their partner's death or impotency. They build large nests and return to them year after year. They are dedicated and loyal to their partners.

In her book, *Native Americans of San Diego County* by Donna Bradley, she says,

> "Most all Native American Indian Peoples attach special significance to the Eagle and its feathers. Images of eagles and their feathers are used on many tribal

logos as symbols of the Native American Indian. To be given an Eagle feather is the highest honor that can be awarded within indigenous cultures." (10)

The Native Indians saw the Eagle as a symbol for great strength, freedom, courage, leadership, and vision. I note that these are the types of energy that my bowl is requesting and the types of energy I want for myself.

It's easier for me to focus on the bowl, which represents a reflection of myself, to uncover some of my deeper needs. I chose to volunteer at a rapture center because I wanted to be near this type of energy. As an American, the eagle represents honor, respect, and dignity. When I acknowledge this, I feel good about myself. My heart is also called to be near my dogs, the ocean, and in the rainforest.

Pause and reflect upon what energy are you called to be near.

REFLECTING UPON DEVIL'S HILL

In the final sanding phase of the bowl, I work on it at ledges under the full moon at Owl's Nest overlooking Peacham Bog in Vermont. Once a year, usually in the fall foliage season, I hike up to the top of the mountain, which resides on the opposite side of this valley, called Devil's Hill. It's my favorite spot in Vermont. During my visits, I pause to notice the changes in the surrounding environment and myself. There are rock cliffs and caves. As a teenager, I explored them with friends. We would crawl around in the crevices. Sometimes we would explore the lower caves on our bellies with headlamps. From the top of Devil's Hill, there is a spectacular view of the valley, Owl's Nest, Peacham Pond, and the rolling green mountains.

I am usually on Devil's Hill looking over here, so today I am gaining a new perspective. When I sit here and look toward my favorite spot in nature, I get a reflection of myself contemplating on Devil's Hill. I consider myself a steward over that piece of preservation land. It gives more to me than I can ever give back. I feel grounded and peaceful when I sit on these mountain ledges. This is the energy that this chanupa bowl and my soul want to capture.

COMPLETING THE BOWL

I complete the bowl while I am under the great redwood trees at Mt. Madonna Retreat in California. I am sitting on a bench in a manmade cave built into the earth. A waterfall spreads out like a lacey white blanket flowing over the roof. The sound of the waterfall is soothing. Nearby, alone in the field, is a gigantic eight-foot silver Om symbol placed on a cement pedestal. *Om* is said to be the first sound of creation and represents the almighty God. In this case, God is sitting in the field watching people come and go. Like any artist, God adores those who appreciate his creations: the dew on the spider webs in the morning, the patches of neon violet flower petals, and the way the sun rays turn the waist-high grass into a field of gold in the late afternoon.

I am doing my final fine-sanding on this chanupa bowl. On the back wall of the cave rests a weathered gray statue from India. Devotees have left flowers and fruits as an offering at the foot of the statue. It is Vishnu, the Preserver, the second member of the Trimurti, along with Brahma, the Creator, and Shiva, the Destroyer. It makes sense that this is the frosting energy that my pipe bowl desires near completion. These glorious pallets of energy are packed in this one pipe bowl for a purpose, beyond what I can conceive. It takes significant patience and care to complete a bowl, and during that process, it becomes an extension of myself. If I offer my chanupa for another person to hold, I feel like they are holding my heart in their hands.

While carving the wooden stem, I called on forty angels, one-by-one, while listening to devotional chants by Snatam

Kaur. Her voice is angelically pure and uplifting. During the process of being created, the female bowl traveled to exotic and beautiful places while the male stem is content to just get'er done at the tent site by the fire.

To honor the White Buffalo Calf Woman, I purchase a fancy and expensive braided bracelet with entwined turquoise and amber stones at an upscale jewelry store in Great Barrington, Massachusetts. I attach the bracelet around the stem closest to the mouthpiece. I have also acquired three white swan feathers that will hang from the opposite end.

PLACING THE CHANUPA TOGETHER

When the chanupa is complete, I go to a sweat lodge gathering with Chief Calvin, who presides over the Native Nations of Manitoba, Canada. I go to his room and offer him some tobacco. I show him my chanupa and ask for his advice.

He says, "For the first full year, smoke the pipe by yourself; get to know it."

The pipe and bowl are wrapped in a dark brown deer hide, which I purchased from a man who goes by the name of Geronimo.

Chief Calvin says, "That deer hide would make a nice pipe bag."

I call this pipe My Personal Pipe. I am the only person to ever smoke and pray with it. I get to know My Personal Pipe and myself better by praying and listening without any distractions.

I invite Feather Maker, a female companion at this Native American gathering, to sit with me on my buffalo robe to examine my chanupa.

As I hold my stem and bowl, it feels complete. I sense that I am being asked, "What is the purpose of the chanupa?"

I reflect upon loving myself, living the truth, sending out prayers, and connecting with my Native American ancestors. I slowly hand the bowl to Feather Maker. She holds the bowl next to her heart.

She says, "I feel energy, like thunder and lightning in my heart."

While she holds the female bowl near her heart, she describes the lightning energy in the masculine stem. Men and women have different needs and ways of expressing themselves, but just like the bowl and stem, we are designed to be together.

I ask Feather Maker to join me in a ceremony to place the new bowl and stem together for the first time. I choose a time when two sweat lodge ceremonies are simultaneously occurring. One is for the men and the other is for the women. She stands close to the women's lodge and I am near the men's lodge. She smudges the bowl and I smudge the stem. There is a straight line between the two lodges, with the fire in the middle. She holds the bowl in front of her at midlevel, and I hold the stem in front of me. We walk slowly toward each other. We meet near the fire and gently insert the pipe stem into the bowl. We can hear soft singing from the women and the deeper voices of the men from their corresponding lodges. I feel in my heart a spiritual bond beyond what we can hear or see. It exists between all men and all women.

I stand firm and hold the chanupa. In my inner vision, there are Native American chiefs sitting around the fire and Native American women creating an outer circle. There is a medicine man with a long, eagle-feather bonnet, dancing wildly around the fire. I honor the four directions as I fill the pipe with kinnikinnick. It's a combination of herbs that includes red willow bark, bear berry, yerba santa, and raspberry leaf.

I visualize the White Buffalo Calf Woman walking out of the woods from the north. I notice she has on her wrist the bracelet that I purchased to honor her. She has accepted the gift. She goes to the chiefs and speaks to them. Then she walks forward and sinks into the fire. The hearts of the Native American chiefs, the pipe carriers, and the women behind them are glowing bright red. I am now listening to the chanupa to honor this beautiful Native American tradition, my ancestors, and myself.

The Native American tradition is tangible and solid. It's like going barefoot to feel the earth, walking slowly and mindfully up to a tree to touch the rough texture of the bark. The blue jay and chipmunk live in the woods, and when somebody walks in their living room, they know it. My Personal Pipe allows me to slow down and reflect upon myself. I ask: *Why is this guy in such a hurry?* When I slow down in this way, my living room expands to include all of nature and the Spirit World.

Here I am smoking my chanupa under a pine tree. When I pray and listen, I become aware of what is going on inside myself. I am a part of nature, and how I treat the earth and all its inhabitants is a reflection of who I am. Spirits dart and move all around this big world, but there is one I should get to know better. It's the spirit that lives inside of me.

I am of Abenaki descent, and the chanupa is a Lakota Sioux tradition. I want to honor and respect them. I feel it's appropriate to include an explanation about the significance of the chanupa from a respected authority like John Lame Deer from the Lakota Sioux Nation. This excerpt is from the book, *Seeker of Visions; The Life of a Sioux Medicine Man* by John Lame Deer and Richard Erdoes.

Blood Turned to Stone

"I held the pipes. Their bowls were my flesh. The stem stood for all the generations. I felt my blood going into the pipe, I felt it coming back, I felt it circling in my mind like some spirit. I felt the pipes come alive in my hands, felt them move. I felt a power surging from them into my body, filling all of me. Tears were streaming down my face. And in my mind I got a glimpse of

what that pipe meant.

"*That Calf Pipe made me know myself, made me know the earth around me. It healed the blindness of my heart and made me see another world beyond the everyday world of the green frog skin (money). I saw that the pipe was my church, a little piece of stone and wood, but I would need nothing more as long as I had this. I knew that within this pipe were all the powers of nature, that within this pipe was me. I knew that when I smoked the pipe I was at the center of all things, giving myself to the Great Spirit, and that every other Indian praying with his pipe would, at one time or other, feel the same. I knew that releasing the smoke to rise up to the sky, I also released something of myself that wanted to be free and that thereby I gladdened all the plants and animals on earth.*" (11)

THE HEALING PIPE

I make my second chanupa a few years after My Personal Pipe. It's in the shape of a disk. I call it The Healing Pipe. I work on the bowl as I live in a screen tent on top of a mountain. I am a volunteer for The Abode of the Message, a Sufi retreat center in New Lebanon, New York. I need a hand-crank drill, and a friend, Devin, who spends a lot of time in nature, appears. He lends me one. That is how it works in the Native American realm. We are all brothers. We are all related. I work on the bowl most of that day. Then I lie down to sleep for the night.

During the night, a black bear comes by to investigate. It leans against my screen tent to sniff inside. In the morning, there are bear claw marks in the side. I felt safe enough and never woke up. It is an honor to have this visitor bring bear medicine to my chanupa. I have been told that a black bear instinctively knows when it needs to eat plant medicine and where to find it. They are natural healers.

The primary intention I place in this chanupa is to bring healing. Friends and I pray together with it. I invite select friends to join me to smoke and pray with The Healing Pipe in a teepee at the Abode.

One friend, Fascia asks, "Why do you need to use a pipe to pray?"

I say, "Just come and see what happens."

I was taught by others who lead Native gatherings that you need to create a sacred, welcoming space, so we had blankets spread out in front of the fire and pillows to sit on. It is not just about praying with the chanupa; part of a pipe ceremony is learning about the way to listen and respect each other. Fascia prayed with my friends and me, using the chanupa.

Afterwards, she said, "I felt something happen. It is a powerful way to pray."

You don't need a chanupa to pray. One needs to pray from the heart, from a place of authenticity, and then listen — really listen — and be open to receive with faith. My Native Brother shared different ways I can even use the chanupa to set a strong intention without praying. For example, if I am facing a challenging situation, I can load the chanupa and set it aside for a few days or weeks before I actually smoke the kinnikinnick and pray. During this time, the chanupa is "loaded," and my prayers are simmering. Often, the intentions of my prayers will start to address the situation.

For me, having the chanupa creates a sacred space. A pipe carrier has a responsibility to honor the chanupa, even if at times they don't honor themselves. A pipe carrier must prove themselves worthy, just as a Knight of the Round Table had to prove he was chivalrous enough. In the legend, the Knights swore a Code of Chivalry. Meaning they promised to uphold the rules given to them. Those include: to help a woman in need and never harm her. Another was: do not be cruel, and grant mercy unto him who asks for it. My friends who are pipe carriers set a living example and share a code of conduct that is similar. It includes: treat all living creatures with compassion, graciously serve others, and strive to live from the heart.

THE UNIVERSAL PIPE

My third pipe comes about in a rather peculiar manner. I am showing Wise Wolf how to make a chanupa. I send him the two pieces of that first chanupa bowl that broke in half. It's a guide for him to see, inside and out. Wise Wolf takes it upon himself to mend this broken pipe. When I receive it back, I am pleasantly surprised to find the two halves cemented together. I take it as a sign and make a stem. This is my third chanupa. I call it The Universal Pipe. The chanupa and I are broadening to accept God in different forms, religions, and traditions.

When I finish the stem, I tie it to a tree branch on the edge of a field to let it wave in the wind. I had been spotting a black bear grazing on grass in this area. Before I leave the pipe stem in the tree, I check out the area for bear signs. I discover the bear was on top of some ledges. I squat down to identify blueberries in some fresh bear scat. I am embarrassed to say that I lingered near the feces with the chanupa stem in one hand. It was a dumb thing to do, especially at this vulnerable stage of energy absorption.

I question if starting with a broken pipe bowl, even though it's mended, is a wise move. Some things are sacred, and once they crack or break, they lose their value. Years later I receive confirmation through a Lakota expert: "I would not use a broken bowl, even if it was repaired by a trusted source. The energy gets out through the cracks, even when they are mended." My best solution would have been to make a new bowl. But I go forward with the mended chanupa, because I don't know any better. Besides, it has sentimental value after my mentor, Wise Wolf, repaired it.

I let the stem swing on a tree branch for a week. Afterwards, I take my first medicine walk with The Universal Pipe. During the walk, I come across animal scat wherever I turn.

I find that of the fox, deer, bear, and moose. There are also animal bones scattered all over. Perhaps it's too late. Have I called in death and an assortment of (excuse the pun) crap into my life? Yes! The Universal Pipe goes on to teach me about the darker side. Let me explain what I mean by the darker side. ∎

CHAPTER 14

Death and Desperation

My grandmother, Hosanna, was a schoolteacher. After my grandfather, Buck, died, she found comfort in studying the Bible. She did not just read the Bible; she grasped hold of each word and chewed on it and digested it as a teacher. I am her student, and when I visit, we dissect her latest Bible passages. When I leave from a visit with her, I am spiritually filled. Her home is a sanctuary for family and friends. They are always welcomed with a smile, an endearing conversation, and a meal consisting of little bits of leftovers. Her couch is also a comfortable place to take a short nap. She is monumental for me as a teacher. She lives to the best of her ability as instructed through the Bible and as guided by the Holy Spirit.

She prays that her two sons will live in harmony. The Lion borrowed $20,000 from her retirement fund. It took years for her to save that much. After several years, she says, "If you can get along with your brother, I will forgive your debt." Her heart is in the right place, but her attempt to buy harmony between her sons seems to be the wrong approach.

Hosanna has devoted herself to Jesus. She prays constantly for her grandchildren, great grandchildren, and friends. She has one nephew, Firecracker, who is in and out of jail. She has taken him under her wing and writes to him regularly. She is probably his only remaining family member that deeply cares about him.

Hosanna held a sharp mind, even in her nineties. She told me in detail about how the windows shook in her house during a hurricane that happened when she was five years old. She enjoys playing different games. Now that she is in her mid-nineties, she has reverted to being more like a child. On occasion, she cries when she doesn't get what she wants.

THE FINAL DAY

At age 96, she had a stroke, and half of her body became paralyzed. Hosanna could no longer talk as she once did, which was rather constantly. When she tried to communicate, it came out as garbled sounds. It left her and family members frustrated. Soon afterwards, she was taken from the hospital to live out her remaining days at an elderly facility called The Pines. I stop by to visit her and often read from Psalms in the Bible. She listens intently and smiles.

After a few months, her condition deteriorates rapidly. There is a large black cat that lives at The Pines. It will linger for a few days in the room of an elderly man or woman before they die. The nurses all know what it means when the black cat shows up in Hosanna's room. She has decided a week earlier to stop eating. She is ready to move on to the next destination, without her body. In her mid-nineties, she spoke with jubilation about when she will be with Jesus. She said with anticipation, "What a glorious day it will be!"

One afternoon, our family gets a call from a nurse explaining that Hosanna is near the end. When I arrive, she is wrapped up in blankets like a cocoon. The Lion and my uncle are in the room with her. It is one of those awkward moments because in our family men rarely express their emotions. Pastor R.I.P. stops by to read Psalm 23, sing a song, and say a final prayer. It brings all of us some comfort. The Lion and my uncle leave to go home around suppertime.

I want to be there so she is not alone when she dies. Time passes slowly. I intend to read her psalm 91, which is one of her favorite passages. It has 16 verses about the safety of abiding in the presence of God, but somehow I end up reading Psalm 119. It's 176 verses known as *A Meditation on the Excellency of the Word of God*.

In its own way, reading her the deep, longer passage is more appropriate as our last teaching. I am her student and her grandson. She was my first Bible teacher and my grandmother. Now, she is dying.

It's 9:30 p.m. and Hosanna is on morphine and going in and out of consciousness. I place my hand on hers and cradle the back of her head. Her body is starting to shut down. Her skin color is turning purple progressively, from her feet up to her head. Nurses regularly come into the room to check her vital signs. Her breathing is rapid and labored. Her heartbeat goes steadily from 26 to 60 beats per minute.

Her blue eyes stare into mine for what seems like an hour. I am staring into God's light. She is filled with love and radiates the presence of God. When a person is dying, the last sense to go is hearing, so I sit down next to her and keep talking. I speak to her as a life coach might during a last session.

I say, "Don't resist. Be soft; don't be afraid. Be aware of everything that is happening and feel it."

Her staring into my eyes brings up a lot of different feelings. It's her only way to communicate and remain connected. At one point, I stare into her eyes and see the reflection of my own eyes. I wonder if she is able to see God in my eyes the same way I do in hers. I am sure it brings some comfort to gaze into another soul just before death. She has moved beyond acknowledging me as her grandson. We are both united as one Spirit of God. My spirit remains in my body. Hers is preparing to take a journey. Just after midnight on Halloween, the nurses roll her back onto her right side. It's the side she favors. Her last breath is more a sigh of relief. She lets out a soft, *"Huhh-hhhh."* The nurse feels her heartbeat and pulse.

She softly says, "She is gone."

She was ready to leave her body. I actually feel some joy for her departure. The nurses roll her on her back, and a minute later, the most incredible Cheshire-cat smile comes over her face. She is in bliss. I think she has just met up with Jesus.

A nurse confirms it when she says, "Those that know Jesus get a big smile after they die. I have seen it before."

As I drive home, I sense her saying, "Thank you! It was easier with you there."

She is there in the light that I saw in her eyes.

I ask her, "What is it like there?"

She says, "I am free!"

It's more like a celebration than an ending. I have some sadness, but I would not call it grief. I feel blessed for the precious moments we shared during her life, even right up to the very last minute. Besides, she knew Psalm 91 well enough to recite it.

> *"Whoever dwells in the shelter of the Most High will rest in the shadow of the Almighty. I will say of the Lord, "He is my refuge and my fortress, my God, in whom I trust."*
>
> (Psalm 91:1-2 NIV)

DESPERATION

Years ago, I turned my home into a duplex rental unit and renovated my guest cottage into a rental home. It provided a decent income, but being a landlord is no fairy tale. At times, it's more like a horror movie. Sometimes, tenants stop paying the rent, punch holes in the doors and walls, move out unexpectedly, and usually leave behind bags filled with foul-smelling garbage. Every job, relationship, or addiction I encounter has a lesson in it. Being a landlord helped purge my anger. A half dozen times a tenant has had the nerve to look me in the eyes and say, "I am not going to pay the rent. I am not moving out!" Then they cross their arms and give me a look that implies, "What are you going to do about it?" I would often explode and do some foolish, violent act that I would later regret.

After years of facing difficult rental situations, I realize that getting angry is not the best approach. Getting angry often causes the other to react immediately. Sometimes, I get the desired results, but it never resolves a situation in a harmonious manner. If I allow time to calm down, I can face a situation with greater wisdom. Each situation is different. If I understand their perspective and mine, then I can often resolve a conflict in a manner so we both get what we want.

I am having a stressful situation where a couple of tenants are three months behind on the rent. I notice the tenants have cut a six-inch hole in the interior and exterior wall of the rental house. Now, their washing machine water discharges directly in the backyard. My level of stress and anger is starting to rise. It takes months to actually evict somebody according to Vermont rental laws. Of course, they know this and use it to their advantage. They decide to stir the pot by using the devil's favorite weapon: they lie. They tell my tenant living in my lower-level duplex apartment, "We have seen the landlord sneak in your apartment at night. He stands above your bed and watches you sleep."

These tenants cannot afford to move out of my rental unit without the funds to place a deposit to rent another home, so I offer them $500 to move out. They look at me with disbelief and say, "This must be a trick!" It's not a trick. I am willing to purchase my peace of mind. I actually pay them to leave.

Around this time, the septic system at my rental duplex gives out. I am wading in crap, literally this time. I replaced it eight years prior for about $3,500, but since then Vermont has passed a new regulation. I must hire an expensive engineer to approve and design it. What in reality costs $5,000 to replace is lathered into a $20,000 project. I am upset about a variety of ways the cost of living in Vermont has increased, so I write a letter to the editor of the Caledonian Record, which is our local paper:

Break Free

There are 3 milestone decisions that changed my life significantly. The first was living without a TV. It set my mind free! The second was selling my car and riding a bike when possible, no guilty acid rain on my shoulders. The third was converting my house to a rental duplex to gain financial freedom.

I am forced to sell my home due to the outrageous costs to live in Vermont; health insurance, heating fuel, and taxes are outrageously expensive, but what broke my back was the new septic regulations requiring a $20,000 mound system. Then a permit arrives after the work is complete stating I may no longer utilize my home as a duplex apartment.

It seems the system is encouraging me to lounge on the welfare system with free food, free medical coverage, fuel assistance, and tax breaks. Why work? For me it's simple, I would rather give to society than be a burden on the system. So I am, like many other middle-aged, skilled Vermonters, moving out of this state. I plan to live in a sustainable community in Costa Rica.

I love this state and this country, but radical change is required. It starts within you. As for those in Government, Lao-Tzu said it well… "If you want to govern the people, you must place yourself below them. If you want to lead the people, you must learn to follow them."

Adios Amigos, 5th Generation Vermonter

BRICK BLOCK

The financial dilemma I am facing is not limited to my rental unit. It seems like every avenue I have invested in is simultaneously draining my finances. My 2nd cousin invented a way to place a simulated brick face with inlaid grout lines on wall and chimney blocks. They are available in all the common block sizes and grout colors and can have the brick face on one or both sides. They can be used in construction for half the cost of bricks, and even up close they appear to be bricks. They are manufactured at cement-block plants, where they produce two or three blocks every five seconds.

Brick Block is a fabulous idea, especially for the United States, Canada, and Latin America. But one needs a team and finances to launch a specialized block like this nationwide. The Lion, along with a great uncle who is an inventor at IBM, and various friends and family members including myself, become board members and investors. Brick Block receives various patents and we manage the business for the next ten years.

Brick Block is unveiled at the New England construction trade show. We are a big hit and have hundreds of leads and prospective projects. A few years later, we have manufacturing plants producing our specialized blocks throughout New England and as far south as Pennsylvania. We ship our product further south. The largest areas for brick construction in the United States are in the deep south.

Brick Block needs to purchase a few new molds to be able to make our products in block plants that utilize a different brand of block production equipment. I take out a $70,000 loan and lend the money to Brick Block. I want them to succeed. To make a long story short, I don't get paid back in cash. I agree to accept stock. In part, I choose to follow the risky financial example set by The Lion. He is in full support of my actions, perhaps in part because he is a major stockholder. In the end, I am responsible for a $70,000 loan to the bank.

THE RAT TRAP

At this point, I have excellent credit, and a dozen credit-card companies have sent offers for cash at 0%- 5% interest.

Like a rat, I take the bait. I am good at playing the credit card game. I pay off the $70,000 loan to the bank in five years. In the process, I accumulate a huge amount of credit card debt. I owe them…$70,000.

After three years, it starts to steamroll, and my monthly payment in loans and credit cards bills are twice what I earn each month. My whole financial world is starting to crumble. I need to make some radical decisions real soon.

I feel like I am running a gauntlet with bill collectors beating me on all sides. They are all demanding that I pay them. I have always paid my bills on time, but I can no longer do it. The thought of not being able to pay all my bills is anxiety-inducing. I constantly feel the stress. I am forced to draw a line, consider my priorities, and decide which bills to pay. There is a bill for the guy who delivered gravel for my septic system. He is fairly low on my priority list until he places a lien on my home.

I am living on the edge of a nervous breakdown. My muscles are wound so tightly that they feel like steel knots. I am in a very dark place. I made some unwise decisions with my finances. Now, I am paying the price. The stress is physically clamping down on my body like a vice. I have to stop and rest every few hours.

In order to keep all possible rental money flowing, I sell *all* personal items of any value: guns and family antiques, like the grandfather clock that my great, great-grandfather assembled. Then I move back into our family home with The Lamb.

To top it all off, I am in the middle of another one of those ugly scenes with a tenant who is behind on the rent. His dad has been a family employee with us for years. Now his son just gave me his spiel, "I am not going to pay any more rent. I am not moving out either." I have already lined up a new tenant to move in at the end of the month. I need him to either pay up or move out. I am angry. I make a big show by banging on the stovepipe. Then I go to punch a cupboard door beside him.

As my punch is mid-air, he bends over at the waist. My elbow accidentally hits him in the eye. He gets a shiner out of it. He immediately drives to the police station and presses charges. As part of my retribution, I am ordered to take a series of sessions with a counselor for anger management.

To make matters worse, the tenant never returns to the rental unit. I am told he is afraid to come back. Eventually, I must place all his belongings in a storage unit. I give his Dad the key along with all the food from his fridge and freezer. Just another day as a landlord!

CHAPTER 15

The Lighthouse

During all this commotion, I am attending the local Christian church led by Pastor R.I.P. I know if I serve others it's time well spent; plus it makes me feel better. They want a youth-group leader. I want to work with youth, but Pastor R.I.P. will not even consider me as a candidate. I assume it's because I am a yoga teacher.

I have prayed about teaching yoga. It's what the Holy Spirit wants me to do. I have even dissected the components of yoga for myself from a biblical perspective, so I can clearly understand where there are controversies. The Bible is clear about not having idols in the form of statues. Some yoga teachers set up altars with statues of various Gods and Goddesses like Shiva, Ganesh or Buddha. Yoga is traditionally linked to Hinduism, Buddhism, and Jainism, so their concepts are infused. I can empathize how this could make a Christian feel uncomfortable.

CRISTO MORPHO FITNESS

One Easter Sunday, I design a Christ-based yoga class called Cristo Morpho Fitness. It comes as a complete download, before I knew there was any such thing as Christian yoga. It includes a time for prayer, worship music, breathing exercises, and sometimes I read healing scriptures while postures are being held. The big difference between a regular yoga class and a Christ-based yoga class is that the focus is on Christ.

During a Cristo Morpho Fitness class, I can feel the presence of the Holy Spirit.

Once I taught Cristo Morpho Fitness to my Integral Yoga class students. They gave me mixed reviews. Jesus brings up strong reactions. Most people either love Jesus or they are radically opposed. Those who are open to a Christ-connection get touched by the Holy Spirit. One woman, who was open, had giggles all through the class. Sometimes the Holy Spirit comes accompanied with tears or giggles.

As a Christ-based yoga teacher, I encounter resistance from pastors who have not experienced a yoga class. They don't want a form of Christian fitness taught in their church. Some fundamental Christians deem yoga as evil. I have heard some outrageously false claims about yoga from Christians. A coworker, who was a Christian woman in her sixties said, "After attending my first yoga class I felt vibrantly energized, like I was young again. I felt so good that I went out and partied that night and the next morning I felt great." She went on to explain how it was her decision to go drinking, but she thought evil spirits from the yoga class prevented her from feeling the effects of the alcohol. Another Christian proclaimed, "Every yoga pose allows an evil spirit to enter your body." Thankfully, there are some open-minded pastors that welcome yoga or Christian yoga into their church.

THE UNIVERSALIST CHURCH

I visit the local Universalist church. I am introduced to Pastor B. I explain to him that I desire to lead a youth group.

He says, "We have been searching for a youth group leader. You can start next Sunday."

I say, "I would like to offer Cristo Morpho Fitness and yoga classes at your church."

He replies, "Sure! There is a big sanctuary upstairs."

It's an old church with a beautiful sanctuary space with high ceilings, huge windows, and a well-worn wooden floor.

On Sunday, I begin as the youth pastor. There are 10-12 bright kids in the youth group. They paint a wall mural in the space where we gather. Then each kid paints an animal with a musical instrument, such as a cat with a guitar or an elephant on the drums. During the winter we have a sledding party at a nearby steep hill. Of course, it is followed by hot chocolate with marshmallows back in the church kitchen. We also meet here to make homemade pizzas. The kids like to play checkers and other games during our free time. I am discovering that these youths are a talented bunch. One is acting in a play (which we attend), another plays the violin, and a few play guitars or drums. We decide to gather in the sanctuary on a Saturday morning for a music jam.

Before I know it, I am elected to be on the board of directors for the church. I get approval and organize a project to clear out the sanctuary for a week, and we refinish the floors. It's a big project. Some local yoga teachers and church volunteers pull together. Now there is a beautifully refinished floor. It seems like a big leap compared to being reined in at the Christian church.

After four months, I am finding the real challenge of being a youth pastor is dealing with the parents, because the kids are all super cool. There was one incident, regarding a youth being told about an upcoming music jam, that became pivotal. For some unknown reason, his mother was strongly against his attending. When I called to inform the youth, his mother answered so I gave her the message. She said, "Don't contact him about it. He doesn't want to go." What she may not have known was that after he missed the first music jam, he was rather bummed out. He specifically asked me to tell him about the next one. He played an instrument and wanted to participate. So I went against her request. I told him about the music jam. Perhaps if he really wanted to attend the music jam and his mother was against it, the three of us could discuss it.

Once she found out I had contacted her son, against her

request, she was livid. She arranged a special board meeting, without my knowledge, to resolve the situation. She had the power to persuade. They had an on-the-spot vote to remove me from the position of youth group leader. What really hurt was that the board did not want to listen to what happened from my perspective before deciding my fate. As a result, I felt banished from their church.

Needless to say, my stint of volunteer service at the Universalist Church came to a rapid end. I was not too upset. Pastor B had done a few things that led me to question his ethics. I left their church for the most part feeling unheard, unappreciated, and unfairly treated.

THE ULTIMATUM LETTER

I never had any reason to question the ethics of Pastor R.I.P., and I hunger to be in a church where I can feel the Holy Spirit during worship again. I humbly go back to his church. After a spell of not attending what they consider "the right" church, I have ruffled some feathers.

Upon my return, a long-time church member gives me a scrutinizing look and sharply says, "What are *you* doing back here?"

Overall, I am welcomed back by the Christian church. I am willing and ready to find my place in this church. I join a home group. It becomes a life support system. I find that the home group is a place to worship with friends, share personal challenges, and recognize how the Bible can guide us through difficult times. I share my financial despair and receive some heartfelt support.

Sometimes I feel uncomfortable at the Christian Church. I don't meet their standards for being a Christian. My spiritual path began with yoga and immersing myself in more of a universal approach. Therefore, I often speak different spiritual phrases. I find it difficult to accept their lack of tolerance toward other religions and the way their leaders verbally bash homosexuals during services and seminars. Basically, I fail tremendously at being what they consider to be a good Christian.

After five years of attending their church, I ask Pastor R.I.P. point blank, "What is it I need to do so you will trust me?"

He says, "I don't believe I can ever trust you. There is nothing you can do." This was quite a debilitating blow. My own father had proven years ago that he didn't trust me, and now my secondary father figure tells me the same.

Their church does assist me in numerous ways, for which I am grateful. I meet with a church elder weekly to receive counsel. He listens, but eventually asks me to stop talking about my financial problems. He doesn't know what to do about my bills or the stress they cause. Finance is not his area of expertise. Then Pastor R.I.P. connects me with a Christian financial advisor, who is monumental in helping me face the reality of my sticky financial situation.

He says, "It's important to tithe and have faith. There is no quick fix when you are in this deep. It could take several years to recover financially."

As fate had it, soon after, on a Sunday, Pastor R.I.P. gives a sermon devoted to tithing.

He states, "When you are facing financial difficulties, it's important to continue to tithe."

I am not convinced that tithing to the church will help my situation when my money is, in effect, coming from a credit card company, which increases my debt. I finally get it while I am driving home. It's about giving regardless of your situation. I turn around and drive back to write out a check for 10% of what I earned that month.

The next time I meet with Pastor R.I.P., he says, "I am doing something this church has never done before. I am returning your tithe check. I feel it was not given with the right attitude in your heart."

This leaves me utterly confused about tithing! It's the beginning of the end. Afterwards, a series of uncanny events unfold at the church. It all ends with what I call "The Ultimatum Letter" from Pastor R.I.P. It is a formal letter that I will paraphrase in a shorter form:

The Ultimatum Letter

We are requesting that you stand up in front of all the church members and openly repent for three things. If you don't want to comply, then we request that you leave our church, the support group, and any affiliation.

1. *Repent that it was wrong to leave our church and go to the Universalist Church.*

2. *Repent that your letter to the editor stating major milestones in your life should have included Jesus Christ. We feel your reference should have been Biblical scripture instead of a Lao-Tzu quote.*

3. *Repent that one cannot renew their mind through a Christian healing session. Renewing the mind happens over time, through reading the Bible.*

The renewing of the mind has to do with what happened after I went to a session with Charles Guest, a Christian Healer for Spiritual Warfare. During the session we address my fear of older men as an eight-year-old. With the help of Jesus, we were able to connect my heart and my mind. It was a powerful healing session. When I came home my head began to throb and burn. It was hot to touch. I became concerned and put ice on top of my head. Then I heard a soft voice say, "It will go away in one hour", and it did. This was my first real healing with Jesus and I was excited about it.

During a time for open testimonies at church on the next Sunday, I said, "After my spiritual warfare session, I felt my mind was renewed." I chose the word "renewed", because I was trying to use some of their church jargon. I never imagined my ignorant misuse of a word would be critically judged as grounds for my removal.

Well, it's not in my heart to repent the three things that Pastor R.I.P. requested to remain at his church. I did not feel that even one of the three things was really wrong. I feel that I have no option, if I have any self-dignity remaining, other than to leave Pastor R.I.P.'s church. This means I will lose the lifeline of support that I received from the home group.

My boat has begun to sink. In desperation, I abandon it. I swim alone toward the shore, shivering from being wet and cold. I am frustrated with this Christian church; our core beliefs and values are different. It's essential that I am part of a spiritual community where my relationships are based on mutual trust, respect, and understanding. Love and acceptance seem far from my reach at this church, but I believe they exist elsewhere.

These awkward issues are bobbing on the surface, circling around like sharks. I am swimming in treacherous waters: nobody to trust, nobody to understand me, nobody to affirm me anymore. I am going through my darkest night of despair. Part of my underlying hope is that the church will stop singing cheery hymns and cast out a lifeline to pull me back aboard. Their merry rowboat filled with Christian crusaders is rowing nearby. I am floundering in the water. My body sinks, except for one hand that is raised up above my head. They have spotted me and extended out a gift in my direction. I anticipate a life preserver, but instead it is an anchor. They give one last plastic smile and shout out "Halleluiah" before they wave farewell. I am swept down…down…down toward the bottom of the deep, dark, blue sea. I feel alone, betrayed, and alienated by yet another church.

THE LIGHTHOUSE

I let go of their anchor and come up gasping for air. In the darkness, I locate the shoreline and swim toward it. I crawl up onto the dry land, exhausted. A storm is starting to rain down. The wind blows the rain in sheets off the ocean. After I catch my breath, I begin to walk along a slippery, dark path. The short scruffy shrubs offer no relief from that wind. I find myself standing on a small cliff, peering out toward the sea. There are no boats in sight; there is no shelter. Whichever direction I turn, I am facing the storm. From my despairing perspective, there is nobody left on this earth. I am all alone. Why am I being broken down, crushed, and bruised, lost and forgotten, abandoned and cast aside?

Then, in the distance I see *Him*. There is a lone lighthouse on a distant island. The light shines across the water. A beam of light exposes a desperately lonely man, drenched in rain, shivering from the cold, longing for the comfort of a friend. Then I realize, even in the middle of the storm, I am not alone. I feel the source of the light radiating. It is peace and love. I recognize it. I have felt it before. His silhouette is in the middle of the fog. I know who *He* is, but more importantly, *He* knows who I am. The church may leave, my finances can be a disaster, my body can be battered, but Jesus is still the same. I stare at His silhouette, looming in the distance. He is surrounded by the light. I take a step forward....

CHAPTER 16

Jesus Calling

I cry out to Jesus. I take another few steps forward, lose my footing, and slip over the edge. I start to slide down the face of the slippery, wet cliff. In despair, I grasp out to reach a branch or a stone — something solid, something real to hold onto. As I fall, I feel my hand wrap around a branch — No it's *not* a branch, it's the wooden stem of my chanupa that I have grabbed. I snap out of the daydream. I am standing on the back porch of our brick house preparing to pray with the chanupas! Spread out upon a table before me are my three pipes and stems, with furs underneath them. The sun is shining down brightly. I can hear the roaring waterfalls from the river below.

I am doing a rather unorthodox chanupa ceremony because I want Jesus to be a part of it; perhaps *His* silhouette from the fog remains with me. I feel it's my last chance to surrender my life to Jesus. I give Him full spiritual authority in all realms. It's a step beyond being a part of any church. It's about desiring a deeper relationship with Jesus. It's a big bold move, which I do willingly. Christ performed miracles, and people are healed by His love, daily. Certainly, Jesus has the ability to straighten out my life. Maybe I need to surrender *completely* before Jesus can fully maneuver in my life.

THE CHANUPA CEREMONY WITH THE HOLY SPIRIT

I have a four-inch pewter statue of Jesus with one arm

nailed to a cross. He is looking toward a dove with wings spread. It is taking flight from His other free hand. This statue represents the peace that Christ brings, along with the suffering He willingly endured. I offer tobacco to the earth and load the three chanupas with kinnikinnick to pray. In my ceremony, I load one pipe to honor the east, one for the south, and one for the west. The statue of Christ stands alone to honor the north for the Holy Spirit.

There is a chickadee sitting in a small pine tree, peeping out a song, calmly witnessing my ceremony. I sing a song to the East, South, and West. I smoke each of the three chanupas…My Personal Pipe, The Healing Pipe, and The Universal Pipe…as I say my prayers. When I am done praying with each chanupa, I kiss it.

I think to myself, *How odd is this?*

I just gave each pipe a soft little kiss of affection. It was like what one might give to a friend on the cheek when they depart.

I sing out, "Hallelujah, hallelujah, hallelujah" from Handel's Messiah to honor Jesus for the north. It was fresh in my mind because I had orchestrated our church home group to sing it.

I make a request of Jesus: "Take charge of my life through the Holy Spirit. Rule with your authority over all the aspects in my life…my finances, my spiritual life, my health, and my relationships." It's a step in faith, for in my heart, Jesus represents my last hope. There is stillness; no visions, no thunderbolts, no tingling in my heart. The ceremony is complete.

But a few minutes after the ceremony, a spirit responds. As I walk back through the kitchen carrying the three wooden stems, I pass the wood stove. There is a roaring fire within it.

A soft whispering voice says, "Throw them in the fire!"

I stop walking. I don't want to listen or obey the voice of *this* spirit. I try to ignore it, yet I know it could possibly be the Holy Spirit responding. I had a vision three years earlier of myself smashing my chanupa bowls and burning the stems. Now it has returned as a haunting flashback.

I reply to the spirit in a questioning tone, "Throw them in the fire?"

I think to myself, *Are you crazy? I can't do that.* I tell myself it's the voice of an unwanted spirit attempting to misguide me. I had never heard a soft whispering voice like this one following any other chanupa ceremony. But this is the first time I have ever invited the Holy Spirit to be a part of the ceremony. I am concerned. I place the stems upstairs in my bedroom and go back for the bowls. I carry all three bowls with a fur wrapped around them.

When I pass by the wood stove, the soft whispering voice speaks again, "Smash them with a hammer."

I respond out loud, "I will not do any such thing!"

Suddenly, The Universal Pipe falls out of the fur. It hits the floor and breaks in half. At that moment, I feel disappointed and dismayed; I know, without a doubt, it's the Holy Spirit. If I am not obedient, then the other two chanupas will be taken away. I am reluctant, but feel I have no other option. I must obey the Holy Spirit. I did ask the Holy Spirit to take control of my life, but this is not what I expected. I grab my Bible to find some confirmation.

> *"I have a message from God in my heart concerning the sinfulness of the wicked: There is no fear of God before their eyes. In their own eyes they flatter themselves too much to detect or hate their sin. The words of their mouths are wicked and deceitful; they fail to act wisely or do good. Even on their beds they plot evil; they commit themselves to a sinful course and do not reject what is wrong. Your love, Lord, reaches to the heavens, your faithfulness to the skies. Your righteousness is like the highest mountains, your justice like the great deep. You, Lord, preserve both people and an-*

imals. How priceless is your unfailing love, O God! People take refuge in the shadow of your wings."

(Psalm 36:1-7 NIV)

A SACRIFICE FOR THE ALTAR

Of course I am reluctant! But I have faith that The Holy Spirit is taking control and making this request for my own benefit. I'm not in a position to judge whether praying with the chanupa is a sin. I have seen plenty of good results from my prayers. Perhaps the Lord is jealous enough to want me all for himself, in His own way. I am willing to comply. Actually, I feel I have no other option than to be obedient, even if it means laying down my chanupas. If I must do it, I prefer to do it with my own hands, rather than having each taken away by some other means. The Holy Spirit, for reasons unbeknownst to me, has made a clear request. I know what I must do.

> "They say to wood, 'You are my father,' and to stone, 'You gave me birth.' They have turned their backs to me and not their faces; yet when they are in trouble, they say, 'Come and save us!' Where then are the gods you made for yourselves? Let them come if they can save you when you are in trouble...."
>
> (Jeremiah 2:27-28 NIV)

I take my personal pipe and the healing pipe and do as I am guided. In a ceremonial manner, I carefully wrap them in red cloth and tie off the bundle. I bury them each underneath a sweat lodge altar.

MY ESCAPE TO YOGAVILLE

I need to leave this town, this church, and this situation. All I feel here relates to misery and pain. A friend is traveling overnight in a van destined for Virginia. I arrange to travel with him. I made arrangements to volunteer at Satchidananda

Ashram, better known as Yogaville, for a few months. Afterwards, I hope to start taking classes at the nearby Liberty University, through a Vermont state grant. I have faith in God to provide a way to pay the bill.

Yogaville gives me a chance to pull myself back together. As part of their volunteer program, I am a LYT (Light) serving for thirty hours a week, usually in the kitchen or housecleaning. There is plenty of structure and discipline built into my routine. I go to daily yoga classes and meditations. Our group meets weekly for scripture studies and community Satsang, and we share as a group, which provides the needed support. I find the teachings from Swami Satchidananda very inspiring.

He says, "The aim of all spiritual practices is to know the real Self, to know the Knower. A very healthy and relaxed body with a calm and serene mind will allow the true light or the true nature of the Self within to express itself without any distortions."

My favorite part of the Integral Yoga classes is the long, guided, deep relaxations. They provide detailed step-by-step instructions on how to relax. They leave my body refreshed and renewed.

The presence of Swami Satchidananda is still here guiding people even after he has left his body. He gives encouragement to his devotees, the yoga teachers, volunteers, and visitors. He helps build up people's confidence in themselves. I never met him in person, but I can feel his peaceful presence.

I often take long walks in the woods. One day, I go to meditate in a cave on a trail near a brook. Before I know it, I find myself rolling in the brook in my underwear grieving, crying, and yelling out in anger to God, "Why did you take away my chanupas?"

In general, a man or woman receives a chanupa when they are ready for it. If it's misused, it can be taken away. I heard of a circumstance where a misused chanupa was even stolen. I understand the immense power in the chanupa. It should be honored and respected.

I wonder, *Was I worshiping the chanupa as an idol?*

Certainly, it's not meant to be worshiped as a God. It's a grounded way to pray from the heart. I feel constantly humbled by not having my chanupas.

Swami Satchidananda says, "All that happens is God's will, not even a speck of dust can move without God."

Eventually, I start to let it go.

The chanupa is one way I found inner peace. Through them I came closer to understanding God, life, and myself. This Spirit of God still lives in me. I am still intact; my heart is still beating. I am still alive. I can live with or without them. Making them taught me lessons, but losing them was a tougher lesson. It forced me to realize that my power to pray resides in my heart and in my intentions, not in the chanupa.

CHAPTER 17

Fearless Faith

At this point, I don't really know Jesus or what He is all about. If I want to get to know somebody, I spend time with them, but how do I do that with Jesus, who is not in the flesh? I have asked Jesus to come into my life. I am ready to explore the Bible and to start a personal relationship with Him. I feel the best environment for this to happen is a place where I can immerse myself in a "Jesus culture." My Vermont grant for classes at Liberty University is approved. God is faithful in providing the funds.

Liberty University is located in Lynchburg, Virginia. The university is a small city with paved streets. There is a huge dome-shaped arena that has a basketball court in the center filled with folding chairs. I gather here with 10,000 other students for assembly twice a week. We begin with several worship songs led by students playing guitar, drums, and keyboards. It has the same rock beat as a concert, but there are some noteworthy differences. The words are to glorify Jesus and God.

At Liberty University, as with most churches, we begin with songs of praise and worship. It's a way to synchronize in harmony with each other. Even more importantly, we get closer to God or Jesus. Many students have their eyes closed. It allows them to focus more on the feelings in their hearts.

Occasionally, I get tears in my eyes during worship. I become overwhelmed by feelings of love toward Jesus or God.

It's mixed at that same moment with the love that I receive. God and Jesus continually love me. But during worship I can feel it and taste it.

When I listen to worship music with 10,000 other people or on my own, it forces me to move beyond my thoughts and worries. I rest in my heart. There is a difference between listening to music and feeling it. Worship music is meant to be felt in your heart. We sing with our voices, but if a song is received or stems from the heart, it becomes a deeper spiritual experience.

I often receive personal guidance through the worship music, through the reading of a scripture, or from those sharing a testimony. I am touched when someone gets up to share how Jesus made a difference in his or her life. There is passion in their voice. *How can I get that kind of passion for Jesus?*

FAITH IN THE BIBLE

My relationship and faith in Christ was shaky until I accepted that the Holy Bible, especially the New Testament, was the truth. I was stubborn and questioned if parts of the Bible were irrefutable.

Jesus said,

> "Do not think that I have come to abolish the Law or the Prophets (referring to the scriptures of His time); I have not come to abolish them but to fulfill them."
>
> (Matthew 5:17 NIV)

Reflect upon what that means!

Jesus is saying, "The scriptures are true and I am here as part of the proof."

I have studied and contemplated The Yoga Sutras, The Bhagavita, the Toa Ching, and the Sufi writings of Hazrat Inayat Khan. As far as I am concerned, they all speak the truth. The primary reason I went to Liberty University was to find out what Jesus was really about. What sets Him apart from other spiritual teachers? In the Bible, Peter and John write that Jesus lived a perfect life, without sin. Jesus made some preposterous claims about Himself:

> "The Father and I are one."
>
> (John 10:30 NIV)

> "You are of this world; I am not of this world."
>
> (John 8:23 NIV)

> "Before Abraham was born, I am."
>
> (John 8:58 NIV)

I understand why some people don't believe in Jesus or what is written in the Bible. What Jesus says seems crazy! Jesus does not claim, as do other spiritual teachers, to show a way to salvation. He states He *is* the way to salvation. (John 14:6) Then there are all the healing miracles and His resurrection. After I pieced together what Jesus did and said, along with a lot of soul-searching, I came to the conclusion that there is no other possibility: Jesus *is* the Son of God.

I don't expect everyone's view on Jesus or the Bible will drastically change overnight. It's my desire that some readers will gain a new perspective and a few eager souls will further investigate the Bible or explore what Jesus is really about from followers who know Him. The foundation that I build upon is that the Bible is true. If you do not believe, and you want to position yourself to better understand my viewpoint, then entertain the possibility that it could be true, for the next few chapters.

Many people have experienced an overzealous person trying to evangelize in a judgmental or unwelcome manner. Why do they do that? Well, they are passionate about Jesus and want to share it, but often they take the wrong approach. I believe what most people who know Jesus desire is for you to experience a relationship with Him. The Bible is certainly a relevant starting point for learning about Jesus. An alternative approach, which I advocate, is to speak about their relationship with Jesus. It's interesting to learn another's heart-felt experience and less offensive to show how scripture relates or provides proof. This is the approach I take.

I find some parts of the Bible, especially the Old Testament, hard to comprehend. In these areas, I ask the Holy Spirit for guidance. Often, what I don't understand is made clear through a sermon, a song, or a casual conversation with a friend. For example, I don't understand why I should "fear God." I was afraid of my real father for years, and don't want to fear God. I have some issues around it and pray to the Holy Spirit for an answer. The Bible uses the word "fear" at least 300 times in reference to God. If God is my creator who loves me, then why should I be afraid of Him?

In the article, *What does it mean to fear God?* by JoHannah Reardon, she writes,

> *"Fearing God is good because it saves us from caving in to our own sinful nature. That's why hearing someone is God-fearing actually makes us trust that person more. If they fear God, they are more likely to keep their word and treat others with kindness. In fact, Romans 3, a classic chapter on sin, says that our chief sin is that we 'have no fear of God at all' (Romans 3:18).*
>
> *"So how does fear of God, who is perfect love, take away fear? William D. Eisenhower puts it this way in his article Fearing God in Christianity Today:*
>
> *"Unfortunately, many of us presume that the world is the ultimate threat and that God's function is to offset it. How different this is from the biblical position that God is far scarier than the world .... When we assume that the world is the ultimate threat, we give it*

unwarranted power, for in truth, the world's threats are temporary. When we expect God to balance the stress of the world, we reduce him to the world's equal .... As I walk with the Lord, I discover that God poses an ominous threat to my ego, but not to me. He rescues me from my delusions, so he may reveal the truth that sets me free. He casts me down, only to lift me up again. He sits in judgment of my sin, but forgives me nevertheless. Fear of the Lord is the beginning of wisdom, but love from the Lord is its completion.

"And, of course, the ultimate example of fear and perfect love working together is Jesus Christ. He warned us at every turn to fear God, not men — and he confirmed that in everything about his life and death. He spoke lovingly but frankly to all and didn't mince words when people needed to face their sin and repent. But he also demonstrated love beyond human understanding when he lived out his words, 'There is no greater love than to lay down one's life for one's friends (John 15:13).' With love like that, what is left to fear but God?" (12)

HOLY SPIRIT GUIDANCE

If I want to get to know Jesus, then I need to get to know the Holy Spirit. Jesus sent us the Holy Spirit as a way for us to stay in touch with Him. This is no ordinary event. The Holy Spirit was sent because Jesus loves us. He can't be on this earth, not right now. Jesus is ruling over the Kingdom in heaven. (Remember, we are all believing the Bible.) Through the Holy Spirit, Jesus and His followers also have power upon the earth.

"But very truly I tell you, it is for your good that I am going away. Unless I go away, the Advocate will not come to you; but if I go, I will send him to you... But

when he, the Spirit of truth, comes, he will guide you into all the truth. He will not speak on his own; he will speak only what he hears, and he will tell you what is yet to come. He will glorify me because it is from me that he will receive what he will make known to you."
(John: 16:7,13,14 NIV)

The Bible explains that The Holy Spirit has characteristics similar to any person. I like to picture the Holy Spirit as our living host, a wise and gentle grandfather who provides intimate services and powerful resources. Our living host does what Jesus would want to do if He was on the earth. He has an engaging personality. He has a range of glorious emotions. He is, hopefully, elated and always good-natured. The Holy Spirit has His own will and desires. One is to comfort and care for His family.

I have been let down by men and women, especially when I have built-in expectations. But Jesus, a.k.a. the Holy Spirit, will not, cannot, let me down. He is there with me. When I feel broken and need healing, the Holy Spirit knows it and wants to aid. He is there to listen, encourage, and comfort me. It is a great comfort to know that during my whole life, someone will be present who always understands and loves me.

Often the cause of my discomfort stems from what I tell myself; I have no friends, nobody loves me, I can't do it, I am not smart enough, strong enough, or handsome enough. When I pause and let the Holy Spirit intercede, He reveals them all ... as lies.

"Behold, You desire truth in the innermost being, And in the hidden part You will make me know wisdom."
(Psalm 51:6 NASB)

The Holy Spirit crashes over me, "I am so pleased with you." He holds me. His voice keeps me steadfast when I am in over my head. He wants me to give Him all my problems. He wants me to rely on Him. He wants my attention. I believe He wants me to lose control. That way, He can take over. He can handle it; I can't anymore. When I rely on Him, it brings me beautiful joy. He really deserves to have what He wants — me.

Jesus is on earth and in heaven. Jesus knew that He had to die on that cross to allow the Holy Spirit to be with us. Through His obedience, He was able to divide Himself to be able to reign over heaven and earth. He is still alive! I never understood how people could get so excited about Jesus. Now, I am becoming one of them. In my case, I first needed a deeper understanding of Jesus and to experience what it means to actually have the Holy Spirit living inside of my heart. Now, I know how much goodness resides in Jesus and the Holy Spirit. It's hard to understand what that actually means if you have never experienced it. One gets access by asking Jesus, via the Holy Spirit, into your life. He needs permission to operate in your life. One needs to invite Him to take up residence in their heart. It can be that simple. The Holy Spirit is available to counsel, comfort, intercede, guide, and give out spiritual gifts.

> *"To one there is given through the Spirit a message of wisdom, to another a message of knowledge by means of the same Spirit, to another faith by the same Spirit, to another gifts of healing by that one Spirit, to another miraculous powers, to another prophecy, to another distinguishing between spirits, to another speaking in different kinds of tongues, and to still another the interpretation of tongues. All these are the work of one and the same Spirit, and he distributes them to each one, just as he determines."*
>
> (1 Corinthians 12:8-11 NIV)

When I have a need for a spiritual gift, I pray for it. I believe that I have received all of the gifts at different times, in varying degrees. Faith dominates as my strongest gift. I have also been given wisdom, but I need to slow down to pray and listen in order to receive it. I often receive my guidance during walks.

The greatest gift is being in His presence. It is a taste of Heaven. We are able to taste Jesus through the Holy Spirit.

When I patiently and persistently pray with faith, God has never failed to provide personal healing. The Holy Spirit wants to protect me from harm and keep me healthy. In order to receive these blessings, I must be obedient to following the guidance given. We often expect a miracle, which does happen on occasion, but more often it requires discipline, patience, and persistence. I believe that being where there is a strong presence of God or Love can bring about healing more rapidly.

When I have a serious problem, I pray. I acknowledge today that I could be more joyful and that I can be more thankful for my blessings. I am writing this because a few people reading this book could be more thankful. You know if I am talking about you because you have goose bumps all over your arms! If that is the case, then right now, put down this book and give thanks for all you have been given. The book will still be here. I had my health, finances, and beloved friends taken away so I could learn to be thankful. Now don't be like me. Just do it.

Pause for a moment and be thankful!

"Rejoice always, pray continually, give thanks in all circumstances; for this is God's will for you in Christ Jesus."

(1 Thessalonians 5:16-18 NIV)

DOUBT

After Jesus was crucified, most of his apostles were gathered in the upper room. They were scared for a good reason. They didn't want to be captured and crucified. Thomas ran off by himself. He knew being with them meant a greater chance of being caught. These are the apostles — the ones Jesus handpicked to follow Him! They saw all His miracles and still they had their doubts. Jesus said to Peter during Passover,

> *"Simon, Simon, Satan has asked to sift all of you as wheat. But I have prayed for you, Simon, that your faith may not fail. And when you have turned back, strengthen your brothers."*
>
> *(Luke 22:31-32 NIV)*

If I understand it properly, Jesus grants Satan permission to sift His disciples like wheat. Jesus knows that Peter must face temptation, but He is praying for him. He loves Simon so much He wants him to reach his full potential.

Even after witnessing His resurrection, they fell back to their old ways. Peter and the others went fishing. Maybe they wanted to return to their former lifestyle because it felt more comfortable. Again and again, Jesus let them know that His life and His resurrection happened to give their life a new purpose and meaning. It was hard for them to change their ways and make their own stand.

But the ascension was the climax of His final forty days. He requested that the apostles gather at Mount of Olives. He told them that it was time for Him to leave this earth. They had witnessed His life and death and resurrection. It was time to receive their final instructions. They were told to be His witnesses and spread His teachings. They were told to stay in Jerusalem until they received the power of the Holy Spirit, which will comfort and guide them in all truth. Jesus explains that He must leave in order for them to receive the Holy Spirit.

The apostles are beginning to understand their purpose or their final destiny. Jesus had shown a living example of how the Holy Spirit lived in and operated through one man, Himself. Jesus declared that anyone who believed in Him with faith would receive authority to heal and perform miracles in His name.

The next book is called Acts for a reason. They finally got it! They began to have real faith. They dedicated their lives completely to Jesus. After they receive the Holy Spirit, they better understood its power and wanted others to receive it. The apostles began miraculously healing people and Peter stood up at Pentecost to say,

> "Therefore let all Israel be assured of this: God has made this Jesus, whom you crucified, both Lord and Messiah."
>
> When the people heard this, they were cut to the heart and said to Peter and the other apostles, "Brothers, what shall we do?"
>
> Peter replied, "Repent and be baptized, every one of you, in the name of Jesus Christ for the forgiveness of your sins. And you will receive the gift of the Holy Spirit.... Those who accepted his message were baptized, and about three thousand were added to their number that day."
>
> (Act 2:38-41 NIV)

Great things happened when Peter placed his faith in Jesus. The same can happen to you and me. There will be temptations and we can count on being sifted, just like Peter. But Jesus is there to intercede for your behalf and mine. All we need to do is *believe*.

After the resurrection, doubting Thomas said he had to touch Jesus to know He was real. Jesus complied.

> "Then Jesus told him, "Because you have seen me, you have believed; blessed are those who have not seen and yet have believed."
>
> (John 20:29 NIV)

THE MISUNDERSTOOD CHRISTIAN

I am writing this section for Christians who have an understanding of and faith in the Bible. They are often misunderstood by other people who have little understanding of Christian lifestyle or the Bible. My hope is that Christians can be better understood. It's easy to talk to a Christian about Jesus, but I am cautious when I talk about Him with people that don't have a connection with Jesus or the Bible. Some people have a lot of resistance toward God or Jesus. I believe the primary cause is spiritual abuse from church leaders, but it also occurs through authority figures in well-intended Christian families.

Ronald Enroth in his book, *Recovering From Churches That Abuse*, explains,

> *"When our trust is violated by those who have been accorded society's respect because of their special role as spiritual caretakers and shepherds of God's flock, the pain, injury, and disillusionment can be devastating. Juanita and Dale Ryan in Recovery from Spiritual Abuse (Downers Grove, Ill.: InterVarsity Press, 1992, p 9-10.) wrote, 'Spiritual abuse is a kind of abuse which damages the central core of who we are. It leaves us spiritually discouraged and emotionally cut off from the healing love of God.'*
>
> *"Spiritual abuse takes place when leaders to whom people look for guidance and spiritual nurture use their positions of authority to manipulate, control, and dominate. Or, as David Johnson and Jeff VanVonderen describe it in The Subtle Power of Spiritual Abuse (Minneapolis: Bethany House, 1991 p. 20), 'Spiritual abuse is the mistreatment of a person who is in need of help, support or greater spiritual empowerment, with the result of weakening, undermining or decreasing that*

person's spiritual empowerment.'

"Most people who are victims of spiritual abuse are sincerely seeking God, either out of a desire to serve him and know him more intimately or out of a deeply felt need to resolve problems. Being vulnerable in their spiritual journey, they would not knowingly subject themselves to pastoral or spiritual abuse. When they later realize that they have been involved in an unhealthy, abusive system, it is understandable that they may harbor resentment and bitterness against the leadership and against God himself. 'Why did God allow this to happen to me when I was sincerely trying to know his will?'" [13]

I try to relate to each person on a level they can understand. I deliberately choose not to discuss Jesus or the Bible with some friends because, frankly, they are not interested or get offended. In this case, it's better that I just show how much I love and care about them. It's not difficult to open up and talk about Jesus after I have established a friendship. Over time, people are naturally curious, and most want to know about my relationship with Jesus, even if it's not their chosen faith. I hope that my actions and the kindness with which I treat others reflects that Christ lives within me.

Imagine how hard it is for a Christian to relate to somebody who has little or no knowledge of the Bible. The Bible addresses almost all of the major issues of life. The Bible is a Christian's foundation of evidence; one who does not accept the Bible as the truth will at times contradict the Bible with their words and corresponding actions. Those who are not Christians will validate their evidence based on their worldly reasoning. Jesus was not of this world. Christians must at times have faith that goes beyond understanding. To debate with a Christian without accepting supporting evidence from the Bible or being of the opinion that part of the Bible is not true, never goes over well.

Once you have established that somebody believes in the Bible, you generally know a lot about their beliefs. At times, it's a real challenge for a Christian to live out Christ's commandments. If you want a genuine eye-opener, then the next time you interact with a Christian, ask him or her to open their heart and tell you what Jesus has done in them or who is Jesus to them. If they have a personal relationship with Jesus then you will know by their experience that Jesus is the real deal. Christians will be delighted to share in this way.

> *"As a prisoner for the Lord, then, I urge you to live a life worthy of the calling you have received. Be completely humble and gentle; be patient, bearing with one another in love. Make every effort to keep the unity of the Spirit through the bond of peace."*
>
> (Ephesians 4:1-3 NIV)

JESUS IS MISUNDERSTOOD

There is a force out there that makes it difficult for some people to accept and understand Christ. Can you feel it? It's rooted in a dark misunderstanding and carries a history of false accusations, prosecutions, and violent acts that claim to be done for Christ. Gandhi said, "I like your Christ, but not your Christians. Your Christians are nothing like your Christ." Jesus knows which actions are acts of love and those that are not. It's no surprise that Christians sometimes feel misunderstood. Jesus was misunderstood almost all the time, by most people, including his twelve disciples.

Jesus loves me and I love Him. Sometimes I talk to Him as a friend and I feel His presence. Other times, I feel all alone, but Jesus is nearby. I know Jesus has the capability to heal the trauma in my heart because I have experienced it. Jesus is a big part of my life and good things keep happening. I am glad about it and our relationship keeps deepening. But my Savior, Jesus, is still a mystery. He operates from a completely different dimension.

When I speak with Jesus in quiet times, He talks back. Once Jesus said, "I am not in love with you." I thought to myself, *What a bummer!* Then, He continued, "I am *madly* in love with you and any person that is making an attempt to follow me."

I asked Jesus, "What do you want to tell people?" Jesus said, "I have five things...

1. "Don't be afraid of me. I am not the (misguided) church."
2. "I am sick of people pretending they know me more than they do."
3. "I would like there to be more hands-on healing in the U.S.A."
4. "If a Christian kills himself, he will not come to me."
5. "Love one another."

CHAPTER 18

Knocking on Heaven's Door

If you surrender to Jesus, then expect to slowly transform into a new creature. It's a process of surrendering one's life to Christ. I believe there is always a little more I can surrender. In my spiritual vision, I go to Jesus and find a door. I knock on it, just like knocking on heaven's door. At first, He does not open the door or respond, but Jesus knows I am there.

I say, "Jesus, I want to have a deeper relationship with you. Will you be my teacher, my guide, and my friend?"

Eventually, the door opens and Jesus says, "Will you die for me?"

Wait a minute. That's a bit too heavy. I visualize myself dying as a martyr for Christ. Ouch! I am not ready to stand up for Jesus to *that* extreme. My life is a precious commodity. In reality, there are few who are willing or able to completely surrender their whole body and soul to Christ in an unharnessed and unashamed manner.

I say, "I am not ready to die for you, but if I get to know you better, then one day I may be ready."

Jesus says, "Come back when you are ready." I leave a little disappointed. I can't explain Jesus in a candy-coated way. Perhaps it is best if we take a look at His words and you decide what He really means. Yes, we need to creak open that old dusty Bible and look at the words in red. The Jesus I am getting to know is not a gentle lamb. He is a fierce lion.

> "Do not suppose that I have come to bring peace to the earth. I did not come to bring peace, but a sword. For I have come to turn 'a man against his father, a daughter against her mother, a daughter-in-law against her mother-in-law; a man's enemies will be the members of his own household.' Anyone who loves their father or mother more than me is not worthy of me; anyone who loves their son or daughter more than me is not worthy of me. Whoever does not take up their cross and follow me is not worthy of me. Whoever finds their life will lose it, and whoever loses their life for my sake will find it."
>
> (Matthew 10:34-39 NIV)

This sounds pretty harsh. Jesus wants a serious commitment.

> "Not everyone who says to me, 'Lord, Lord,' will enter the kingdom of heaven, but only the one who does the will of my Father who is in heaven. Many will say to me on that day, 'Lord, Lord, did we not prophesy in your name and in your name drive out demons and in your name perform many miracles?' Then I will tell them plainly, 'I never knew you. Away from me, you evildoers!'"
>
> (Matthew 7:21-24 NIV)

You mean I can go to church and tithe and read the Bible? But once in heaven, I might not be let into the Jesus club. That is an upset! What do I need to do?

> "Therefore go and make disciples of all nations, baptizing them in the name of the Father and of the Son and of the Holy Spirit, and teaching them to obey everything I have commanded you. And surely I am with you always, to the very end of the age."
>
> (Matthew 28:19-20 NIV)

A disciple is one who will embrace and assist in spreading the teachings. If I believe in the teachings of Jesus, that seems pretty reasonable. I will gladly share His teachings with others. What is the best way for me to go about it?

Jesus picked out twelve ordinary men that were willing to follow Him. Life unfolded; Jesus was Himself. He often taught the disciples and other people during ordinary everyday events: they ran out of wine at the wedding; He meets a woman at a well, because He is thirsty; the temple taxes needed to be paid; a woman was caught in the act of committing adultery; and His friend, Lazareth, died. My point is — opportunities arise.

Now, about baptism. Jesus is asking us to dunk underwater in the name of God, Himself, and The Holy Spirit. To a conventional adult, this ceremony might seem bizarre. But Jesus also told us we must look at everything with fresh eyes like innocent children.

> *"And he said: 'Truly I tell you, unless you change and become like little children, you will never enter the kingdom of heaven. Therefore, whoever takes the lowly position of this child is the greatest in the kingdom of heaven. And whoever welcomes one such child in my name welcomes me.'"*
>
> (Matthew 18:3-5 NIV)

When I take a childlike perspective, I am ready to dunk in the pool. It helps knowing Jesus did it first. There was also the criminal being crucified next to Jesus, who was not baptized. The fact that one believes in Jesus seems more important than the baptism.

> *Then he said, "Jesus, remember me when you come into your kingdom."*

Jesus answered him, "Truly I tell you, today you will be with me in paradise."

(Luke 23:42-43 NIV)

I felt the reasons for my being baptized were more symbolic. Let's seek an answer from Got Questions Ministries. *What is the symbolism of water baptism?*

> *"Water baptism symbolizes the believer's total trust in and total reliance on the Lord Jesus Christ, as well as a commitment to live obediently to Him. It also expresses unity with all the saints (Ephesians 2:19), that is, with every person in every nation on earth who is a member of the Body of Christ (Galatians 3:27–28). Water baptism conveys this and more, but it is not what saves us. Instead, we are saved by grace through faith, apart from works (Ephesians 2:8–9). We are baptized because our Lord commanded it. (Matthew 28:19).*
>
> *"Water baptism is a beautiful picture of what our Lord has done for us. As we are completely immersed in the water, we symbolize burial with our Lord; we are baptized into His death on the cross and are no longer slaves to self or sin (Romans 6:3–7). When we are raised out of the water, we are symbolically resurrected — raised to new life in Christ to be with Him forever, born into the family of our loving God (Romans 8:16). Water baptism also illustrates the spiritual cleansing we experience when we are saved; just as water cleanses the flesh, so the Holy Spirit cleanses our hearts when we trust Christ."* [14]

LOVE YOUR ENEMIES

In order to learn or teach all of Jesus' commandments, we

need to study the Bible. Let's examine a few of His principal commandments.

> "'Love the Lord your God with all your heart and with all your soul and with all your strength and with all your mind'; and, 'Love your neighbor as yourself.'"
> (Luke 10:27 NIV)

One imperative reason He came was to show us how to love one another and how much He loved God.

> "You have heard that it was said, 'Love your neighbor and hate your enemy.' But I tell you, love your enemies and pray for those who persecute you, that you may be children of your Father in heaven. He causes his sun to rise on the evil and the good, and sends rain on the righteous and the unrighteous."
> (Matthew 5:43-45 NIV)

Jesus introduced a new paradigm. The workings of God are a mystery. If God really sent Jesus, as His son, in the flesh, don't expect to be able to figure out Jesus. That is not what it's all about. There is a bigger purpose. God wants us to know how much He loves us. Jesus came to show us how much He loves God and us. The Pharisees, and many of us, from pride, fear, or ignorance, do not want to accept Jesus or His love.

I believe the broken ones were healed by Jesus because He loved them. His love was directed at the broken ones for a reason: They were open and able to receive it. Actually, He was overwhelmed with compassion. Love emanated from His presence, healing manifested because sickness and disease were obstacles in the way. The woman with the bleeding traveled thirty miles to touch His cloak and then she was healed. Many people went out of their way to seek out Jesus, probably because they heard about the miracles. But what Jesus was and still is offering is healing through His love.

If you have been broken or suffered immensely, you are a prime candidate to receive His love. It will probably not manifest in the way you expect. In all honesty, you may need to be broken down even more before you are ready. One must be ripe. Most of the hardcore followers of Jesus have been broken down, beaten, and pummeled. The Holy Spirit or the love of God flows through the cracks and scars in their bodies, just like Him. These Brothers and Sisters that specialize in love, naturally spend their time with the broken-hearted, those inflicted with diseases, the homeless, prisoners, widows, and orphans. When Jesus said, "Love your enemies", it was meant to include your extended family, the clerk at the grocery store, your local police officers, and any annoying coworkers. In short, every single nasty person who crosses your path. If you really *love* them, you no longer see them as being nasty. You sympathize with them; you treat them with kindness.

We can't impart the teachings of Jesus unless we are living in the light of Love. As I get closer to this light, the line of religion and people's everyday (non-violent) actions being right or wrong begins to fade. It is more about loving people for who they are, not what they do. People raised in other cultures have different values and customs. We should expect them to think and act differently. It is the sad truth; many Christians are not fully living in that light. But it's essential that we learn to revere God and cherish each other.

WORLD HARVEST OUTREACH

I want to share an example of a church that I attend in Chambersburg, Pennsylvania, that has successfully fostered an environment of love. Relationships with each other and with the Holy Spirit and Jesus are their primary focus. They go on regular missionary trips to the Ukraine and Costa Rica, where they have established some beautiful relationships.

There is no need to state their rules. They live them and

you learn their protocol after attending a few gatherings. Only a few guidelines exist. One is to be yourself. It takes some people a year or more to be comfortable in their own skin. Their second rule is no coffee in the sanctuary. They don't want to stain the carpet. They enforce it in a light-hearted way with the coffee police. They don't need a lot of rules or a complex governing structure, because the Holy Spirit rules over this place with love.

Their worship team resembles the Bethel Church format. Each gathering for worship or a discussion is fresh and alive, because they follow the Holy Spirit's lead. It's not always apparent what will happen next, but a theme generally appears. It is common to see a man or woman step up onto the stage during worship to share a word, a personal breakthrough, or join in a song. Actually, the whole church is part of the worship team. There are many from the younger generation. They are usually up front by the stage doing lively dancing and dynamic praising. It can become blissfully ecstatic. Sometimes they spill up onto the stage. They become united, as one spirit in worship.

Occasionally, someone in the worship team or the multitude breaks down in tears. A lot of stuff comes up when you are in the presence of the Holy Spirit and this much love. Those in need are soon surrounded by hugs and caring, warm hands. I recall one of the young female singers weeping, because of what the Holy Spirit was pressing upon her to deliver. She is given fortitude by a few young women who run up and place hands on her back. She knows what she has to say is significant. Once she regains her composure, she valiantly grabs the mike and screams, "YOU'RE NOT DEAD! YOU'RE NOT DEAD!" When you have been really broken, it feels like the life has been sucked out of you. I was feeling bleak and lifeless. She went on to remind me, along with the whole worship team: *We are Alive!* Jesus gives us life and He is alive in us. Sometimes, we need a slap to wake up, so we can fully live and love as intended.

For many people there is fear of being intimate. As babies, we were hugged and held by our mother. We loved being intimate. We cried out for it sometimes. Touch is essential for our being able to thrive emotionally as a child, and as an adult. Along the path, some of us were taught that being close is forbidden. We are sometimes told in a relationship: You can't touch me, you can't be near me, you can't speak to me, and you can't hug me. Maybe it was another church or a community that sent the message: "you don't fit in" or "we are not comfortable with you". I believe after it happens a few times, we start to lose hope. It sends a message that "you are not worthy of being loved" and "you need to stop being intimate". In order to break the chain of lies, we need to be able to trust and respect other people, our church community, and be confident in ourselves.

At World Harvest Outreach, the leaders or "Fathers" set an example for all the "Sons". They are the first to repent and ask for forgiveness. Jesus wants to annihilate the wall of judgment we have created. In most cases, the wall was unknowingly built through society. As children, we learn to emulate our parents and friends. People still discriminate against race, religion, and women. It often reveals itself in the form of sarcasm or bias jokes. We need not blame ourselves, but if we are aware of our own blemishes, we can take responsibility. That means we need to learn to love every single person for *who they are*; not how they look, what they do, their different beliefs, or their past.

Take a moment and consider whether you have shown favoritism or resistance to people according to: gender, race, religion, age, physical features, income, intelligence, opposing beliefs, or temperament.

If we are able to selflessly give and receive love, it will be reflected in our traits as described in "the fruit of the Spirit". In other words, don't try to be kind, just be loving and you will possess kindness.

> "But the fruit of the Spirit is love, joy, peace, patience, kindness, goodness, faithfulness, gentleness, self-control; against such things there is no law."
> (Galatians 5:22-23 NASB)

The King James Version uses the word longsuffering. It's an excellent word. We can show our love by hanging out with friends and family when they are hurting. We don't need to teach them, preach to them, or try to fix them. All we need to do is be with them, with love in our hearts. The secret is to focus on loving them so much that we forget about ourselves. Just remember, we are not trying to heal ourselves or them.

RENUNCIATION AND ATTACHMENT

It seems like I had everything good in my life taken away. Maybe it was to make space for something better (like God or Jesus). Perhaps, I needed to learn to not be so attached. Renunciation is all about relinquishing or surrendering something that you once enjoyed. The ultimate renunciation is of self, one's separateness from others and the world.

Let's seek an explanation from a teacher close to my heart, Swami Satchidananda. He is the founder of Integral Yoga and Satchidananda Ashram. Swami Satchidananda writes,

> "Either you renounce completely, or lose everything. Both are the same. If you don't renounce and you are a sincere seeker probably the world will temporarily take all away from you. That is another reason why people who are really after God suffer so much and seem to lose everything one by one. Don't think

by wanting God, you will have everything. No, if you want God be ready to lose everything. He will take it away because He wants you totally. He doesn't want you to run after other things." (15)

I believe that is what happened to me. God wanted me to surrender everything, in essence my whole life, to Him. I am pretty stubborn. It took fifteen years to break me down.

God took it all away: My finances, my wife, my health, my cameras, and even my cat. My, my, my, this all seems about me, doesn't it?

Swami Satchidananda writes,

"To keep the mind tranquil, we have to free ourselves from anything that we might call ours. It includes the body, mind, intelligence, ego, everything. Nothing is mine. Nothing belongs to me. It all belongs to God. And ultimately, I, Myself belong to God."

When I first read this quote and contemplated surrendering myself completely to God, I began to cry.

I thought to myself, "What good will my body be to God?" I cannot sit down for very long; it causes pain in my back. Well, God knows about my back, and He will accept me or you in our currently-perceived, pathetic conditions. Through His love we can find healing and a purpose. His love is everywhere, especially inside Jesus and the hearts of other people. But finding love never happens as we expect. God has a tailor-made plan for each of us. Jesus is part of God's plan for me.

Swami Satchidananda continues with this subject in a booklet called *Everything Will Come to You*,

"Renunciation means 'well given up.' But in this case, it's not that you give up completely. What you give up is the notion that you are this and you are that.

> It's an understanding. You don't have to become somebody. You don't have to get it from somebody. What it means is that you come 'to know yourself' who you really are. This understanding cannot be given to you by somebody else."

At this moment, I am in Costa Rica and a fabulously brilliant colored Toucan has perched a few feet away on a tree limb. I am in awe of the pure majestic beauty in the rainbow of colors on his chest and tail feathers. God is always this close. When I focus on God or my inner peace and let go of anything that I call mine, then I am a more compassionate and loving person. God, peace, or truth reside deep within me; sometimes it gets covered up.

Swami Satchidananda continues,

> "Attachment is based on just you and yourself. This is selfishness. When you are free from selfish attachment, you become a better instrument to serve everybody. Because you see yourself in everybody, everybody's pain is yours, everybody's suffering is yours. A total unattached person is one who can best serve, because he or she doesn't think of personal gain in doing anything."

Swami Satchidananda encourages his students to give up their attachments to everything (not necessarily things) for a reason.

> "You get the Kingdom. Because you left everything and got the Kingdom are you poor? No. Then you become the owner of everything. The Bible assures you, if you stop running after things, you will get the Kingdom and everything else will be added too. What a wonderful teaching. Everything will be automatically added. You don't have to ask, 'Can I get this? Can I get that?'

No. Everything will come to you."

SEEING THE LIGHT

Surrendering my all to Jesus is probably not as demanding, after I have had everything taken away, because I feel less attached. But the thought of allowing Jesus and all His love to shake up my world is still frightening. Despite all my hardships, the Holy Spirit has led me through safely to Jesus. He must have been present during my darkest moments, when all my spiritual battles took place.

Jesus has done the work for me. He died, in part, to forgive me for anything that violates the ideal relationship between myself and God. The Bible is clear about deterring those methods that I thought were giving me power. Some call it sin. It's an old archery term that means "to miss the mark." I am going to take aim at Jesus. His terms are crystal clear...Take all of me or nothing.

"Whoever is not with me is against me, and whoever does not gather with me scatters."
(Matthew 12:30 NIV)

The words of Christ seem unrelenting. Jesus draws a line, and those who dare cross it step into a new realm; they will never look back. He is radically bold and in your face, but His love for God and the diligence He shows for us and for His followers is exemplary. Jesus is serious about His request. I need to be willing to give up my life. I think about when Jesus said, "Come back and knock on my door when you are ready."

Only a king with the authority and power to offer something more valuable would dare make such a bold statement. It truly is a narrow gate, and few can pass. I think of all the healing that took place in my heart through Jesus. I know I can trust Him more than any earthbound man or woman. I know Him well enough to make this decision, but my ego still doesn't like the idea of losing my life. Am I willing to serve Jesus all the days of my life? Will my new "Life in Christ" be better? My mind keeps coming up with excuses.

I shift gears and focus on the *love* in my heart. I extend trust and humble myself, even though I don't fully comprehend Jesus, the Messiah, Son of God. I am going to have faith in Him so He can live, breathe, and operate through me. My answer resides in my heart. Yes! I am willing to give my life for Jesus. I love Him and I know He *madly* loves me. I know He is willing to die for me. In fact, Jesus died for us all, so in effect He has already died for me. He has already done it! Why am I hesitating? If I must die for Jesus, God please let it be a noble death: not an aneurysm, a car wreck, or slipping on a bar of soap in the bathtub.

I am ready to return and knock on His door. I stand outside and proudly say to Jesus, "I will die for you."

The door opens and I step inside. Then the door shuts with me on the inside. It feels different. He really is the King of Kings. Jesus is a tough Master.

I let go of my thoughts about how a relationship with Him should appear. I surrender my hopes, dreams, and ambitions into His hands. If I can do this, then I am free. I do feel lighter, like a burden has been lifted. Jesus is in the spirit, and I am in the flesh. It is kind of exciting, like a first date. All I need to do is be myself. I have given Him my all. I must be patient. Jesus is working in my life. He knows what I want and what I *really* need.

My new plan is pretty simple… I will follow His plan. I pray and quietly listen. I sense the presence of Jesus and keep Him in the corner of my eye.

Jesus says, "You will feel no more suffering or pain." I believe it's true. Once in His world, I feel that I can rise above my pain and suffering. Standing inside the quiet place near Jesus, I can sense that one day a fierce battle will unfold. Jesus will be riding on that white horse. I will be charging in on Jesus' side.

Perhaps the battle has already started. Actually, it was going on inside of myself for fifteen years. Thankfully, I saw the light. I realize now; it's easier to join Him than to resist. Today is a good day to join with me on the same side as Jesus.

If you believe in Jesus and want the Holy Spirit, just ask Him.

CHAPTER 19

The Guide

We all attain spiritual growth by living in this world. It is enhanced if we live with love in our hearts and cultivate awareness. Relationships of love may, in fact, be the greatest teachers. When love is the main focus, spiritual growth is a side-effect. God gave us roles as a mother or father, grandmother or grandfather, boyfriend or girlfriend, brother or sister, friend or co-worker for a well-intended reason: to experience being loved and to express our love toward each other. Most of us need not venture on a quest to find more spiritual growth. We just need to pay careful attention to the beloved ones in our lives. Part of our journey in learning how to love one another includes feeling pain and suffering. Our losses allow us to feel human vulnerability.

The Swan Song section is a love story. The gamut of emotions I felt during that relationship included: envy, rage, panic, guilt, playfulness, bliss, affection, and compassion. We all go through an array of feelings in relationships. At one point in my relationship with Swan Song, I was experiencing a lot of confusion, so I went on a ten-day silent retreat. It led me to a place of peace. Afterwards, I had more confidence in myself. My faith in Jesus also brought me comfort. I made a bold decision I had not even considered prior to the retreat, because I was able to listen to my heart.

What if, during those transitional points in our life, we took a pause and went on a guided retreat? What if we just set an intention to be in our heart and just listen in silence for 3 or 5 days? What if we press in closer to our chosen faith and do spiritual practices that assist us in receiving guidance with clarity?

An ideal time to do a retreat is before or after a life transition. You could be facing an illness, heading into a new job, moving to a new location, or contemplating your next step in a relationship. If one clears their slate and gets a fresh perspective, they will better know who they are, what they need, and what their attitude is. Through proper guidance and prayer, one attains mental clarity, a deeper emotional connection, and spiritual preparation. By contemplating a future or past scenario, without being emotionally attached, a degree of insight is revealed. Often we don't grant ourselves enough silent time to absorb the current feelings in our body, heart, and soul. We plug into the next project or relationship and then wonder, *"Why am I in this same sticky situation again?"* It is better to face our inner fears while peaceful and relaxed during a safe retreat setting. Then we build up resilience to face the stress-dragons with courage.

A spiritual retreat can be a time of advanced spiritual growth through introspection, awakening, or letting go. The key components are silence, meditation, relaxation, and spiritual practices. One intentionally changes their patterns and detaches from the world, which leads to a fresh perspective. This is a time for transformation and to gather inner power and fortitude.

GUIDED RETREATS

My favorite type of retreat is a personal guided retreat. I prefer these because they provide one-on-one guidance, but if one does not want to fly solo, then group retreats can be satisfying. It's recommended to have a guide while on retreat because one can enter into altered states of consciousness, and deep emotional issues can surface. Besides, it can be overwhelming for the mind to be silent for an extended period. A guide will offer instruction, support, and act as a protective spiritual shield. The best retreat guides will work with your intentions and choose practices to reinforce them. The most common length for a retreat is 1, 3, 5, or 10 days. It's best to start with a one or three-day guided personal or group retreat. After several shorter retreats, spread out over a few years, then consider a five or ten day. One can even be guided on a thirty or forty-day retreat. That takes considerable preparation. During a longer retreat one can dive beneath the surface and examine their core beliefs. When one gains an understanding of why they made certain decisions and how their beliefs led them in a direction, it can shake up their whole world perspective.

Autumn is my favorite time for a retreat. Nature is shifting and letting go of the leaves before the stillness of winter. There is a personal rhythm that one can tap into during a retreat that entices a deep personal connection with nature. Being in nature is the ideal environment for a retreat.

Hazrat Inayat Khan wrote,

> *"To the eye of the seer every leaf of the tree is a page of the holy book that contains divine revelation, and he is inspired every moment of his life by constantly reading and understanding the holy script of nature. When man writes, he inscribes upon rock, leaf, paper, wood or steel. When God writes, the characters He writes are living creatures."* (16)

I experience regular guided retreats at The Abode of the Message in New Lebanon, New York. Their retreat guides are familiar with all the major religions and accommodate to allow one to deepen their own chosen spiritual path. They have wooden huts with heaters, excellent food, and enjoyable walking trails. During a retreat, there are no outside conversations and no writing in journals. The reading of a few spiritual passages is encouraged and often revealing. The focus during a retreat is an inward moment-by-moment journey into the heart. It may sound simple, but a lot of internal shifts transpire and it can be a life-altering experience.

The standard retreat includes a morning and evening meditation; a time for slow, mindful walking in nature; a check-in time with your guide; breathing practices; and usually, chanting a few selected names for God.

REMEMBERING THE NAMES OF GOD

Wazifa is the Sufi practice of reciting and meditating on one or more of the 99 names of God. It's a Sufi tradition, and the words are Islamic. Yet, we all know and hold the names of God in our hearts. Repeating these names of God aloud or silently is a powerful healing tool. For example, Ya Nur means "light." When this word is spoken, whispered, or thought, it manifests. As you remember the name, its divine transmission flows into your heart. It can deeply transform and heal. It's a powerful practice to promote the conscious emergence and continual awareness of those divine qualities in one's own life. It's a means of connecting to, and being a vehicle of, the divine presence. Pir Vilayat Inayat Khan, in his book *Awakening*, explains,

> *"If a peaceful person comes into the room, someone might say, 'It is wonderful to see a peaceful person.' The dervish, however, would say instead, 'Isn't it wonderful to see Divine Peace coming through this person?' What they mean by this is that the human personality has the potential to become the vehicle of the Universe's archetypes. This is the intention behind the practice of wazâ'if... to connect a specific quality in oneself to its source..."* [17]

When I repeat a wazifa, I speak the word from my heart

and recall the meaning. The depth of my intention is more important than the number of repetitions. It's a different way of praying. When the proper wazifa is chosen, I often experience a feeling of ecstasy. Sometimes there are uncontrollable tears which correspond to blissful joy or act as a channel for an emotional release.

In yoga, they repeat a mantra, and Catholics repeat the rosary. It's a similar ritual; I hope that people of different religious traditions can acknowledge our similarities instead of dwelling on the differences. It is incorrect thinking to believe there is only one right and acceptable way to pray. God didn't just create one religion, one language, or one color of skin. But we are all one human tribe.

MAKING NATIVE AMERICAN CRAFTS

During my retreat, I like to do some light stretches in the morning sun and take a catnap after lunch. I also find it brings me inner peace to make a Native American item. Usually, I know well in advance what I will make and gather all the supplies before my retreat. Sometimes, someone will give me an item from nature, like a turtle shell. Often, I will be inspired to make it into a gift, such a turtle-shell rattle. When it's done, I give it back to them. I like to make Native American crafts and give them away as gifts.

As a guideline, I make Native American crafts with hand tools — no power tools — so my energy goes into it. I start by offering tobacco and then sage myself, the tools, and the pieces. The sage is used to purify everything. Each piece of leather, bone, stone, shell, or wood tells its own story. As the designer, I bond the pieces together; I am a part of it. Once it's complete, I smudge it again with sage. But this time, my intention with the smudging is to make it sacred. A sacred item should not be set upon the ground. It should be respected. Usually it is stored in a box, basket, or suitcase surrounded with sage, cedar, or sweet grass. Otherwise, there is no wrong way to make a Native American craft item. Anyone can do it. Just listen to your heart.

Each Native American craft I make represents a stage in my life. During one of my first retreats, I made a rattle from a small branch that fell from the giant sycamore tree I call the Almighty One in Shakomako. The wooden handle is covered in black leather, and the shakers are made of large, ear-shaped pods with seeds inside. They fell from a tree that I stood under during my initiation into the Sufi order. The Sufi order does not insist that one initiates; in fact, they don't even suggest it. When I felt ready, I asked an accomplished Sufi teacher I admired to initiate me.

I remember staring intensely into the eyes of the Sufi teacher, Aziza, as she said the opening invocation created by Hazrat Inayat Khan as part of my initiation:

Toward the One,
The Perfection of Love, Harmony, and Beauty,
The Only Being,
United with all the Illuminated Souls,
Who form the Embodiment of the Master,
The Spirit of Guidance. [18]

In a mystical way, I could see the past lineages reflected in her eyes. There was a vast spaciousness that went back in time. Deep calls to deep. It is a bit spooky, but rather cool. When I use the rattle, it reminds me of my initiation.

During another retreat, I attain 99 round, stone beads of amethyst, malachite, and smoky quartz to make prayer beads. I chose each type of stone for certain qualities it possesses. The amethyst is for healing. The malachite reaches the inner feelings of a person and reflects what is there, be it negative or positive. The smoky quartz is commonly used as a powerful Native American stone to protect and clear negativity. At the starting bead, I attach an eagle-head bead carved by an Alaskan Native. I purchased it during the summer I was a canoe guide. When I use these prayer beads, they are more powerful than anything I could buy.

THE GOOFY SUFIS

It's common practice to keep to oneself what transpires during a retreat. One can never fully express with justice the magnitude of a self-transformation experience with mere words. Attempting to describe it may actually take away from the experience. It was my nature to break or bend every retreat's rules, perhaps to better understand it, or it might have been just for fun.

There are various denominations of Sufis. I am part of the Sufi lineage called the Chishti. The tradition of this order is traced from the time of Abraham. But within the larger Sufi circles, we are called the Goofy Sufis. When I first met the mountain-retreat coordinator, Nevin, he came up to shake my hand, dragging one leg and groaning. He was just kidding around. He would greet me and other coworkers by waving his hands on his head like they were moose antlers. I am well-accomplished at, and proud to uphold, our reputation for goofing off.

During retreats, I have spoken when I needed to be silent, read a book, received a massage, entered a sauna, ridden a bike, checked my email, and traveled to town. Afterwards, I realize all these retreat guidelines are for my own benefit. I have grown to respect them. This said, I, the rule-breaker, will break the rule again and share glimpses into my personal retreats.

WISE WOLF ON RETREAT

It's the break of day at the top of the mountain. I walk slowly along the forest trail. I am observing the great oaks and the mostly-bare maple trees and how they are spaced apart symmetrically, like soldiers dressed in camouflage. A gray squirrel and a few blue jays are in the tree branches, part of the costume worn by the forest. I feel that the trees can sense my footsteps as I tread on the dark brown earth beneath them.

I inhale and take a step. With my exhale, I take the next step. I feel my heel and toe touch the earth. My steps are like whispers. I am still enough to hear my heart beat four times between each step: *thump...thump...thump...thump*. The orange sunrays peek through the leaves, and a few golden beams spotlight down upon overzealous grass patches. The shadows near the tree trunks show a dark contrast, and broken twigs lie randomly scattered about. I can smell the moss draped on the northern side of each tree. I slowly step forward on the path out into the rays of sunlight. It shines on my hands and cheeks. I pause to feel the warmth and welcome it on my skin.

In the distance, I hear the gentle, deep tone from a set of wind chimes. *Ding...dong. Ding...dong*. There is a gigantic set of chimes dangling at the top of the retreat mountain. They are here to represent the elements of the wind. I see the four shining, silver bars, like elephants' tusks, hanging down from forty feet above, where they are tied to a branch of a giant oak.

I slowly, step by step, make my way to the giant chimes. I stand underneath them and slowly gaze up. The gigantic chimes are suspended directly above me. The sound reverberates through my cells. When I move slightly to the right or left, the perfectly resounding tone is distorted. I remain still in my chamber. The energetic tone is thick, like warm chocolate being poured on my head. I feel it drip down my arms and chest before it forms a small puddle around my feet. I am tempted to stoop down and take a lick. But I remain still.

I look down another trail. There is the silhouette of a man walking in my direction. As he comes closer, I can distinguish that he is wearing slightly weathered jeans, leather work boots, and a blue sweatshirt with the hood over his head. The cloth veil over his face glistens. It is tucked in under his hoodie to cover his face. But I know him by his walk. One hip is tight-er and slightly pulls out. His short steps, combined with his white beard behind that veil, resemble that of a wizard. He is my mentor, Wise Wolf. I am glad to see him here. He is on the mountain as a participant in his own ten-day retreat.

As he approaches, I smile and expect him to acknowledge me. He knows I am here. It is obvious. I hold back the urge to give him a big bear-hug. That is how he usually greets me. Yet, Wise Wolf peers straight ahead; he is focusing intensely within. Perhaps this walk in his heart is melting the trauma and stressful hours he spends as a hospice worker. His retreat time is precious. He holds every drop of energy compassionately. He continues to deliberately step forward, as if a cement statue has broken free from the mold to take its first few slow, silent steps. There is not so much as a nod as he walks past. I am mesmerized by his slow, mime movements. Or is it the inward concentration?

I reminisce about our past mentor meetings; how he would sit on the edge of a chair, listening intently. Once he said firmly, "Why are you beating around the bush? If you have something to say to me, just say it!" He was right. After that day I did. He was the first man older than myself that didn't scare the crap out of me. I felt he trusted me, and I trusted him. I was comfortable enough to talk about anything with him. This meant a lot. It was a breakthrough, because both The Lion and Pastor R.I.P. had instilled the belief that they would not trust me.

Wise Wolf was there to listen during my darkest moments. I confided in him that I sometimes had mixed feelings about being on a spiritual path that involves yoga, Native American traditions, and Jesus. I find that many Christians are offended by my involvement in Native American traditions or yoga. They expect me to follow Jesus, exclusively.

Wise Wolf said, "All these paths come together within you."

I desire to obey the Holy Spirit. When I participate in yoga or Native American traditions, Jesus and the Holy Spirit are right beside me. If I am not sharing them as part of my truth, then I am offending myself. The Holy Spirit wants me to be myself. Some people may not be pleased with my not following Jesus, exclusively. It is not my role to make them happy. Regardless of what others think, I need to respect and love myself, every day. The real question is: *Can they love me for who I am?*

When one initiates in the Sufi order, they are supposed to have a guide for life. At one point, my guide said she would guide me on retreats, but could no longer be there for personal advice. After that, Wise Wolf unofficially took over. It was clear that he cared. He was more than just a mentor. He is a friend who shares wise counsel. He teaches me more with his silent intention than he could with words. During the moment Wise Wolf passes, I realize the levels of depth that one is capable of attaining on a silent retreat. I continue to watch Wise Wolf out of the corners of my eyes, without turning my head, until he disappears.

SILENCE

Silence is mystical. It's rather ironic that I am attempting to convey the deeper meanings of silence with words. Imagine a house with a family in the country. During the day, they are all active and talking. At night, on the outside, the surroundings become quieter and darkness settles in. The stars appear above and some creatures, like the owl, start hunting. This owl is not hunting mice; it is swooping in to gather up their words. Now, the family is cozy and asleep in their beds. They are all giving their bodies and minds a chance to rest. While asleep, they are all at peace. Silence is touching the recesses of their souls. While being silent, they let go of their worries from yesterday and plans for tomorrow. They all wake up refreshed and ready for another day.

Silence is always there, even during the daytime, sometimes trapped beneath the commotion. During a silent retreat you retain the silence from the night all through the next day, even while you are awake. Wise Wolf was holding silence, even on the inside, deep within his organs. Without being weighed down by thoughts, words, and concepts on the inside, one can live more in the present moment. When inner silence is achieved, retreatants become more curious about their surroundings. They move more slowly, with fresh eyes to examine the outside world. Something as common as a fern blowing in the wind becomes fascinating.

Our inner heart resides with God in stillness. In this place, we are unified through a deeper sense of knowing. We are able to know and love ourselves. We gain a fresh perspective. Our attitude shifts. What we thought were problems are no longer such a big deal. When silence is held for extended periods and contained properly, it shatters our preconceived notions.

CHAPTER 20

The Forty-Day Retreat

I follow in some big footsteps when I commit to a forty-day retreat. In the Bible, Elijah (1 Kings 19:8) and Moses (Exodus 24:18) fasted for forty days. Moses did two back-to-back, and at least during the second one, had neither food nor drink. But probably the most renowned forty-day fast was done by Jesus.

Immediately after being baptized with the Holy Spirit by John the Baptist, Jesus fasted for forty days and nights in the Judean Desert. The temptation of Christ is told in the Gospels of Matthew, Mark, and Luke. During his fast, the devil appeared to Jesus and tempted him three times. Jesus refused each temptation and the devil departed.

> *"Then Jesus was led by the Spirit into the wilderness to be tempted by the devil. After fasting forty days and forty nights, he was hungry. The tempter came to him and said, 'If you are the Son of God, tell these stones to become bread.'"*
>
> (Matthew 4:1-3 NIV)

It is important to note that the devil remarked, *"If you are the Son of God"*. He wants to question the identity of Jesus. Jesus is solid in His identity. If we understand our true identity, then the devil has no recourse. Satan's power is limited and temporal. He really only has power when we give him the authority. I believe this happens when we exhibit a lack of faith or believe his lies. Jesus has authority over Heaven and Earth. If we realize how the Cross, the Incarnation, the Resurrection, and the Ascension set us all (not just Christians) free, then we can live and love, fearlessly.

THE HOLY SPIRIT AS MY GUIDE

As a 44 year old, life is a dream. My beard is turning white. I felt the desire to do a forty-day retreat for three years before it manifested. When the time came, I sought out a Sufi guide. There are only a few qualified to guide a forty-day retreat. One qualification is they need to have been guided on a forty-day retreat themselves. When I contact one and get no response, I take it as a sign; I should seek alternative forms of guidance.

I know it's imperative that I have a guide, or at the very least, check in with somebody regularly. I speak with my two mentors and they make themselves available by email or phone, but neither is officially qualified to guide a forty-day retreat. I decide to check in once a week at a men's support group for sexual integrity at a local church. I can share with them. But I stay mindful about not talking too much.

I am not expecting my forty-day retreat to be easy. The devil, or undesirable spirits, tempt me. Jesus, Moses, and Elijah were guided by listening to God. I will do the same, but I will rely heavily on the Holy Spirit as my primary guide.

How will the Holy Spirit guide me? Certainly, I will pray and listen. I always pay attention when a similar message appears through three independent sources. When this happens, it's probably the Holy Spirit or God. I trust the Bible and other spiritual scriptures as confirmation. I find that wisdom and a compassionate heart join together as a team for my final filtering process. That is how I get my guidance.

There are different levels of intensity when I feel the Holy Spirit, but usually it's a tingling sensation. I often sense the presence of the Holy Spirit during worship or when I receive guidance in a prayer or passage. When I give a person a message directed by the Holy Spirit, I feel the presence. It does not need to be a Christ-related connection. The Holy Spirit often works through me when I teach a yoga class or participate in a Native American ceremony. I conclude that the Holy Spirit or God's presence guides us all, regardless of our religion or beliefs. Jesus broke down many barriers. God's truth, light, and love are available for every soul to claim.

I need to remain firm in my own identity. I have an identity in Jesus. I have an identity in Native American traditions. I have an identity in yoga. If I am to deny any part of who I am, then I am not living my truth. But a controversial question that some Christians ask... *Does Jesus condemn those who practice yoga and participate in Native American traditions?* Jesus broke down walls of intolerance. He has room for everyone. In the past, I tried to deny or conceal parts of my identity from others who may not appreciate how it melds together within me. I know some people will love and accept me for who I am, others will not.

ANGER SURFACES

The night before my retreat begins, anger starts to surface. There are three professionals that I felt did me wrong. I had an unnecessary hiatus hernia operation. I blame it on the surgeon. Then, I was given antibiotics for six months by another doctor, to eliminate the *possibility* of Lyme disease. The antibiotics raised havoc with my stomach, immune system, and liver. The last professional was a healing-touch counselor in New York. I went to him for healing. He diagnosed that I had a male/female energy imbalance. At one point, he asked to rub my sexual organ. I awkwardly consented. Afterwards, I felt I had been sexually molested. It left me feeling even more confused.

I turn a leaf and accept full responsibility. I ask Jesus to help me find forgiveness to heal the anger. My mind slips to view past relationships, financial insolvency, emotional turbulence, and sexual abuse. I grieve for deceased family members, pets, and friends.

In our culture, it's not commonly acceptable for a man to cry. I take thirty minutes to consciously cry out my pain. It starts off with a fake sob that grows to be a deep, heartfelt, genuine cry, with tears. I regret that I am not utilizing my God-given gift to take more photographs. After all the crying, I feel better. Now I am ready to begin my forty-day retreat.

MY DAILY RETREAT PRACTICES

I will be doing this retreat in my home. I place a sign on the door that says "Observing Silence" for any visitors. I spend much of my retreat time in a spare bedroom. It resembles a retreat hut. There is a large white candle on a shelf, blue carpet on the floor, and two windows, but otherwise the room is empty and free from any clutter. The wall is tongue and groove pine boards. Some of the knots in the boards resemble distorted ghost faces.

I set a strong intention to do specific retreat practices every day. Each evening, I cover my head with a veil to keep my focus inward. I light a thick, white candle and repeat my two chosen names for God from the Sufi tradition. My index finger and thumb roll over the 99 stone prayer beads that I made. I repeat the first wazifa: "al-Qahhar," the one who overcomes all obstacles and is victorious over any opposition. It is to encourage the pursuit of one's purpose by practicing mastery.

My head is facing to the right side. It begins to roll downward, with my chin near my chest, then up and over to the left. Next, I glance up toward the ceiling. The cycle ends with me facing downward in the direction of my heart as I say the last wazifa: "al-Ghani," the one who is self-sufficient, without need of anything and completely satisfied. It is to encourage creativity and to be confident in one's abilities.

I transition from saying my wazifas out loud (Dhiker), to saying them more softly, as a whisper (Fikr), and as the ultimate variation, I repeat the words in my mind, as a thought (Fikr-Asir). I can feel a subtle resonating vibration generated, even after the words and thoughts have ceased. This is the energy and power in a wazifa that resides beyond the sound.

The third chant I repeat two or three times a day. It's the word "Cristo Morpho." I define it to mean, "Christ Transforms." "Cristo" is Christ in Spanish, and "Morpho" is from the Blue Morpho translucent butterfly that frequently meanders along the brooks on our property in Costa Rica. I say "Cristo Morpho" as I walk slowly in a circle around the room with the 99 stone beads in my right hand, as an abacus, counting out the repetitions. I listen to the words and feel the sound vibration, which resonates from my throat. My goal is to repeat "Cristo Morpho" 10,000 times over forty days. It seems insurmountable, but little-by-little, day-by-day, from December 12th to January 20th, I persist.

THE COMPASSION OF BUDDHA

The Holy Spirit is my main guide, but I also pick out forty universally-known spiritual teachers. I request guidance from one each day. On the first day, it's Buddha. I call on Buddha to be present as I sit to meditate for thirty minutes. During my meditation, I feel intense peace like never before. I am held in the silence and stillness of pure compassion. When standing under a starry sky, one gets a sense of the vast expanse of the universe. The stars spread out beyond our vision, but one can grasp that stars exist in other infinite galaxies. Imagine this comprehension of the stars as compassion that extends towards every blade of grass, insect, and life form on the earth. This is how much compassion resides in Buddha.

FOCUS ON THE CURE

On day 3, my guide is Swami Sri Yukteswar. He is The

Guru that entered me for ten days. He says, "Christ is your chosen guru."

On day 5, I pray with Angel Ariel about how I can help the environment. I send a $25 donation that goes toward the release of wild wolves in New England.

On day 6, the Sufi teacher, Hazrat Inayat Khan, is my guide. The focus is on healing. He says, "Focus on the cure; never the illness or pain, for then it will only grow. Genuine healing requires confidence, concentration, and faith."

I begin to allow ten minutes each day to focus on the gold cross that The Lion gave me, as a way to build up my power of concentration. I spend some time each day affirming that I have a strong vibrant body, a good memory, plenty of energy, and the ability to express my emotions.

MY REQUEST TO MAKE A CHANUPA

As I mentioned, I like to make Native American items during my retreat. I would like to make a new chanupa under the authority of the Holy Spirit. I need to have a dialogue with Jesus and the Native American chiefs before I begin such a controversial undertaking.

I have a large piece of black pipestone and one piece of a cherry limb left from a tree on my property that I cut down and milled. I made a promise to that tree that I would use all the wood. I made a chest the same dimensions as the Ark of the Covenant to hold my sacred items, and the remaining lumber was used to build two large bookshelves.

I gather in a spiritual powwow with seven respected Native chiefs. It may be a vision in my mind, but each event has a purpose and I take seriously the signs given through my visions. This group is called together to decide if it is in my best interests to make and own a chanupa again. In my inner vision each chief rides in on his horse. They travel from different regions of the United States and Canada. I place nine different animal skins for seats around a fire circle. Red Cloud leads the horses to the water and comes to the circle. He stands in front of the buffalo robe. Ten Bears, who is covered in black body paint, goes to the bear fur. Shooting Star, who represents the Northern Alaskan region, chooses the cougar. Black Elk goes to the elk skin. Last of the Mohegans, who represents tribes that have already vanished in this country, prefers a bobcat. Red Cluster goes to a fox skin. I tell the chiefs we are expecting Jesus and the White Buffalo Calf Woman to arrive, but we can all sit down. There are two furs remaining; one is a white rabbit fur and the other a sheepskin.

A thunderbolt strikes the ground and Jesus is walking toward us across a field. Then a White Buffalo appears near him. He turns to face what has changed into the White Buffalo Calf Woman. They walk solemnly together to our circle and sit down. All those gathered are fully present and listen intently as I explain how my three chanupas were taken away when the Holy Spirit was invited to rule over my life during my last chanupa ceremony.

Jesus explains, "This act was requested to show obedience to me." Jesus knows of my love for the Native traditions, the chanupa and the White Buffalo Calf Woman.

Jesus asks, "Can a man have two masters?"

I make my request to the group to make another chanupa. I explain that I desire the power of the Holy Spirit to reign as the ultimate authority over and through it. Red Cloud protests and is not in agreement to give their power over to Christ's authority.

The White Buffalo Calf Woman speaks, "The power of Jesus is greater than our medicine. We know that when the third White Buffalo appears, our Native nation will shift. It is a merger so our people and their wisdom will live on."

She takes the bracelet I had purchased for her off her wrist and passes it to Jesus.

She continues, "My allegiance is with Him. Under His love is the power we all feel for one another, as a brother and sister."

She passes a chanupa around the circle. Each Chief smokes the chanupa and then in time, speaks to the group, while they hold it. They decide as a group to allow the Holy Spirit pipe to exist. I can make another chanupa and be a pipe carrier, but there are certain stipulations. Chief Shooting Star blows the pipe smoke across the stars in the night sky.

Jesus, who is last in the circle, speaks, "God willing, the Holy Spirit will live in this pipe and I will rule as an authority. If at times, I do not act, then the White Buffalo Calf Woman shall, as in the past."

I offer the skins each is sitting on and a bundle to each, as a token of my appreciation and respect.

(I had a longstanding debate with myself about including the making of the new chanupa. I will receive condemnation from some Christians for being a pipe carrier again. For me, it is more important what Jesus wants. He wants me to be free; that means fully being myself. Jesus fully respects and honors Native Americans and all of their traditions. The greater tragedy is for me to conceal my truth. I need not hide any part of my identity. I am not the man I once was. I am a son of my Heavenly Father; I am that I am.)

QUALIFICATIONS TO TEACH

On day 8, the yoga guru, Neem Koroli Baba, is my guide. It's amazing how the character and personality of some guides comes forth. I spend about one hour each day as directed by the guide of the day.

Neem Koroli Baba says in a grumbly voice, "Chant for one hour, then seek my guidance."

I chant along with music by Krishna Dass and Snatam Kaur. They both chant from the heart, and one can feel a loving vibration in their voices. His guidance reveals that whenever I want it or need it, I can take in a loving vibration through chanting.

I feel that this forty-day retreat is a prerequisite for becoming a spiritual teacher. During this retreat, I plan to complete my last requirements to become a certified yoga therapist. My desire is to teach people with chronic conditions.

I ask Neem Karoli Baba," What must I do to be qualified to teach people?"

His response is, "Listen to God."

I decide to ask the same question to some of my other guides. Swami Satchidananda says, "Speak the truth and care deeply for others; live in a high state of consciousness; have an area of spiritual expertise."

Another says, "Do not be attached to your results; live as an example of your teachings; and be there when you are really needed."

The yoga teacher, B.K.S. Iyengar, says, "It's important to have a lifelong commitment."

They all have slightly different perspectives; when taken as a whole, they all add a piece to make the pie complete.

On day 11, I begin to work on the new chanupa. It shall be called "Quddus". The word Quddus comes from the Arabic root Qadusa. Qadusa carries the meaning "to be pure, holy, and spotless."

There are going to be three bowls in this one pipe. One large bowl in the middle I will call the "Holy Spirit" section, and one smaller one on the end I will call the "God" section. A cross will be mounted on top of the "God" bowl. In one of the T intersections forming the cross, will be the third bowl, which represents Jesus. In effect, this one pipe will have the trinity of the Father, the Son, and the Holy Spirit. I will attach the pewter statue of Christ on the cross. It is the statue of Christ I had on the day of the ceremony, after which the three chanupas were taken away. I feel joy that what was once taken away by the Holy Spirit will now be returned, not as three separate chanupas, but three chanupas in one. It will be better than I could have imagined.

In my agreement with the Native chiefs, there are conditions to allow Christ and the Holy Spirit to operate through my chanupa, such as, "I will not touch my lips to any other chanupa." Jesus requests that I read the gospels while I make the bowl, to absorb them into my heart and transfer them to the pipe. The elements are strongly under the direction of this pipe, and I believe the "God" bowl has the innate ability to control the weather, if I am ever guided to pray in that manner.

On day 12, I feel emotionally and physically wiped out. Thoughts and speech make no sense. I want to cry.

On day 19, I burn a hole through the piece of cherry wood for the pipe stem. My metal rod is not long enough to reach the full length, so I need to come at it from both ends. I use the wood stove in the kitchen once the coals are red hot. I am questioning if I can be precise enough to meet in the middle with a straight hole. These things cannot be rushed. It is cozy to have a fire, with snow on the ground outside. There is the smell of smoke, because I have the front door of the stove open. When I break through, I peer through the stem hole as a telescope to view the full moon. It is perfect.

On December 24, Swami Shivinanda is my guide.

He asks, "If you are told a lie by all, why will you believe me when I tell you differently?" He has a good point. I allow myself to question whether what I have been told by other people is true.

I want to do something special for Christmas Eve, so I repeat all of the 99 beautiful names for God 17 times.

On Christmas Day, my guide is Mary. I want to honor the mother of Christ. She guides me in her way to honor my own mother. I told The Lamb I would visit with her on Christmas Day for a few hours. She comes to my home, and we have a cup of tea and play Scrabble, her favorite game. I have a great meditation on Christmas Day, perhaps because the world is focusing on Christ and giving in the spirit of love.

A MILESTONE

Day twenty is a milestone. It's New Year's Eve. I am halfway. I have a dream about my past wife, Forevermore. We are sleeping together in my parents' bedroom in our brick home. She talks about teaching Spanish students how to dance the tango, and then leaves the room. I wake up distraught and all emotional. It has been fifteen years since I have seen her. I thought I had worked through all my stuff with Forevermore. Now she comes back in a dream.

My intention is to go deeper in the remaining twenty days of the retreat. I want the stuff to surface that is lodged deep down in the crevices. It seems to have already begun to surface around my separation with Forevermore.

As a way to express what I feel and find closure, I write a letter to Forevermore and send it to her mom. I would prefer to send it directly to her, but I have had no contact with her for the last twelve years. I don't even know where she lives. I have doubts that her mom will even give her the letter. Regardless, I feel it will bring some healing to share how I feel with her mom.

I explain in the letter what went on in my head and my heart...how it all led to our divorce. This happened fifteen years ago; I guess it took me a long time to process it. I can't change my past, but I can live and heal in the present.

We both took what we thought was the easy way out. It took years for me to move on. I can't remove every trace of Forevermore from my memory. Actually, I still love her in my heart. I find comfort in knowing it's possible that I could feel the same intensity of love again, even if it's not for her. There is grace enough and time enough in this life for a second chance.

CARING FOR THE HEART SESSIONS

During the second half of my retreat, I do one session a day in a Christian counseling workbook called *Caring for the Heart* by John Regier.

The big session for me is on bitterness. Can I actually forgive The Lion? What I hold against him is damaging to my body and spirit. I need to find inner peace around it. It's not hurting him one little bit. Jesus comes to heal my heart. When this happens, I feel lightness in my shoulders as my burden lifts and floats away.

"Bitterness is like drinking poison and waiting for the other person to die."
— Joanna Weaver

NANI AND GLITTER

I do sessions for every woman with whom I have had a relationship. During my college years, I had two girlfriends simultaneously, Nani and Glitter. I told each of them about the other, but I downplayed the situation.

Nani lived in Vermont and was a sweet country girl. She liked to babysit, bake cookies, and wear flannel button-down shirts. Glitter lived for the bright city lights. She was the life of the party and wore the latest trendy black skirts. I met Glitter at college.

Once Nani came to visit me at college, and while we were eating in the dining hall, Glitter spotted us and cruised over to our table.

With a big fake smile she said, "Hi, I am Glitter," as she nonchalantly threw a glass of water in my face.

She continued to express hostile and jealous feelings.

Nani gave me a stuffed rabbit named Hoppy. When Glitter found out it was from her, Hoppy's fate was sealed. The first time I came home to rescue Hoppy, he was tied around the top of the chimney. The next time, my roommate's Ford pickup, which he called the Demon Dog, had a rear tire parked dead-center on Hoppy, squashing his rabbit body as flat as a pancake. The last time Glitter took Hoppy, it was as a hostage; I never saw him again. He was given to some neighborhood kid that passed by on a bike.

I juggled two girlfriends for more than a year. I found no good reason to change my wicked ways. I thought I had the best of both worlds, but I was being insensitive to their feelings. I lacked integrity in my relationships with women. In my conscience, I felt it was wrong, but inside my head, my father gave me his approval through his actions.

During that summer, I met Forevermore. She said, "Listen Jack, you're not going to date me if you have other girlfriends."

I got the message fast. I was not going to let what happened with Julia, whom I had a crush on in the seventh grade, happen again. There was no hesitation. I immediately went and told Glitter and Nani that we were over. I was extremely fond of Forevermore. I wanted to be with her. I thought we would last forever.

Glitter and Nani both deserved better treatment from a man. We were all young and naive. I didn't know I was instigating a messy triangle, but as I reflect back, it's clear. After my heart-healing session, Jesus cleared away the debris. I sympathized with how my selfish actions hurt Glitter and Nani. I contact them both to ask their forgiveness for treating them with a lack of respect. Now they are both married and have kids. Nani responds, "You are forgiven! It was over fifteen years ago. We have all moved on."

FRIENDS FOREVER

On my wedding ring, Forevermore personally had engraved the words "friends forever." The engraving deeply touched me. I had the thought...*Once she was my wife, and now she does not even want to be my friend.* When I realized this a few years ago, I became angry. I took a hammer, and with tears in my eyes, pounded my wedding ring until it broke in half. This was the first time I really began to process and feel the pain from our divorce.

In my sorrowful, brokenhearted condition, I mailed the two broken pieces of my wedding ring back to Forevermore. In my warped way, I wanted her to know how much it hurt not being her friend. I didn't consider how it would make her feel when she received it. It's one of the few actions I truly regret. If I ever speak with her again, I will ask for her forgiveness. But after that incident, she ceased all communication.

In my "Caring for the Heart" session, I get in touch with how she probably felt when she received the pounded wedding ring pieces. On this day, I cry uncontrollably for a few hours. The sadness that resides in my chest found a way to release after I began to care more about her feelings. It's a little late, but now I understand why she stopped communicating with me.

While I am crying, The Lamb attempts to call me, even though she knows I am on a silent retreat. She leaves a message inquiring how I am feeling. It's her nature to care about others. She could sense that I was feeling some intense emotions. God knows everything that is happening. He cares and loves me as a loving parent. God lives in The Lamb's heart.

After my session with Forevermore, I feel the whispering voice of God say, "Your time with her is done. There will be another that you will love as dearly."

REMOVING THE DARK SPIRITS

During the course of the "Caring for the Heart" sessions, I work to remove the dark spirits of envy, pride, lust, lying, stealing, deception, sarcasm, and hypocrisy. I become aware of the spiritual battle and how I was influenced in subtle ways. I have my own inner battle between the darkness and the light. The light beckons with a kind and loving smile. The darkness seeks to manipulate and control. The problem is pretty common; I like to do what makes me feel good. I need to be able to discern what is actually beneficial. In small doses, acts that are not beneficial seem harmless, but once the door is open, it does not shut as easily. Over time, they compile together and it can destroy the person I was meant to be.

We have the freedom to choose our own destiny. What we think are trivial decisions may actually be more important than what we consider to be the crucial ones. I ignorantly gave over my power to the darker spirits through inappropriate thoughts, desires, and actions. I was oblivious to how pornography, inappropriate music, and dowsing were affecting me. When the veil was lifted, it was a revealing moment. I took control and reclaimed my power.

This battle takes place in my home, on retreat, and out in the world. I choose what I want to watch, read, or take in through my senses. When I watch a movie or go to a concert, I am influenced by it. I delete songs on my computer or throw away the CDs with any lyrics that reinforce these darker forces. Artists like Jim Morrison or Bob Marley, who openly promote drugs as part of their image or in their lyrics, are no longer welcome. One song can trigger that old familiar feeling of going to a party or getting high. Christians call it a familiar spirit. I don't need it or want it anymore.

We all want to be happy. I rely on an array of addictions when I am deficient in pleasure. I may crave certain types of food or have a desire to shop, watch a movie, or be online. It's scary to face my own demons, but if I don't confront them today, they will continue to rule over my life. In order for me to find harmony and conquer this adversary, I need to get grounded, draw a line, slip into the flow, reclaim my identity, get closer to nature, and enjoy intimate relationships. It includes sharing and caring for others. If I want to be loved by my family and friends, I need to treat them accordingly.

> *"Treat others the same way you want them to treat you."* (Luke 6:31 NASB)

I give thanks to the Holy Spirit for insights into how I had been led astray. The scriptures and spiritual teachers are here to guide us toward the truth. The enemy's favorite tool is to lie. You can count on it. The whole glorification of alcohol, drugs, sex, cigarettes, and violence is an illusion created by the dark forces. If I had lived without any alcohol or drug use, I would be healthier, richer, and wiser. How can people say it's alright for them and then not expect their kids to be like them? If one lives their own truth, then their kids have a genuine example. Let your actions glorify those around you. (It is easy to say, but not so easy to do.)

APHRODITE, GODDESS OF PLEASURE AND PROCREATION

I am tempted by one undesirable spirit. It's my own fault. I invite her in. If the devil is going to tempt me, it will be with a sexy woman in a red dress. On day 28, I choose Aphrodite as my guide. She is the Greek Goddess of love, beauty, pleasure, and procreation. Her Roman equivalent is the Goddess Venus.

You might ask, "Why in the world did you pick the Goddess of pleasure and procreation as your guide?"

Yes, I should know better. It's like my subconscious secretly leads me to find new forms of sexual temptation. It's relentless. Aphrodite does not guide me with love and beauty, as I desire. She comes as a wild sexual fantasy. She wears no red dress. I am unable to resist her.

Luckily, I am getting vital support from the men's sexual-integrity group at the church. It is way too agonizing for me to explain Aphrodite to my brothers in Christ, but even if they didn't understand, they would have given me support. It's best that I just don't visit Aphrodite, ever again.

SEXUAL INTEGRITY FOR MEN

By attending a men's sexual-integrity group, I am waging a personal battle. When I realize other men face similar sexual challenges, I empathize, and my situation becomes more...human. We each write a purity statement. Some guys carry their purity statement in their pocket or repeat it when facing sexual temptation. It's a powerful tool that draws the boundaries. It's your personal beliefs, affirmations, and intentions that revolve around sexual integrity. Words are more concrete than thoughts when it comes to a spiritual battle. I memorize my purity statement because each sentence has power and a purpose. When I am being tempted, I would like to say I always wield it like a sword. But the truth is, I don't always wield it. When I do, it helps.

My Purity Statement

I resolve to do God's Will.
I am protected by God's grace.
I am pure in my thoughts and actions.
I will fear no evil, for God is with me.
The male and female body is a sacred temple.
Sexuality is a gift from God,
for a man and woman to express their love.
I will set an example of how to live the truth, as guided by the Holy Spirit, the Bible, and Jesus Christ.

THE POINT OF NO RETURN

Each person is different, and there are different triggers or patterns that emerge in every addiction. An alcoholic or cigarette smoker will feel the urge for a fix when stress increases. My triggers can be stress, boredom, success, isolation, or watching a movie with a sensual scene. I do my best to avoid or be cautious during these times. At these times a blinking yellow light flashes:

***** WARNING *****

It means I am near the point of no return. If I reach this point, then I most likely can't turn back. When lust hits hard, I need to get my fix. It's the point after an alcoholic takes that first drink. Sexual addiction can be confusing because sex is a natural act. But when one seeks sex for anything other than a way to express love to a partner, it becomes distorted. This is what leads to sexual addiction. It's all about having a pure intention. For example, a side effect of sex is that it can relieve stress, but if your reason for having sex is to relieve stress or fall asleep, it indicates a problem.

The hard part about an addiction is when I fall off the wagon. I need to get back up with my pride all bruised and climb back on. I may go years without a problem and suddenly…. *WHACK!* It happens. I may think I am beyond needing support and get careless about my triggers. To retain my stronghold, I need to keep the door with the beast locked and bolted shut. In effect, I slam the door on lust. I vow to change my ways, but in the real world, that door can wiggle open with time. One day, there will be a knock, knock, knock on my door, probably when I least expect it.

CHAPTER 21

The Lion's Den

Three years later I am at The Lion's house for ten days as he stays at his summer camp on the lake. It seems like a good quiet place to write a few chapters of my book. My landing in The Lion's Den is not a random occurrence. It has happened for a reason. I have not seen him much over the past few years because I felt a need for space to heal with minimal stress. My life has been fairly peaceful. As I settle into The Lion's Den, some of my childhood memories come back to haunt me.

I look at a large wall hanging of an English hunting scene. When I was a child, it hung on his office wall at home. In this scene, four men are sitting around a table drinking coffee and enjoying breakfast. They are dressed in red suits and tall black leather riding boots for fox hunting. One man stands apart from the others. He is leaning against the fireplace. As I look closer, he resembles...The Lion. He holds a whip under his arm. His conversation commands the attention of the other men in the room.

The scene of the men reminds me of our hunting camp, more so when my grandfather, Buck, was alive. Family and friends were welcome to visit, and often they would end up spending the night. In the morning, there would be a big breakfast with bacon and eggs, toast cooked over the fire, fresh coffee, and tall tales. Stories at camp followed a natural progression; the last story told is slightly more impressive than the prior. The stories tended to be exaggerated over time, and the facts inflated exponentially by the number of beers consumed.

REMINISCING ABOUT THE LION

I reminisce about my interaction with The Lion during my younger days. When I was eighteen, I packed my 1937 Pontiac full of my belongings, including a drum set, and headed out to travel across the USA. It was a time when one would expect some encouragement from a father. I was heading out as a young man to explore the world, on my own, for the first time.

The Lion's parting words were, "You won't make it on your own. The world is a cold and cruel place."

That statement made me angry. But I dared not show it in front of him. I took it as a challenge. I could survive in this world. I clenched my jaw and made a vow. "I will work hard enough, long enough, to be rich enough and tough enough to survive in this world." The Lion probably made a similar vow as a young man. I was told that after he quit college, his father told him to move out of their house, go get a job, and make something of himself. The Lion used to say, "I will outdo my father."

After high school, I was persuaded to go to college to get a business degree. The Lion promised I would have a huge yearly income. He told me the exact amount I would be making. He did the same thing with Gadget when trying to persuade him to attend Vermont Technical College, but he declined the offer. He didn't want to have to pay back the loan. In my case, he wanted an heir to take over his empire: the family business. At the time, I was slightly hesitant and did not want to go to college. For many years, he tried to sell me on the concept, "Money is the most important thing in life."

The Lion did pay for my first four years of college. His car was used as collateral when I went for a semester abroad in Australia. I was responsible for the loan payments. While living in Seattle with Forevermore, I was struggling to find a decent job, and The Lion wanted to purchase a new car. This meant both of our loans needed to be refinanced. He said, "I refinanced *our* loan to help you out. Now you can pay it off faster." I was not involved in the decision, and found out that my loan payments were doubled. I took on a night job counting inventory in order to make the payments.

My grandfather Buck was always helping people. He would deliver items, and as a mechanic, he could fix about anything. He was so accustomed to helping others that he made up a few funny quotes. One is, "If you help somebody out, then the next time they need help, they are going to think of you." Buck had another quote that applied to my loan situation, "If you *really* want to help me, then don't help me."

Most of the real problems my brother and I had with our father revolved around money. The Lion was a businessman, and it was his nature to make a profit. Family was not immune. Gadget purchased a home in his late twenties, and The Lion was the cosigner. Then The Lion convinced him to switch roles and become the cosigner so he was listed as the owner. He explained it would benefit Gadget's taxes. When The Lion was in financial trouble, he sold Gadget's home. According to Gadget, he had made $35,000 in payments but never received any cash from the sale of his own home. The Lion could be underhanded in a subtle way. Gadget was rather pissed off about that one, but eventually he forgave him.

Once, I could not come up with the money to pay my property taxes. I knew The Lion had loaned $700 to another manager. I figure being his son and an employee for the past eight years has built up some goodwill. I work harder and am paid less than the other managers.

I ask, "Dad, can I borrow $1,000 to pay my taxes?" He replies, "Son, these times are hard and life is tough!" Then, as if to console me, he repeats a Shakespeare quote from Hamlet. He says, "Neither a borrower, nor a lender be." I knew what he really meant. He was a big-time borrower. At one point, he owed over three and a half million dollars to various banks. And he was also a lender. He was just not a lender to me.

If I had been given time to make a decision as to my inclination, I would have probably studied photography. God gave me a gift for taking pictures. I recall a moment when I was in Kluane National Park, high on a mountaintop with a herd of wild Dall sheep. The lighting was perfect, so I was able to position the Dall sheep with snow-capped mountains in the background. When I have a camera, I see life's beauty through God's eyes and I can capture it. I want to do it so I can share the photos with others. The camera and I had a sacred contract. It allowed me to express creatively who I was. For me it's as natural as the way a niece or nephew grabs hold of your leg and gives it a hug.

I must pay my taxes! The only asset I have is my camera equipment. It breaks my heart to sell it, but I feel like I have no other option. I place an ad on the Internet. It sells fast to a Chinese buyer. Then the camera equipment is stolen on route. It never reaches its intended buyer. Insurance pays for it, but I feel like God took it back. Our contract was broken. I make another vow: "I will never borrow or ask for any assistance from The Lion for the rest of my life."

THE SOFT SIDE OF THE LION

Many years after I sell my camera, The Lion starts to acknowledge that I have talent as a photographer. And The Lion graciously, without hesitation, has offered his home. He says, "I am glad to have you come stay in my house; while you are there, feed my dogs." It has worked out so far. I really need a place to stay, and I like to write when nobody is around. Maybe The Lion is being human and his heart is not all stone.

Once, he purchased hip waders for Gadget and me to go fishing with him and Buck. It was probably Buck's idea. We went to a secret spot known as Horn of the Moon. The Lion is not the type to walk in the woods, and I never saw him hold a fishing pole. But he bought us hip waders and went with us. Horn of the Moon requires a hike up the brook to reach a mountain pond. We were instructed to walk slowly in the marshy bog. One wrong step and you will slip out of sight in the muck. Buck had a fly-fishing rod. I watched him pull in a nice rainbow trout. I didn't catch a fish, but it was a memorable day.

If I think hard, I can recall family trips and other fun times, but these did not leave deep ruts in my mind like the painful memories did. Once I was working for the family business as a manager, he made it a point to share all his challenging business scenarios. He would call me first thing in the morning. He wanted me to learn how to deal with similar problems if I ever took over the business. His heart was into teaching me. Once, I asked him how he was going to deal with a difficult situation. He replied, "I don't know." I was dismayed; how could he, The Lion, not know the answer? He had never been this vulnerable or this honest before. It did not show weakness, but wisdom. His decisions were a matter of the right timing, and sometimes he just needed more information before he could make a good decision. He was a sharp businessman for many years.

In his behalf, The Lion and I would often play ping-pong in the basement or toss a baseball in the front yard. He even helped coach the peewee baseball team in our hometown; underneath his rough coat, he cared for and loved his kids.

THE BRADY BUNCH

I am rudely awakened to another part of his underlying nature, and mine, while I am thumbing through the channels of his television. I stumble upon the Playboy channel on his satellite network. I am surprised there are not any blocks or codes. Anybody can watch it. Of course, I immediately stop on *that* channel.

The scene starts off innocently. It is a take-off on the

Brady Bunch. Cool. There is a funky, multi-colored van and the whole family living together, but the actors are all over 18. I am intrigued. I used to watch the show. So far it's clean. There has not been any flesh shown. It quickly shifts when Greg brings his girlfriend up into his groovy bedroom with the lava lamp, and they undress.

Cindy is in a high-cut skirt with her trademark pigtails. She is out in the front yard flirting with the milkman. I want to change the channel, but I cannot do it. The hook is sunk into my flesh. After a few minutes, Cindy is having sex with the milkman on a lawn chair. Why am I watching this?

I can't bring myself to change the channel. Instead, I detach and observe my feelings. I really feel for the women and men that work in these porn flicks. I wonder, what do they tell their spouses and kids? Love is lacking. Their acting is cold and uninviting. The sad truth is I have gone for years without watching any porn and today I watch it for 20 minutes. The inevitable *knock, knock, knock* came on my door. I opened the door and invited *lust* to come sit beside me in the living room.

RETAINING SEXUAL INTEGRITY

I set up my home to remove these fleshy temptations. I don't even own a television. Now, porn is staring me in the face. I am right back in The Lion's Den, where it was first conceived. I should have expected it. The Lion may not be aware or willing to acknowledge that porn is an issue. I am not blaming The Lion for my sexual addiction. Every man is accountable for his own actions. But now that porn is readily accessible, I must dance with the devil. I don't have many options. I turn to a Christian friend who is aware of temptations that exist in pornography for support; otherwise I will be hooked and reeled in again and again.

I phone up Cowboy, who was my housemate when I attended Liberty University. He understands my helpless feeling and situation. I desperately ask, "Will you be my accountability partner?" He replies, "Yes, of course." It's a simple but powerful solution. I call him each night and let him know if I did or did not turn on the Playboy channel that day. He prays for me. I know my limits and prepare myself for a weeklong battle. I have numerous reruns of the Brady Bunch scenes stuck in my mind. Of course, I have the desire to turn back on the Playboy channel, but I don't do it. It would be awkward and embarrassing to tell Cowboy that I turned on the Playboy channel.

Soon after watching the Brady Bunch porn flick, I feel shame and guilt. It happens every time. I compassionately forgive myself. I pray to Jesus for strength to overcome my addiction. I think of the women in my life that were affected by my past sexually addictive behavior. How much did the pornography magazines and movies affect my failed marriage?

John Regier, the Christian counselor who created Caring for the Heart Ministry, says that a man involved in pornography is only capable of loving his wife at a 3% level. One will not give or receive love normally until they get adequate counseling to heal any trauma received or inflicted as physical, emotional, or spiritual abuse.

A good wife or a woman with integrity will keep her man accountable. She will have the courage to speak out against porn and will not tolerate movies with strong sexual content. Recovery from an addiction can be a long process. For me, it requires spiritual transformation and faith in the healing power of Jesus Christ.

I pray that Jesus will help me avoid pornography. Part of me desires to watch porn, while another part despises it. I need to be strong and make a stand for myself. My accountability partner and men's support groups have a vital purpose, but more important are my own actions. Joe Zychik writes,

> "If you want to overcome sex addiction, don't expect a group to save you. You overcome sex addiction or any other problem through your own, independent,

self-reliant choices." [19]

All week long, I face the beast. I slay and conquer it. It is a victory!

T.C Ryan's says,

"I worked long and hard at recovery before experiencing the sustained sobriety and growing serenity I longed for. To overcome my intimacy wounds, I focused on interpersonal relationships. I had two sponsors and worked with two therapists. I attended sex-addiction recovery groups, and I began a confidentiality group for clergy. I discovered how important being part of a healthy community is for genuine life change."

He goes on to explains what the sexual addict needs,

"Something greater than reasoning, something stronger than self-will, and something more interventive than messages to make different choices. The addict needs truth and community, support and love, and the healthy reintegration of their life." [20]

VISUAL STIMULATION

Women and men are programmed differently. Most women desire intimacy and affection from a man, especially before becoming involved in a relationship. That means a guy who genuinely listens and cares. Most men are visual creatures; all it takes is a flash of some bare skin, and the primitive triggers get activated. Because of my past programming, I am hypersensitive to any female flesh, be it on paper, video, or on a woman. As a man, I must be extremely disciplined and careful about what I place in front of my eyes if I want to live a pure life. It took me years to reprogram my lustful thoughts. Now

I look upon a woman as a sacred creature with a divine spirit, mind, and body.

In Costa Rica, I go to the R rated *American Pie* movie with a date. I have no clue what the movie is about, but it's the only movie that we had both not seen. When it starts to get raunchy, I begin to writhe in my seat. I can't stand watching it. I awkwardly tell her I want to leave the movie and invite her to go with me. She does not want to leave the movie, which is her option, but she feels greatly insulted because I did. After I leave the movie, I wait outside of the theater for her. Later, once she has cooled down, I explain why I loathe sexual scenes and how they are disrespectful toward women, but she really doesn't get it.

I share this example because it's hard for a woman to fully understand sexual addiction and how lust can adversely affect a man. I urge women who believe their partner is struggling with sexual addiction to listen to them. Allow some compassion and forgiveness. Pray for and encourage your partner to make decisions and actions with sexual integrity.

CHAPTER 22

The Chains that Bind

I forgave The Lion for most of what happened in my childhood, but I still have some bitterness around how I feel he took advantage of The Lamb. After he moved out, he gave the family brick home to his wife. He agreed to make the remaining payments and provide her with a car and some spending money. When his business was expanding, he asked her if he could refinance the house for an $85,000 loan with the remaining equity. When I asked The Lamb about the loan, she replied, "I was led to believe that you would take over the business. I think you were led to believe that, too! Had I known that would not happen, I would not have gone along with the loan." In the end, she gave her consent, and also allowed The Lion to charge on her credit card.

He paid $15,000 toward the loan but eventually fell months behind and then stopped making the house and credit card payments completely. The bank started to foreclose on her home. She needed to sell her home to get out of the mess. The only way The Lamb could stall for more time was to file for bankruptcy.

> *"For the married woman is bound by law to her husband while he is living; but if her husband dies, she is released from the law concerning the husband."*
> *(Romans 7:2 NASB)*

Let's get a visual image: two ships, one is a man and the

other is a woman, both sailing along. They sail where they want and when they want. They get married because they want to sail together, as a team. The symbol of the spiritual bond of marriage between the two is a ring. There is a ring on the foredeck of one boat with a long chain bolted to the stern of the other. It is a commitment. They need to sail in the same direction. One cannot head into a storm and the other head away. They both either weather a storm or avoid it. One ship may take a hit and the other may remain unscarred, but it will slow them both down. If one ship is hit hard and begins to sink, then the other boat can still float around, happy as a clam — until the chain pulls tight, and then…*plop!* They both go out of sight.

Given their situation, I encourage The Lion to divorce The Lamb. He says, "I can't do it. Half of all I own would go to her." Well, spiritually they are bound and they both sink. The Lamb might have gone down harder than The Lion because she could not see the chain being pulled tight.

The Lion's pride never allowed him to file for his own bankruptcy. But his actions placed his legal wife in a position where she had no other option, even though she only owed a sliver of his total debt. During his financial crisis, he borrowed from a half dozen friends and made it a point to pay them all back, with interest.

I unexpectedly run into The Lion in town. We have lunch together. His face is weathered; he's heavier set around the middle; and his stature resembles a battle-worn king sitting down to dine. We talk about the last episode of his burdensome financial saga. He tells me that his financial situation has improved. It takes some gumption, but I ask, "Have you considered sending $50 or $100 a month to The Lamb for the money that you owe her?" He flies mad, "I don't owe her anything!"

He does not show any remorse or any intention to ever pay her back. He justifies not owing her by explaining that he provided for her financial needs for many years. (Isn't that what a husband is supposed to do?) Anyhow, it breaks my heart and God's. Marriage is meant to be a vow to protect, support, and honor your spouse. Now that his fortune is basically gone, he has no good reason to not divorce her.

It's a difficult situation. It is probably not my business, even as a son, to try and fix what I perceive as my parents' problems. Perhaps it is better that I pray for them and hand their situation over to a higher authority, like Jesus. He shared His view on marriage and divorce. Jesus was *not* in favor of divorce, at all. But He makes an exception in situations where there has been sexual immorality.

> "Some Pharisees came to him to test him. They asked, "Is it lawful for a man to divorce his wife for any and every reason?"
> "Haven't you read," he replied, "that at the beginning the Creator 'made them male and female,' and said, 'For this reason a man will leave his father and mother and be united to his wife, and the two will become one flesh'? So they are no longer two, but one flesh. Therefore, what God has joined together, let no one separate."
> "Why then," they asked, "did Moses command that a man give his wife a certificate of divorce and send her away?" Jesus replied, "Moses permitted you to divorce your wives because your hearts were hard. But it was not this way from the beginning. I tell you that anyone who divorces his wife, except for sexual immorality, and marries another woman commits adultery."
> (Matthew 19:3-9 NIV)

THE PURE HEART FORGIVES

God's grace helps those who help others with a pure heart.

The Lamb spent most of her life serving her family faithfully. Family members and relatives loan her some money to help her get by until her home sells. Three different family members offer to let her live with them. Against all odds, in a slumping market, her big brick home sells for a fairly decent price in the middle of the winter.

She immediately pays back about $120,000 for the loan, interest, late fees, credit cards, and bills accrued from her bankruptcy proceedings to clear the debt The Lion imposed upon her. The Lamb has a humble amount of money left over after selling her home, but it's not enough to buy a small home, which was her dream.

She sent The Lion a statement, but makes no legal attempt to get reimbursement from him. She paid his bills after losing her home, going through bankruptcy, and absorbing a ton of stress and emotional pain.

When I ask her about it, she smiles and says, "I have forgiven him." I say, "Are you serious?" She says, "Yes, I have forgiven him for his actions, but I have not forgotten his debt."

The Lamb has put into action what is probably one of the most important teachings of Jesus and I can't get it! I am blown away. I have not yet forgiven The Lion for what he did to her.

I watched all the suffering The Lamb went through. I even went to a bankruptcy lawyer with her. I saw her cry and I did my best to give her emotional and financial support. Even when The Lamb had to live frugally, she held her head high. She possesses real inner nobility. I am immensely impressed because she is beyond allowing money, or the lack of it, to affect her personality.

As her son, my perception is that she has been taken advantage of and treated unfairly by The Lion. I know The Lamb and The Lion, and I have completely different perceptions. The Lion holds a grudge and has a mental list of people who he feels did him wrong. This method devours the spirit. This is how everybody lived before Jesus came along. Then He set an example of a higher order of truth called forgiveness. Jesus was faithfully obedient to God's will to demonstrate divine forgiveness. He embodied it when his blood was shed on the cross.

There is power in feeling wounded and betrayed by some act that happened in the past, but healing cannot exist on that plane. Forgiveness is much more powerful. It leaves behind all the blaming, guilt, and excuses. Forgiveness happens in the present moment, and when you forgive somebody, for whatever reason, you crucify the perception of feeling betrayed. This allows one to ascend to a higher order of truth.

I feel rather humble because The Lamb naturally knew how to forgive. I ask myself, *"Why is it harder for me to forgive The Lion than it is for her?"*

I guess my pride stems from being her son. I perceive there was a great injustice done to my mom. Perhaps I need to learn to love myself on a new level. The Lamb is teaching me a big lesson. I know if I do not forgive The Lion then it will only hurt me. Maybe forgiveness is more of an act of self-love.

THE LION'S LESSONS

Once, while at a retreat, I sent The Lion a letter expressing how I experienced some deeper healing around father and son issues. I wrote how I forgave him for ignoring or not allowing me to express my emotions through my childhood and adult life. I wrote about the importance of being honest to his children and how the lies he told me were traumatic.

I ask him on Father's Day, "What are your thoughts about the letter I sent you?" He replies, "I thought it had some emotional stuff in it, so I never opened it. I threw it away without reading it."

Of course, I feel rejected and hurt. When I was younger, my father seldom showed that he cared about how I felt emotionally. I believe it was difficult for him to feel or express emotions toward certain others in his life, primarily his wife and two sons. The Lion was not always shown much compassion or understanding from his father. I feel for him. I know deep down he loves and cares for my brother and me.

A shift occurred after he became semi-retired. He began to soften. He even said, "I did some immoral things in my past." Acknowledging this is a big step for him. Now that we're both grown adults and live far away, he wants us to come and spend some time with him at camp. We both do. There is hope for my Dad (and other parents), but I needed to come to accept him, as he is. Now, he even says, "I love you, Son" when I am leaving.

I believe one big factor is that he gets regular practice expressing how much he loves his girlfriend and his daughter. He proclaimed, "My priority during my financial crisis was to save my home and the camp on the lake, so my (current) family can enjoy a quality life."

I recently learned that when he was a senior in high school he had a scary dream about his best friend, Egils Aivars Mezaraups. Egils had dropped out of high school to join the Marines. In his dream, he saw a huge wave spill over the deck of a ship and slam Egils around on the boat before sweeping him overboard. The Lion was shocked when he found out… it actually happened. Egils was dead! They found his body near Bermuda. He was only twenty years old. It shook The Lion up immensely and his death had a huge impact upon him. The Lion felt depressed for several months afterwards and attended few classes during his senior year.

Life sends each of us different challenges, and we must bear them with the fortitude and patience, as Jesus did. Even now, I don't fully understand all the hardships The Lion has endured. I had idolized his high school years. I thought of him as a great athlete and leader, who never let anything phase him. In reality, he went through some tough emotional times. He actually was dealt and felt more pain then most kids, and that somehow makes him even more human. It is easy to preemptively pass judgment, even though I don't know all the facts. I know that life's trials test the character of a man. We must each carry our own cross.

> *King Solomon wrote, "In this meaningless life of mine I have seen both of these: a righteous man perishing in his righteousness, and a wicked man live long in his wickedness. Do not be over righteous, neither be overwise — why destroy yourself? Do not be overwicked and do not be a fool — why die before your time? It is good to grasp the one and not let go of the other. The man who fears God will avoid all extremes."*
> (Ecclesiastes 7:15-18 NIV)

God is at work and He shines hope on every soul. The Lion's younger girlfriend is the primary provider financially. Now it's his role to take care of their daughter. I commend him because he affectionately loves and cares for them. He has even started to take better care of his health. He stopped smoking, drinks less hard liquor, and is eating better. He goes to his daughter's basketball games, a softball tournament, takes her to dance classes, and joins her to play the piano for a duet recital. He has the time, being semi-retired, but in this new family scenario, he has made family a priority over money. He *wants* to spend his time with them. Perhaps he realizes his time with his daughter is limited.

I admire his example of a better functioning family. This second time around, God is in The Lion's life teaching him how to love and care for a family. Having found *real* forgiveness for The Lion, I see him in a new light. There are many good qualities in The Lion that are noteworthy.

The Legend of The Lion

The Lion is a beast of power,
A formidable king that rules over his land.

Have no fear, he is glad to meet you at any hour,
He is the first to extend out his mighty hand.
Chairman of the Red Cross, Leader of the Band,
he hands out opportunity, as a job, which will be grand.
Owner of the fancy bistro, lakeside camp,
and shiny Cadillac,
he is the growing envy for what most men's lives do lack.
He trained me, with rigid discipline, as a Lion would,
showing there is no difference, between the bad and good.
Learn to hire, when to fire.
Find out every person's niche,
Let them do it, delegate.
Run the meeting, don't be late.
Interrogate, when the facts are fresh and new.
Read every paper, dissect every word, as a clue.
Don't hold back on greasy food, fickle friends, or having fun.
Be in the parade, join that club,
hold a barbeque out in the sun.
He gave to me a snowmobile, motorcycle, bike, and car.
Taught me how to drive,
shift the gears, without letting them jar.
Weekend travel, dinner out, and vacation trips.
He was the one to provide the funding and pay the tip.
He coached me in baseball, taught me how to dive.
If it were not for him, I would not be alive!
I take for granted my good life. College bills paid,
clothes appear, an invite to camp, where friends all hunt deer,
(Wait, that's not what I meant, in our case,
friends all drink beer.)
The Lion shows me how to live on top, appreciate classical
music, don't sweat the car dents; learn of life from our past
presidents: Roosevelt, Kennedy, Hoover, and Abe.
Each left an impression, which for the Lion is sharp.
All worthy men leave behind, as he will, his mark.
I often feel I stand, as the Lion once did,

ready for battle, ready to give.
It used to upset me, but now I don't mind.
I've placed our past where it should be: behind.
I am the son of a Lion. It's my fate.
There is no need to falter. I accept it as great!
He claims to never get enough in this life.
The woman you love need not be your wife.
Better, he says, to go without sleep,
than miss one moment, which is profound or stirringly deep.
He is my father. I am proud.
I let him know, in his way,
for a Lion is born to roar out loud! ■

Part III
Swan Song

The swan song in ancient Greek is a metaphorical phrase for a final gesture, effort, or performance given just before death or retirement. The phrase refers to an ancient belief that swans sing a beautiful song in the moment just before death, having been silent or not so musical during most of their lifetime.

THE CAST

I have given pseudonyms to the key characters in Swan Song. This allows some discretion, and the fun names reveal a bit about each person's distinguishing trait.

Cetan Luta	Red Hawk
Wicahpi Ska	White Star
Old Medicine Man	Wicahcala
My Beloved	Swan Song
Swan Song's Partner	Chief Thunder Cloud
Teacher of Native American Traditions	My Native Brother
Red Hook Internet Date	Pandora
Past Life Daughter	Feather Maker
Past Life Son	Lost Son
Liberty University Housemate	Cowboy
Omega Life Coach	Nora Queesting
Omega Male Friends	Eric the Viking & G. I. Joe
Omega Female Friends	Sunshine & Terracotta
Omega Fairy-like Friend	Blossom
Omega Akashic Record Reader	Krystal Baal
Omega Meditation Teacher	Althea
Althea's Husband	Huck Finn
Sweat Lodge Friend	Walking Bear
Abode Female Friends	Izabella & Fascia
The Shaman	Charcoal
My Dad	The Lion
My Mom	The Lamb
My Brother	Gadget

CHAPTER 23

My Native Tribe

For over a month, I have had a series of dreams about a past life when I am living in a Native American tribe of Indians in the sky-wide plains out west. I am sitting around a fire circle with all my relatives. The smell of smoke lingers on my woven blanket. In the air it mixes with the other comfortably familiar smells: the dusty earth and pipe tobacco, a deer stew mixed with spices, wet dogs and horse sweat. Our tribe is a vibrant family. We radiate with love and warmth. I relate to each person in our circle through the blood that flows in my veins, a gentle touch, and a small, steady smile.

Nearby sits my sister's husband playing with my nieces and nephews. There is joyful light in their eyes. They smile and giggle. Our way of life is interwoven with nature. It is fresh, wholesome, and alive. We are grateful for every breath, every bite of food, and every relationship. Not just between the souls in our tribe, but also with the relationships we hold with the deer, the birch tree, the earth beneath our bare feet, and the sky above, where the blue jay flies.

My name is Cetan Luta. It means Red Hawk. I was given this name because I have a keen eye. I spot animals far in the distance. The red-tailed hawk is my totem protector. I honor it with tobacco, but more so with my respect, for it will swoop down and grab a rattlesnake without fear. I carry three red-tailed hawk feathers wound together with sinew. They are tied in my hair when I hunt so that I, too, will be without fear.

I am returning from an afternoon of autumn hunting with my older brother and two other warriors. Up ahead, two trails meet and our paths will part. We stop to divide up our game. My older brother pats my shoulder and says, "Next time we hunt rabbits, you stomp on the pile. I will shoot them. Then I can go home with two rabbits." My arrow was deflected by a branch and one rabbit scampered away. I smile and reply, "Why do you need two rabbits when you have no wife?" He snickers and replies, "I will find a wife before your arrow finds that missing rabbit." We depart laughing. The path on the left is a shortcut to the river. I walk down it carrying two drooping, brown rabbits. The lush green tree line of the forest gives way to a field of waist-high golden grass. It blends with the color of my buckskin clothing with its hanging braided strands.

For generations, as long as we have known, the women have designed our clothing and sewn in the brightly-colored seed-bead design of the eagle. We also honor the eagle by painting it on the side of our teepees. It distinguishes our people from the distant tribes beyond the pine-scented mountains. I walk tall and proud to honor our ancestors. They taught me how to walk softly in all circumstances: from heel to toe when hunting, and by listening to every person around the fire before blurting out my thoughts. Many ancestors are gone. Now they live in the stars.

I bend down on one knee to clean my hands. Then I cup water in my palms to refresh my face and quench my thirst. I stand up and pause to admire how the golden grass waves in the wind and how the sun sparkles on the river. My eyes soften when I peer in the direction of the winding path beside the riverbank. It leads to our teepee. There awaits my wife and our two kids: my family.

My wife is Wicahpi Ska. Her name means White Star. She was born in the middle of the night. An extremely bright star flew across the sky that night. Her brown eyes are fawn-soft. Her touch is tender, like a warm summer wind. During the day, she joined the other women to gather roots, berries, and nuts in the baskets they had woven. Both she and I have warm thoughts, anticipating our reuniting in the late afternoon.

Wicahpi Ska comes into view. She is gathering water farther up the river by filling up the preserved stomach and bladder from harvested animals. She is singing a beautiful Native song. I silently step closer so I can listen to her sing. I watch her with a soft smile. Her voice is enchanting. My heart beats faster when I am near her. She always dresses carefully. Today her hair is flowing wild and free, without any braids. When she notices me, the singing stops, our eyes meet, and her smile instantly fills me with joy. We softly embrace. She exclaims in our Native language how it is a pleasure for Cetan Luta to find her by the river. I respond in kind, flirtatiously saying the pleasure is more Cetan Luta's because now he is near Wicahpi Ska. She squints her eyes and smiles again. We walk back along the trail, with my arm wrapped around her shoulder. In her other hand she carries the pouches of water.

Our two young, brown-eyed children, a boy and a girl, ages six and eight, dash out of the teepee. They must have heard our voices. I lean my bow against the teepee and place the two rabbits down. I scoop them both up in a huge bear-hug. I let out a jovial shout, and my daughter shrieks back playfully. My son is pointing down at the two dead, floppy rabbits. I set him down and squat beside him to explain how we tracked the rabbits into a bush pile. Then his uncle stomped on the pile to scare them out. I make a funny face and stomp my feet. I slowly make the motion of pulling back an arrow, then jerk my hand around to point at the target. I make a *whish* noise as I open my fingers wide to let the invisible arrow fly. My son is amused. He mimics my actions and we watch him until an outburst of laughter envelopes us. In our tribe, we don't hold back the urge to laugh or cry. We learn the merits of hard work and know there is also a time to play. This is what it means to live and to die. We are like the changes in the seasons.

One day, during my dream, a great tragedy strikes the tribe. The women are crying and wailing around the fire. Wicahpi Ska is torn apart, distraught, completely beyond herself with screams of agony from deep within. I don't know the cause, but even I am feeling great sadness. Later in the next dream, it's partially revealed: a warrior had died. He startled a grizzly bear. It grabbed him and gouged his back. Its powerful claws killed him.

This same dream continues day after day until the time is right for the medicine to speak. When the medicine speaks, it guides me to go for a long walk in the woods. I cross over two brooks and come to an old logging path with tall pine trees on either side. Two chickadees are chirping high above in the branches. I look up at them. Two feathers slowly float down. I hold open my hand and they both land on my palm. It's a significant sign. Native medicine is in the air.

> *"Native American 'Medicine' is not the same as the modern medicine that we think of today. It is not a pill or a procedure or anything else that can be used to improve one's physical health. When Native Americans refer to 'Medicine', they are referring to the vital power or force that is inherent in Nature itself, and to the personal power within oneself which can enable one to become more whole or complete."* [21]

MY DEATH SONG

I appear on a dirt road near an old white farmhouse. Behind it, there is a large, circular, back field that scales up the hillside. Floating in the middle of the field is an island of tall, striped birch trees.

Sadness for the death of the warrior in my dream still lingers. I am trying to figure out why his death is so significant.

We feel connected in some arcane way. That warrior was close to me.

Suddenly, my eyes lock on a coyote walking down the middle of the road, heading in my direction. They usually run away. But something is peculiar about this one. He stops to stare in my direction. Perhaps this coyote can sense my sadness. I am not a threat and I am not afraid. He angles off up into the field. Then he walks a wide half circle and sits down on his haunches, a mere thirty feet away.

Now I am feeling even more sadness. It is becoming overwhelming. I squat down by a small pool in the brook. At that moment, I realize why Wicahpi Ska was so devastated. The warrior who died was her husband, Cetan Luta.

But, wait a minute! She was *my* past wife. It was *me* that died. I sense that Cetan Luta was my same age, in a past life, at the time of his death. The medicine has been waiting to reveal his death on the corresponding day.

I sense the whole tragic scene from my past life. It all happened dreadfully fast. I was following deer tracks into thick brush. The grizzly bear was startled. It came rushing toward me. There was no time to react or defend myself. I felt a sudden shock as it clasped around my back. Then it gouged me with its huge front claws. My life ended swiftly — too swiftly. Something was missing!

In a ceremonial manner, I take mud from the brook and smear two lines down the sides of my face. I begin to chant in a Native language. As I do, the coyote in the field throws his head back and begins a series of yelps, then he opens his mouth wide and lets out a high-pitched howl. A bush is lined up directly between us, so I only see glimpses of him.

I believe this coyote actually wants to join in my ceremony. A coyote will sometimes howl when they are alone and searching for the pack, but joining me is inconceivable. What an amazingly-bizarre honor to chant with a wild animal, especially a coyote. But I am too caught up in my chanting and feeling the emotions to be overly concerned with the coyote.

My whole universe is opening. I am in a surreal, dreamlike state. I have somehow overlapped another dimension of time. Every sound is magnified. The songs of the birds in the far corner of a field fill my ears with angelic voices along with a sweet golden harp. I am smothered with the smell of spring flowers. My vision is soft and blurry. It feels like I am in two different places. One is definitely not in this earthly realm. There is a timelessness. It feels like a curtain has lifted and I am in heaven.

As the warrior Cetan Luta, I never had a chance to sing my death song. I died too suddenly. Yes, that's it! I need to sing my death song. A death song is to take away fear and give courage when a warrior is facing a deadly situation, usually before heading into battle or during a severe illness. Maybe there are other reasons for it in the Native afterlife. This is what he needs. That is what he is missing! I start to chant Cetan Luta's death song in his Native American tongue.

While I slip into this microcosmic universe, Cetan Luta's soul finds solace. I believe this window in heaven has opened up on earth to allow his soul to freely pass. Now he can continue to travel, as intended. I am assuming he is on a beautiful journey back to the happy hunting ground. I can sense the presence of a medicine man entrusted to watch over Cetan Luta's soul. He is more than a witness. He is calling forth medicine to make all of this happen. I believe that he is somehow connected to that coyote. I can't see him, but I can feel him. It is possible he could even be…inside that coyote.

Broken Circle

A dream, a vision of the circle that is broken.
The wailing of hearts still rings in my ears.
The cries are not for me but for the love of life.
I watch a child pick a flower and smile.
I am in awe and give thanks for the keeping of my relatives.

*For many years, many lives, the promise is kept.
Release the medicine man that is entrusted
to connect the circle once again.
When the stars are in line, the spirit goes forward,
overlapping the past.*

Once I stop chanting, the coyote trots away to the corner of the field and disappears. I stand alone for a moment. I am absorbing all that has just happened. Cetan Luta's death song is a big piece of the puzzle. I slowly walk home. I go into the bathroom and look in the mirror. To my surprise, from the corner of each eye, wide, mud-smeared trails are streaming down the sides of my cheeks. They appear to be tears from Cetan Luta. They don't look like mine.

From this day forward, my dreams of the Native American tribe cease. But they continue in visions, and his past life continues to seek completion through cherished people that I meet in this life. Some of my new closest friends were, without a doubt, part of my past life within that Native American tribe. Our past and present lives will soon start to merge and the broken circle will be mended.

WICAHCALA REVEALS THE SACRED NAME

Months later, in a vision, I see my Native American tribe again. My Native blood-brother has taken in my wife and raised my two kids, as is the custom. She learns to love him in her own way, and he provides for her. But her heart yearns with a passion to be with her first love: Cetan Luta. When she misses him, she stands under the stars to feel his presence.

Wicahpi Ska prays with a pure heart to the medicine men for their spirits to be reunited. The medicine men live in the stars, beyond time and space. They look down upon their people to protect and provide for the needs of their souls.

Some Native Americans have two names; one name is never made public because of the power it would give another over them. The secret and sacred names are meant to only be known by the individual and the medicine man who watches guard over that person during life and beyond. Cetan Luta had trusted Wicahpi Ska so much that he told her his sacred name. It was Ohitika, which means "Appears Bravely."

One night, while Wicahpi Ska was praying under the stars, the old medicine man called Wicahcala appeared. He said, "Your heart is pure and your prayers are heard. The spirits of Cetan Luta *Ohitika* and Wicahpi Ska will be reunited." She was overjoyed when she heard his words. Only the medicine man that watches over Cetan Luta during his life and beyond would know his sacred name. It didn't matter to her if it happened in this life, or the next, or in the spirit world. She found hope and comfort in knowing that one day her spirit would reunite with Cetan Luta. ■

CHAPTER 24

Pandora's Box

I am searching an internet dating site to find my true love. After a score of horrendous dates, I begin to refine my Internet dating criteria. One day, I enter the keyword "yoga." Up pops one woman named Pandora, who lives in Red Hook, New York. We email and then speak on the phone several times. She is pleasant, intellectual, and funny. Eventually, we meet at a quaint B&B in Manchester, Vermont. We spend a charming weekend getting to know each other.

Before her arrival, I conceal several Rumi poems among the fields and flower gardens. Each has a clue leading to the next. We agree to be silent for our first walk. I lead her innocently to the first card. The silence allows us to be ourselves. We can accept each other without the clutter of trying to say the right words to meet some preconceived, self-imposed expectations. The final item in her scavenger hunt is a briefcase-size love letter. It is overflowing with sappy romance that shall never be repeated.

Later we walk on the mowed path that winds along a bordering river. I playfully bolt off the trail into the chest-high grass like an excited teenager.

Pandora grabs her cheeks and screams, "Are you crazy? You're going to get ticks all over. You'll catch Lyme disease!"

I reply, "Yes! I am crazy!"

I did not get Lyme disease.

We sleep together in the same bed. Neither she nor I want

to stir up passion on our first night together. I suggest to her, "Let's draw an invisible line down the center of the bed and agree not to cross it." She agrees. I show her where the line is. I tell her, "I do not even want your little toe to sneak over to my side."

Pandora laughs. We both put on our pajamas and say goodnight. We each stay on our side of the bed.

Before I left my home, I had waded into a nearby pond and pulled up a pink water lily by the roots. I give it to her in the evening. I am a bit disappointed because it closed up. It was so beautiful floating on the pond. But the next morning it opens up brilliantly. Maybe there is hope for us.

The next week we discuss my moving in. It's not practical to date when we live five hours apart. We agree to live together even though we only met a month earlier. It's an impulsive decision, probably based upon the disillusion that we desperately need to find a mate to quench our loneliness. I pack my car and cruise down the interstate. I am anticipating that some sort of romantic relation will blossom.

I misplaced her directions, so I have to use my spiritual radar. I turn off on what I believe is her exit, then take a series of winding back roads that bring me directly to Pandora's lakeside home. It is a sunny picturesque day. She is standing outside in shorts with a cute halter top. She has red, curly hair down to her shoulders, and her cheeks are rosy and peppered with freckles. She gives me a big smile. I give her a big hug.

The inside of her nest is plush and cozy, filled with creature comforts. Friends often comment on the sweetness of her charming décor. She lived in Manhattan for twenty years and brought with her all the sophisticated charm. In the living room sits an ivory-colored replica antique chair with wooden ball and claw feet; on the floor is an entourage of oriental rugs, and on the walls hang several oversized angel paintings. Their eyes seem to be watching my every move, wherever I sit. There is a triangular-shaped, multi-level, gold-rimmed coffee table thick with layers of knickknacks from her world travels during her dance career. On the sofa and flowing onto the floor is a fountain of designer pillows in all shapes and sizes; some are silk with fringes. They never seem to find a proper home due to either their overabundance or their royal, flamboyant, flirtatious nature.

In the upstairs bedroom stands a flawlessly-smooth, dark cherry, sleigh bed with a pillow-top mattress. It is covered with layers of overstuffed down comforters and four pillows. Tassels hanging from antique lamps sway back and forth on each bedside table, and a huge picture window offers a nice view out toward the lake.

A few eccentricities catch my attention; one is what I consider to be a rabid gathering of what we both soon begin to call "stuff". Stuff is defined as bookshelves overflowing with new unread books, compact discs, and videos still in the cellophane wrapper. My assumption is that Pandora dove headfirst into mainstream materialism to fill the gap. Clearly, no man had been in her life for the last several years.

Pandora's zeal for gardening is evident from the rocks she has tenderly placed to resemble a serpentine coastline spilling out from the forest edge, complete with floating tulips, bell-shaped gardenias, and dancing daffodils. Her artistic arrangements rival those in Central Park. Pandora grew up near that park, and it is where her mother still lives. A statue of St. Francis of Assisi, holding a bird bath, kneels in an opening among the flowers. In his prayerful manner, he is calling out to the birds and squirrels. They are regular visitors each morning, along with deer that nibble on her plants, much to her dismay. She uses a little red wagon to deliver her compost and potting soil. This is when her inner child, dressed in overalls to keep away all the ticks, can happily play among the petals and bulbs for hours.

The first few days of living together are filled with the excitement of getting to know each other. However, by the third day, I begin to break out with itchy eyes, a sore throat, and a cough. My skin begins to crawl and confusion sets in. I am emotionally a wreck. For no apparent reason, tears stream down my face. It is not normal. Pandora thinks I am overly sensitive to what she suspects is mold growing in her home. I uncover that, prior to my arrival, she had thrown out green-spotted living room curtains and two pasty-green wicker bookshelves.

We decide to tackle the mold and merrily spend that evening listening to Barbara Streisand's Funny Girl as we scrub the walls, woodwork, and vinyl couch. Of course, Pandora knows all the lines and sings out, accompanied with the occasional animation from the Broadway show. With a new dehumidifier constantly sucking up gallons of moisture, we think we have defeated the mold. Unfortunately, the villain only laughs with a sly grimace at our attempt to fight an invisible foe with caustic chlorine.

Eventually, the mold compromises my whole immune system. I become sensitive to fresh paint, new carpet, and even dust. My symptoms progressively worsen. I decide that before I completely lose my mind, I had better move out. The mold eventually blesses all her stuff by laying a claim on every piece of paper, fabric, and wood. She refuses to leave her sanctuary, because it had been fine for the past four years.

MY RETREAT SPACE

I rent a spacious apartment in nearby Shakomako. It was an old train depot renovated with modern skylights, hardwood floors, and exposed beams. It has a history as a milk storage house for local farmers. Now wealthy horse farms surround the area and deer graze in abundance. I walk across the miniature covered bridge spanning a babbling brook out front. I have found my place of peace and tranquility. I call it My Retreat Space. I feel even more at home when I learn that this spot had been the wintering grounds for a Native American village.

A week later my reality is jolted. At seven a.m., Pandora arrives in a state of hysterics. She is dressed in her cherry-printed pajamas, banging on my front door with her cat in tow under her arm. By now, I am fairly accustomed to her emotional outbreaks, but this one is a notch above. She is babbling uncontrollably, coughing, and swearing.

She declares, "I can't…I won't ever live in that mold-infested house again. I awoke with burning, swollen eyes. I had to pry them open. I was barely able to move. I felt paralyzed. My legs were all numb…my fingers were tingling."

With wide eyes, I say, "Oh my goodness! Pandora!"

Pandora rapidly says, "I could hardly breathe. In a weak and dizzy state, I stumbled outside gasping for fresh air."

She was in a condition that medical experts call "anaphylactic shock." She should have rushed to seek medical attention. Instead, she comes to my sanctuary, with tear-filled sobs, and asks to move in with me.

At this point, I ask myself what good can come from Pandora moving into my home with her cat and all her toxic, moldy belongings.

Well, I cannot turn her away. She is my friend. I say, "Pandora, mi casa es su casa. You can stay in the spare bedroom." She moves in later that day.

We begin living together again. Pandora is sweet and charming as she dances and prances around singing her repertoire of Broadway show tunes. When we play chess and she begins to lose, the chessboard is suddenly shaken or she throws the pieces at me with a sassy smile.

We go on long, silent walks in the mornings. It's my favorite time to be with her, because the silence allows me to keep my sanity.

I tell Pandora, "You have ten chattering monkeys that live in your head, and silence will give them a rest." During our silent walks, I hold up the number of fingers that indicate how many monkeys I think are living in her head that day. She smiles and laughs at my nonsense.

I became close friends with Pandora, but it never blossoms into a romantic relationship. We never fell in love. There were no sparks. But she led me to an awesome spiritual retreat. That's where I find my tribe. And it was there that I meet my beloved. ■

CHAPTER 25

My Native Brother

OMEGA INSTITUTE

Pandora had worked for a spiritual retreat called Omega Institute in Rhinebeck, New York. Omega is a pioneering spiritual center that provides an eclectic collection of vanguard retreats. Hundreds of renowned spiritual teachers have imparted their knowledge. I dare say, just being there raises one's level of consciousness. When one stays for extended periods, such as the 150 volunteers, your "stuff" comes up. Volunteers and guests going through life transitions are drawn to this place, like children to an ice-cream shop on a hot summer day.

Before Omega purchased the place, it was a Jewish summer camp called Boiberik. It still retains that fun-summer-camp feeling; the kind you get when friends gather around a campfire with a guitar. It contains a beautiful lake with hammocks under the pine trees, a beach for swimming, kayaks, and rowboats. There is no better way to spend a sunny afternoon than lying lazily in a boat, chilling out, or chatting with a friend. I like to go to a spot called Turtle Cove and just float under the clouds.

Nature trails lead in loops up to the highest ridges. Scattered in the woods are a few homemade benches; nice places to sit and meditate. The trails cross over a bubbling brook and along the way you will probably pass by a few fairy huts made of sticks. (The fairies are usually bustling in the forest, but you can always leave a note.)

At the farthest side, near Kansas Road, there are several mounds consisting of hundreds of bowling-ball-size stones. They were thought to be ancient ruins from earlier dwellings. And I must mention the grandmother tree: she is near the sweat lodge site. She must be given hugs and offerings, regularly. It is an altar of sorts, decorated with necklaces, shells, candles, and gemstones. These little rituals are a big deal. When you're going through stuff, it helps to let go of something physical.

Omega does not operate during the winter season. The bonds created in one summer at Omega are strong and heartfelt. Hugs are the trademark at Omega. Even the coldest hearts soften after enough hugs. Everyone is accepted.... Gay or straight, young or old. If your hair is blue and you have seven body piercings and a dragon tattoo, that's cool! Omega is a place to experiment with different facets of yourself. Just let your love continue to flow.

At the end of the season, the volunteers say tear-filled farewells. Everybody gets one last hug and a promise to stay in touch as they exchange cell numbers and Internet connections. Half of the volunteers go to exotic places during the winter season and they rarely find the time to stay in touch.

MY NATIVE BROTHER

Pandora introduces me to a couple at Omega who specialize in Native American traditions. They soon become a major influence in my life. The guy I call My Native Brother is not a Native American (he is a dark-skinned Italian), but he instantly treats me like a brother. I consider him to be my first teacher of Native American traditions. His girlfriend, Swan Song has a beautiful voice. I cherish her as well, like a sister.

During one of our first encounters, they come over to my place to join Pandora and me for dinner. Upon entering, Swan Song hands me a bouquet of wildflowers, along with a warm smile that fills me with joy. My Native Brother takes out two hoop bands of sage wrapped tightly in red cloth. He had used them in one of his past sun dance ceremonies. Swan Song lifts her brows and says to him discreetly, "Are you sure you want to give those away?"

He looks at me and explains, "These are sacred items. I want you to have them." He explains how they were used at the sun dance ceremony. I am greatly honored. My Native Brother begins to teach me, often through his actions more than his words. I can tell that his gift has tremendous personal meaning. That makes it even more valuable.

After dinner, My Native Brother begins to tell us about a medicine man he knows. He explains, "He is the great grandson of Crazy Horse. He recently went to prison and needs our prayers."

My Native Brother is a pipe carrier, which means he prays with a chanupa, also known as a peace pipe. He honors me by asking that I pray for this medicine man in my own way.

He invites Pandora and me to join them for a sweat lodge ceremony. It would be my first one. There is an inexplicable connection that occurs whenever My Native Brother, Swan Song and I come together. It feels like we have been together, as friends or family, for years. Our spiritual connection is unsurpassed whenever it involves the Native American realm.

My Native Brother mentions that he wants a rattle. When he speaks about it, my body tingles all over. I am inspired to find him a rattle. I search online and acquire a Southwestern artifact buffalo rattle that is used as a noise-maker in ceremonies and dances. This rattle measures fifteen inches long and is decorated with deerskin leather, beads, feathers, and flint. It is hand-painted and crafted by a Navajo artist, who has signed it.

THE ALMIGHTY ONE

The morning before the sweat lodge ceremony, I pray deeply for someone I don't know. It concerns addictions and letting go of past ways. Crows are flying around my backyard chaotically. I feel the spirits in the air. I leave early to help prepare the sweat lodge. Pandora stays at home. She is hesitant to participate, fearing that she will be sensitive to the smoke.

A few miles down the road, there is a gigantic, historical sycamore tree that measures forty feet in circumference. I call it "The Almighty One". On my way by, I spot a bald eagle flying toward the tree. It's rare to see an eagle this far away from the Hudson River. It's a powerful sign. I pull over to watch as the bald eagle lands on a branch close to the top of The Almighty One. It surveys the vast land beneath for a few minutes and then soars down to glide above the winding river. I notice a red-tailed hawk taking flight from a tree near the river. It appears to fly out from beneath the shadow of the bald eagle.

Around this time, back at home, a picture falls off the wall. (It might have had some assistance from Pandora's rowdy cat.) The picture is of a Lakota village, with a prayer at the bottom. Pandora stops to pick it up and reads the prayer. She takes is as a cue to come to the sweat lodge ceremony.

The Sioux Indian Prayer

O' Great Spirit
Whose voice I hear in the winds,
And whose breath gives life to all the world,
Hear me. I am small and weak.
I need your strength and wisdom.
Let me walk in beauty, and make my eyes
ever behold the red and purple sunset.
Make my hands respect the things I have.
Make my ears sharp to hear your voice.
Make me wise so I may understand
The things you taught my people.
Let me learn the lessons you have hidden
In every leaf and rock.
I seek strength, not to be greater than my brother,

but to fight my greatest enemy – myself.
Make me always ready to come to you with
Clean hands and straight eyes.
So when life fades, as the fading sunset,
My spirit may come to you without shame.

THE SWEAT LODGE CEREMONY

The sun shines down. The woods are covered with a thin blanket of snow, except for a few exposed patches. My Native Brother and I ceremoniously place the rocks that will be used inside the sweat lodge upon a flat row of logs that compose the second layer. The first layer consists of four logs equally spaced at right angles to allow air flow for the fire. It looks like a miniature log raft. It needs to support the weight of all the rocks and the fire without falling over. Prayers accompany the first seven rocks. We take turns by holding a rock above our heads with both hands to honor the four directions, Father Sky, Mother Earth, and the Spirit within. He uses sage to smudge the rocks and the inside of the sweat lodge. We carefully stack split logs on top in a teepee fashion a few layers deep. He offers tobacco to the fire, then lights the birch bark on the bottom ablaze. The fire burns for three hours until the rocks are red hot.

It is always nice to stand around a crackling fire. It's not quite cold enough to see our breath, but the warmth feels good. While we're waiting, I give the buffalo rattle to My Native Brother. He opens his gift slowly. He says, "The lightning on the side is a thunder being. I have a strong connection with it."

Next we prepare the sweat lodge. The dome-shaped, willow-branch frame is about three feet high and twelve feet in diameter. The intersections are all tightly wrapped with faded red fabric. The frame was probably built within the last year, but still remains sturdy. Swan Song cuts an old carpet into pieces to cover the cold ground for flooring inside. Then the three of us cover the outside frame with more than a dozen wool blankets. We start down low and go around in a circular pattern. Rocks are used to hold the edges flat against the ground. The second layer of blankets overlays a portion of the bottom layer. It is pleasant for the three of us to be working together. Swan Song smiles as she works. My Native Brother is lively in spirit. He is definitely in his element.

My Native Brother assembles the door flap. One edge of a blanket is attached to a four-foot stick. Two ropes tied to either end of the stick are tossed over the top of the sweat lodge and secured on the back side.

My Native Brother says, "No light should peek through or our prayers will escape." He crawls inside the sweat lodge. We fold down the door flap. He taps on the blankets in a few spots and his muffled voice directs us to where light is seeping in. Swan Song and I adjust the blankets from the outside until it meets his approval.

Pandora arrives. She doesn't join us in the sweat lodge, but five other friends arrive who will. I meet Shawn for the first time. I have a feeling it was him I prayed for that morning. Swan Song produces a bag filled with colored fabric for making prayer ties. She kneels by the fire on an old blanket and cuts three-inch squares from red, yellow, black, white, blue, and green fabric. She spreads them out. We all take one piece of each color. She instructs me to place a pinch of tobacco in the center of each and silently say a prayer. My Native Brother stands aside, deliberately looking up to the sky, then down before he completes each prayer tie. His face reflects how each prayer is formed with a firm resolve. Then he wraps them up tightly and ties them all on the same string with three inches of space between each one. It makes a row of colorful prayer ties. I follow his lead. We hang them around our necks. Once inside the sweat lodge, we will drape them over the rafters.

There is a pit in the center of the sweat lodge. The dirt from the pit is used to form an altar outside, between the fire and the lodge. Upon the altar mound we arrange our sacred items: eagle talons, eagle feathers, a golden eagle wing, a bear-fur bag, and a piece of buffalo fur from the sun dance. A three-foot stick is jabbed in the center with a few necklaces and rings draped around the remaining short branches. The chanupa is cradled with the bowl on a fur and the stem resting in the Y of another short branch. Settled at the base of the altar is a deer skull, each quadrant is brightly-painted with the four colors of the Native insignia.

I am told there is a spirit line that travels directly from the fire to the altar and then into the sweat lodge. After the fire is started, this line is not to be stepped across during the sweat lodge ceremony. I visualize a multi-colored snake four feet in diameter slithering up a nearby ravine and down into the fire.

My Native Brother and Swan Song bring out their chanupas. They honor the four directions and pray to the Great Spirit who created this world. My Native Brother explains that the sweat lodge is like a clamshell. One hand of the Creator rests above and the other hand is below the ground, with us inside. The hot rocks will be placed in the center. He insists that we wear clothing to show respect, as if our grandmothers were sitting nearby watching us.

When anybody leaves or enters the lodge, they say, "Mitakuye Oyasin" to show respect. It's a traditional Lakota Sioux phrase, which means, "All are related." It reflects the inherent belief of most Native Americans that everything is connected.

Just before we enter, a grizzly, white-bearded, giant of a man appears. He introduces himself as Walking Bear. A small bundle of sage held on an abalone shell is lit. An eagle feather is used to sweep the smoke. Shawn smudges up and down the front and back of each participant. I stand with my arms out in a cross. The smell of sage fills my nostrils. I lift each foot to allow the sage to touch the bottoms. He motions for me to turn around to smudge my back side. When Shawn is finished, he taps me on the head with the eagle feather.

We enter in a clockwise direction. My Native Brother goes in first with his drum, then the women in their skirts, followed by the men in swim trunks or shorts. Shawn and Walking Bear remain outside to tend the fire. They will join us after they bring in the first round of rocks. They use a pitchfork to pull the red-hot rocks from the fire. They are carefully set on a shovel and brushed off with cedar branches to remove any burning ashes. Shawn slides the first red-hot rock inside the doorway on a shovel. Normally, deer antlers are used to grab and place the hot rock from the shovel to the center pit. Unfortunately, we have no deer antlers. Someone forgot them. The situation is discussed between the two fire keepers and My Native Brother. They decide to use the shovel. My Native Brother blesses the first seven rocks by touching them with the end of his chanupa before they are placed in the center pit. The blanket-flap door is pulled closed. We remain still for a moment, enclosed together with the glowing rocks in the center.

My Native Brother leads rounds of drumming and singing, and we take turns sharing our prayers. Swan Song sings a beautiful Native song. Her melody allows me to forget about everything, as if I am being held by the Mother of all Creation. Walking Bear is well-versed in his prayers. It all seems quite familiar to him. He even brought his own rattle, which he uses during a few songs.

Inside the lodge is the sweetest, darkest dark I have ever experienced. It feels like I am back in a womb. After water is poured from a wooden ladle onto the red-hot rocks, steam rises. As we breathe in, the warmth fills our breathing passage on the way to our lungs. I focus on the sensation of the heat. We begin to sweat and pray.

Walking Bear yells out, "Grandfather, it is I, Walking Bear. Hear my prayers…"

It's remarkable all the different names people have for God. No doubt, He hears us whether it be Wakan Tanka, Great Spirit, Grandfather, or Creator.

During the first three rounds, we pray for healing for our friends, family, and the earth. Prayers are formed in the heart, float out through the lips, and are released for others' hearts to acknowledge, embellish, and support. I believe our prayers are also heard by the spirit of the medicine man, who enters the fire and tunnels down the line past the altar to nestle in the hot rocks, waiting to receive our prayers.

During the fourth and final round, we pray for ourselves. They bring in fifteen rocks. It feels like my chest is melting. Every rug and every piece of clothing is drenched in sweat. At first, I gasp. My desire is to escape the swelter, so I get down low. Then I realize, it is better to just surrender and bathe in it. We are being purified by the sweat that pours off our skin and the prayers that come from our mouths. To be more explicit, we are sweating out our prayers.

When Shawn prays for his recovery from substance abuse, I am instantly aware that it was him for whom I prayed this morning. We really are all connected. Right now, we feel like one sweaty ameba. We have distinct prayers, but underneath they stem from our basic desires and needs for our bodies and spirits. We all feel similar emotions, our own pain and pleasure, and we empathize with each other. We are connected with all humanity, but with these eight women and men in this sweat lodge, I have created a memorable bond. I feel comfortably loved for who I am amongst these new friends. I have found my tribe.

At the end of the fourth round, the blanket door is folded open and rested on top. The moon has risen and the planet Venus is shining brightly. There is stillness in the air. While inside the sweat lodge, we hear the hoot of an owl. My Native Brother strikes a match and lights his chanupa. After saying his prayers, he invites us to say ours. The chanupa is gradually passed around. We watch as our prayers rise up toward heaven with the smoke. It's the first time I am invited to smoke and pray with a chanupa. It's a sacred moment. The best way I can keep it sacred is to keep this moment for myself. It is truly ineffable...one of those moments that each person will experience in his or her own way. ■

CHAPTER 26

The Native Medicine

One morning, after a fresh rain, I walk in the woods that once were the Native American wintering grounds of Shakomako. I spot ten deer in the field and locate a great horned owl's nest with fluffy white offspring inside. I gather some feathers, deer bones, and stones that I place together in a circle to perform a ceremony. I chant in a Native American tongue as I dance around it. Afterwards, I squat down and close my eyes. I have a vision of myself sitting in a circle with some Native American chiefs and the White Buffalo Calf Woman. I use tobacco to honor the chiefs and then I make a request, "I want to learn about Native American medicine." They pass around a chanupa and when it's my turn, I take the invisible chanupa and inhale. The Native American chiefs are patient and talk among themselves.

One chief looks me in the eyes to give their response. "First you need to complete our sacred rituals."

In part, learning Native American traditions holds the secret to Native American medicine. If my request to the chiefs had been to become a carpenter, then their response would probably be, "First you need to build several houses."

The Lakota Sioux have kept their traditions and rituals active and alive. The sweat lodge, the peace pipe, and the vision quest, dominate as the most common rituals in this day and age. There is a sun dance ritual that involves four days of powerful fasting, prayer, and dance. It's physically grueling and demands hardcore faith from those who are invited to participate. My Native Brother has participated in the sun dance ceremony a few times.

Over the years, I have been guided through visions from the medicine men, the Native American chiefs and the White Buffalo Calf Woman. I have learned a lot from my friends involved in the Native American traditions. These nature-based rituals teach ways to get to know yourself through prayers and patient interactions with your Creator. The people I have met at powwows and Native gatherings have always been kind and warmly invited me to participate. Their activities include drumming and dancing, learning to track animals, sharing in a circle with a talking stick, or just listening to stories around the fire.

JESUS HAVE MERCY ON ME

Occasionally, I get the desire and guidance to chant a phrase.

One day I am repeating, "Jesus, have mercy on me." I say it out loud for one hour as I slowly walk up an old, winding, logging trail in the woods. Near the mountaintop, I stop saying it because my mouth has dropped open. On the path, staring at my face, is an eight-point buck skeleton. It is hanging suspended by its antlers caught up in a three-inch sapling. It's eerie to be in the presence of this deer skeleton. The ribs are intact and the front feet are dangling off the ground. It is loaded with a story about life and death.

I presume it was on its hind legs, feeding on leaves, when his antlers became caught in the fork of the sapling. The sapling is flexible enough that it can bend back and forth, but strong enough to not break. I imagine the insurmountable suffering this grand animal must have endured — the horrifying moment when the deer realized that its large rack was locked in tree branches. There must have been an immediate shock and a frenzy to break free — a natural desire to place its front feet back on solid ground. I imagine there must have been leaping, gasping, and snorting during its struggle. Any other deer nearby would have been distraught by its slow, gruesome death.

At some point, the buck must have realized that he could not escape. He was hung on a tree. His fate was sealed. Did the buck experience a moment of surrender and peace? Did the buck grow weak from the struggle and eventually starve? I imagine that even the tree, being alive, sustained some trauma. This tree had no intention of capturing this great animal and holding it captive until its death. Life sometimes grabs you like that and hands you over to death, without an explanation.

Then I notice coyote chew-marks on the rib bones. I paint a picture in my mind of coyotes howling as they surround this huge buck during the night, to tear chunks of flesh off his carcass. If the buck was still alive, he would surely have been in a panic. Perhaps the coyotes brought mercy. Either way, his flesh ultimately gave back to feed the circle of life.

All the scenarios of how the buck died flash through my mind, but the overriding thought is of Jesus. Remember, I have been chanting "Jesus have mercy on me" for the past hour. There are many symbolic parallels between Jesus Christ and this buck. This deer allowed me to empathize and come to terms with the suffering that Jesus experienced on the cross. They were both pinned to a tree, for no real reason, forced to suffer and give up their lives. Neither of them were crazy in favor of the whole ordeal. Because of their deaths, others lived more bountifully.

Jesus said on the cross, "Father, forgive them, they know not what they are doing" and "Father, into your hands I entrust my spirit." Although I am not sure that deer can forgive, I can assume it held no grudge against the tree or the coyotes. Granted, Jesus was willingly allowing God's will to unfold, while the Buck seemed to be an innocent victim of unusual circumstances.

I reach up and unhook the buck from the tree. I can see, touch, and feel the buck. At that moment, Jesus becomes as real as the buck. I place his body to rest on the soft earth; then I give a sigh of relief for myself, the buck...and Jesus.

> *"Later, Joseph of Arimathea asked Pilate for the body of Jesus. Now Joseph was a disciple of Jesus, but secretly because he feared the Jewish leaders. With Pilate's permission, he came and took the body away. He was accompanied by Nicodemus, the man who earlier had visited Jesus at night. Nicodemus brought a mixture of myrrh and aloes, about seventy-five pounds. Taking Jesus' body, the two of them wrapped it, with the spices, in strips of linen. This was in accordance with Jewish burial customs. At the place where Jesus was crucified, there was a garden, and in the garden a new tomb, in which no one had ever been laid. Because it was the Jewish day of Preparation and since the tomb was nearby, they laid Jesus there."*
>
> (John 19:38-42 NIV)

I could sense the compassion that Joseph and Nicodemus must have felt as they tended to Christ's body in a manner that showed dignity and respect after such notorious abuse and injustice.

The buck and Jesus were powerful beings, but both of their fates were held in God's hands. Here I am alive. Certainly, less influential and powerful than Jesus. Yet God cares and provides for all my needs day by day, just like theirs, until my final day of reckoning. Will I go out as a victim of circumstances or willingly go without regrets, forgiving others and trusting in God?

MOVING OUT WEST

My Native Brother has made some difficult decisions. For

personal reasons, he made the choice to leave Omega. He decides to move back out west, far away from Swan Song. She will stay at Omega. She expresses with difficulty that she wants to be free from their relationship. As a friend, I witness a few dramatic scenes as their relationship is painfully torn apart. It doesn't feel like it is my place to explain the basic dynamics of their relationship. But for the sake of the story, I will share my perspective and what I witnessed, as their friend.

Swan Song and My Native Brother shared a deep bond of love for each other during the years they spent together. My Native Brother did not want to let go of their relationship. During the next month, he tried to control Swan Song's actions from afar by requesting that she not spend time with other men. To my astonishment, he mentioned my name specifically. Yikes! The situation became heart-wrenching for both of them. I believe that Swan Song wanted her freedom, but loved him, and she couldn't have both. Their relationship was coming to a bitter end.

I go to comfort Swan Song in her tent. She is about to call My Native Brother on the phone. She is lying in bed completely unraveled, hugging her chanupa and sobbing. It shocks me to watch her hold the chanupa (a rock and a stick) so close. I am learning there is more to the chanupa than its appearance. It seemed better equipped to comfort her than I. Perhaps holding the chanupa and praying allows her to get in touch with her emotions regarding My Native Brother.

PAST LIFE CONNECTIONS

I made the decision to stay in the area and volunteer at Omega Institute for the summer. I set up an elaborate 12x24 foot tent site at a location near a pond a few miles away from Omega. I confess, one reason I made this decision was so I could be near Swan Song. I am becoming rather fond of her. Our paths cross again and again at Omega, as if we are the only two people living there. We smile at each other, and each time we meet, she fills me with joy. I feel comfortable around Swan Song, as if we had known each other forever. Our connection grows in a magical way that feels fresh and alive.

One bright sunny day, I am sitting alone on a stone wall near my campsite thinking about Swan Song. I fall into a vision concerning the previous dream I had of the Native American tribe out west. In my vision, Wicahpi Ska (White Star) and my real Native brother were together. He took in Wicahpi Ska and married her after I died, as is the Native American custom. At that moment, it strikes me: Swan Song is my prior wife, Wicahpi Ska, and my native brother-by-blood came back as My Native Brother in this life. This vision revealed the past life connections between Swan Song, My Native Brother, and myself.

I remember how after Cetan Luta (Red Hawk) died, Wicahpi Ska prayed to the medicine man, Whicahcala, for our spirits to be reunited. Her prayers had been heard and were now manifesting in our present-day lives. It is utterly amazing! My Native Brother and Swan Song are together, just as they were after my death as Cetan Luta in our past lives. The circle continues, except now in a modern-day scenario. My Native Brother teaches me the Native American traditions as he did in my past life. Then soon afterwards, his relationship with Swan Song dissolves. This explains why the bond between the three of us is so magical.

I wonder…*Could it be my destiny to reunite with Swan Song?* It seems My Native Brother knows something is going on between us. Could it be possible that the prayers of Wicahpi Ska are manifesting, unbeknownst to Swan Song?

KIDNAPPING SWAN SONG

I feel it is time to reclaim my past wife, given her modern day consent, of course. It appears that her relationship with My Native Brother has run its course. It seems she is now available. I go to Swan Song's tent early one morning during her day off.

In a playful way, I say, "I am here to kidnap you."

She is just waking up and is in favor of this kind of fun.

She drowsily exclaims, "You can kidnap me — after I take my shower!" She takes a leisurely shower, then I whisk her away to nearby Burger Hill. It's a Native American sacred site, so we bring our ritual drums. When we are together, it feels like I am being held in an eternal hug. There are many feelings in my heart that stir and swirl. We are like two innocent children playing in the field. And it's a gorgeous summer day with an azure sky and whispy white clouds.

She has the gift to feel the Spirit World. I have the gift to see it. Together, our two worlds blend seamlessly. When I play my drum and sing a Native American song, warriors appear in my vision. When she sings, she feels an outer circle of women swaying to the left and right. When we sing and play the drums together, then the men and women both appear. The men and the women come together to support and nurture each other. We share a precious moment and finish our morning escapade by praying with her chanupa.

SWAN SONG'S CHANUPA

Swan Song has a chanupa that My Native Brother gave her. It's difficult to keep it burning when she smokes it. Perhaps it's because the stem is plugged and needs to be cleared out. She has put it off for many full moons, and the pipe continues to speak to her about it. In my experience, the chanupa is an extension of the holder, even more so if they make it. If a chanupa is received as a gift, the owner places their energy in it when they hold it, make an alteration, or pray with it. Swan Song's clearing out of her pipe stem can be symbolic of clearing out clutter in her life. I believe she desires to make her own decisions and stand as a woman in her own power. During most of her adult life she has had a boyfriend, so her decisions were made in conjunction with him. Sometimes this required a personal compromise.

We spend a weekend with some friends at Wise Wolf's home, talking about establishing a community on land that I recently purchased in Costa Rica. As part of our intention setting, we have a sweat lodge ceremony. Afterwards, the sacred fire continues to burn. Swan Song takes out her chanupa. It is the perfect time to clear out her stem. We go over the steps, then I squat down and sit on the ground a fair distance away to watch her. I want to give her plenty of space. This is the first time she has ever worked on her own pipe. She puts on thick gloves and heats a rod by placing it on red-hot coals. Then using long pliers, she reaches in and grabs the hot rod. It's important that she does all the work herself. I enjoy watching her kneeling down by the fire as she works. I have a small smile as I watch her. She is beautiful. I feel proud to be her friend. She emits confidence. She is the only woman I know that prays with a chanupa. She quickly pulls out the hot rod and inserts it in the pipe stem. She resembles a pioneer packing down his powder musket with the rod. She occasionally stops to inspect her work and peers through the stem like a telescope. Once, she looks up to notice how intently I am watching her. I receive a quick glance and a smile. But her focus is on clearing out the debris that is blocking her pipe.

As she is working on clearing the stem, it starts to rain. This is not that unusual. It rained while we were in the sweat lodge. She keeps on working in the rain. This is the time for her to dig in a little deeper, even if it means getting wet. Suddenly, it starts to hail. These are not aspirin-size snowflakes, but hail the size of golf balls, the kind that dent your car hood with a loud *ping!* During the hailstorm, Swan Song and I both run for cover under the roof of a shed. It's May 20th and we had been in t-shirts most of the weekend. Hail was the last thing we were expecting.

I believe magic erupted from her heart and the chanupa when they were both finally free to breathe. I am glad I was there to support her healing. It was a tender moment to witness her reclaiming her power. Miracles just happen when Swan Song and I are together. At the very least, something beautiful and unexpected manifests in nature. After the hail stops, the sun shines long, golden rays upon her, and in the distance a beautiful rainbow appears. We both pause and look up as an assortment of swirling neon colors race across the sky in a huge arching bow.

THE EAGLE HANG

I am disappointed to learn that Swan Song has not completely ended her relationship with My Native Brother. It seems to drag on forever. He has been living out west for a month. My Native Brother has planned to participate in the sun dance ceremony, and Swan Song is going there to provide her support. I hope that during her visit they both get clarity regarding their relationship. The ceremony could be his chosen way to let go of Swan Song and mark the end of their relationship.

During the sun dance ceremony, women wear dresses. Before she leaves, I purchase Swan Song a traditional-patterned dress to wear. I love buying Swan Song gifts. But this one is also my way of sending him a message. I am waiting impatiently for their relationship to end. What happens next I regret. I inappropriately use the power of the Native medicine for my own selfish reasons.

I use My Native Brother's old sun dance hoops to connect with him on a physical and spiritual plane at the sun dance ceremony. I give thanks to him for watching over Wicahpi Ska in his past life and Swan Song in this life. I speak to his spirit to let him know in no uncertain terms, "I am back in the flesh and desire to be with Swan Song. I am praying that today during the sun dance ceremony, you will let go of her and make the final cut in your relationship."

During the sun dance ceremony, the participants dance for three days without food and water. They receive spiritual nourishment through friends that pray for them. The sun dancers must go beyond their physical strength and rely on faith. At a designated time, two ropes are looped to two pegs that are slid through two piercings on either side of a sun dancer's chest. The other end of the rope is attached to the top of a cottonwood tree. Traditionally, they dance toward the center tree and then pull away. On their third attempt, they use all their strength to break the skin that holds the pegs.

Another variation is to place the ropes through a loop on top of the cottonwood tree. Then men lift the opposite end of the ropes and the sun dancer is lifted off his feet. He is suspended by the ropes attached to his chest until he is either lowered or breaks free when the skin on his chest tears.

My Native Brother did this variation with what is called an eagle hang. When they lift the ropes, he holds himself suspended with his arms extended, forming a cross. He is not willing or wanting to let go. Minutes pass. Eventually, he bounces and flops to drop down to the earth. As I connect with him from afar, I empathize and feel fragments of his pain. My Native Brother loves Swan Song, and the hurt in his heart is greater than those two ropes suspending him in the air.

SunDancer

I watched, as you came out
Walking with your head down, tears
In your heart
Wondering, always wondering.
We sang you a song, the wind and I
But you did not hear
We sing together, always
But no one hears.
I watched as you came forward
And sat down
Looking, always looking.
I danced in your eyes

But you did not see
I waved my arms and waited
As my leaves rustled about you.
It was not until you fell
And looked up
That you saw me, heard me
And recognized me.
I am the SunDancer
My leaves, rustling in the wind
Are my songs
The sun and the moon
My eyes.
It was not until you
Found me and
Acknowledged me
That you gave me life.
I am the SunDancer
I dance in the sun.

@Wayne Scott of Swan Lake First Reserve of Manitoba, Canada

CHAPTER 27

The Melodrama

I arrange to pick up Swan Song at the airport after she has been away for over a week. She shares with me the details of the sun dance. I surmise he finally let go of her. Even though I still have amorous feelings toward Swan Song, my life has taken an unexpected turn.

Once Swan Song had left, I began to hang out more with an endearing, fun woman who is 20 years younger than I. Swan Song had been all excited about introducing her to me. One day, she insisted that I go to the art room. She went in and told her friend, who came to meet me on the porch. Her adorable companion stood in the doorway and swayed as we spoke. She was as cute as a kitten. One could not help but want to hold her close. When we are together there is a lot of warm bliss in the air. It is fresh and exciting. She is innocent and wise beyond her age. I call her Feather Maker because she is always making gifts with feathers dangling down to give away to friends. She and her gifts are filled with love. She is Asian with long, black hair and a wide smile. Her voice is husky, and when she ends a sentence, she lifts it up a note. I find that appealing.

So we start to hang out in her tiny tent. She keeps it really neat and clean. There are white plastic bins for all her clothes. She likes to burn incense on her altar. She made a glittery, celestial mobile that hangs in the middle of the trail at the intersection leading to her entrance. One needs to bow down to pass under it. She planned it that way so any visitors will honor her home. She has a single bed with a cushy comforter. One evening we ended up side by side, cuddling on her small bed. That part was unexpected. But it felt really nice for both of us. She has no barriers and is not in a relationship, so I spent the night. We both enjoyed being held and sharing intimacy.

It has been ten years since my divorce, and for the first time, I find the courage to open my heart. Perhaps because she is a younger, playful woman. She walks holding my pinkie, and at those times it feels like she is my long-lost daughter. She had a heart operation as a baby. It is as if her heart has stayed open since that day. One day, she was across the field and looked my way with love overflowing from her heart. I could feel the burn. She has a lot of love to offer, not just for me but for everybody. She wants to be a nurse, which suits her well. She is compassionate and upbeat.

Feather Maker and I often go to be with Swan Song in her big, cozy tent. Another friend, Lost Son, occasionally joins us as we sing songs, share our day, or pick out a card from her animal or Native medicine deck. When Swan Song and Feather Maker are together, they curl up like two kittens. I find it a pretty laid back and comfortable scene. Sometimes we all hang out in our pajamas. When the four of us are together, it is like we are a family again. Maybe in some bizarre way, Lost Son and Feather Maker were our kids in our past Native American lives. And now it has spilled over into our present life. Sure is sweet to all be reunited.

I have come to believe that the souls that we love and trust the most from our past lives come back in this life to teach us the really hard lessons. During these moments we don't understand what is really happening, but we have chosen them to inject the most difficult pain and profound healing into our life. During the process, we have some immensely unpleasant emotions arise. But underneath it all, we love them.

Of course, I enjoy hanging out and cuddling with Feather

Maker, but it's not our destiny to be together for more than a few months. I sense that our age difference is an embarrassment for her. After an unpleasant experience, her ability to trust men is limited. But she is young, free-spirited, and pliable. I let her know she can trust me. After a month, she has a breakthrough. She is more confident and getting bolder around the guys her age that she finds appealing.

But my heart still cries out to be with Swan Song. I am closer to her age. There is something eternally magical about being together. It could last more than a lifetime. Swan Song knows I am affectionately involved with Feather Maker. Feather Maker is aware of my fondness toward Swan Song. It is so obvious. If I make an advance toward Swan Song now, it will be a risky maneuver.

There had been a few tender moments that Swan Song and I shared together, but they did not indicate a genuine romance. Once, I went to visit Swan Song in her tent and stayed until 2:30 a.m. There was a fierce rainstorm outside. I begged her, "Please let me sleep on your floor. Just this one time!" She refused to consider it, and in her serious, deep voice said, "Go home, now!" The coyotes howled in protest as I stepped out of her warm, cozy tent into the blustery rainstorm.

AN UNEXPECTED SURPRISE

Feather Maker and I are still affectionately involved when I visit Swan Song in her tent one lazy morning. Swan Song and I lie down on her bed to talk. And she loves to cuddle. I sure am willing. Yeah, we are a bit impulsive and risqué, but we're just cuddling. It begins to unfold as a stirring, soft, puffy-white-cloud dream. We are in each other's arms. It feels like heaven.

Suddenly, the tent unzips and Feather Maker pops in. There is a deadly silence. We all absorb the impact. The charged emotions of guilt and betrayal come flowing into the tent like burning lava meeting the ocean. Cuddling Swan Song while still involved with Feather Maker was a disastrous mistake. We all feel the consequences. Our hearts are all being ripped apart. Feather Maker looks daggers at me. It's clearly over for Feather Maker and me. The trust I had previously accumulated is now worthless. It vanishes in two seconds flat. She looks emotionally devastated and will never trust me again. She turns and quietly leaves the tent.

The next few moments are awkward. Swan Song and I both feel it. What felt so right a moment ago has disappeared. It has turned to shame. I leave her tent with my head hanging low.

I try to talk with Feather Maker, but it is in vain. It is too late. I lacked the courage to tell Feather Maker that my heart yearned to be with Swan Song. I should have had the guts to initiate closure with her, regardless of the outcome with Swan Song. She is a casualty of my brutal carelessness. I never intended to hurt her. I feel like a lousy shmuck. She deserves to be treated with respect. Instead, I impress another searing-hot brand on her heart. It's a typical one, worn by many women: "TRUST NOT A MAN".

It's a pity that we can't learn lessons about love without getting hurt or inflicting heartbreak. The pain, along with the elated feeling of being in love, lets us know that we are human and fully alive. My heart feels the two extremes: a mix of joy about finally being with Swan Song, and sadness for the way I mistreated Feather Maker.

SWALLOWING POISON

The next day, on the way to her tent, I am anticipating embracing my beloved Swan Song again. I am having divine thoughts of being in her arms. I unzip the fly of her tent to enter. I peek into the tent. She is lying in bed in all her beauty. Her dirty blond, wavy hair is somewhat messy and unkempt. To me, she is adorable in her silky pajamas. My body is ready to unfold next to hers, but my dearest beloved is not smiling back. I suddenly notice that she is lying in bed next to a hairy, bare-chested man. I find he has a big, detestable smile on his face. It takes me a second to realize that Swan Song is embracing our friend, Lost Son. It's now my turn to swallow the poison. My heart is like a crackle-glass vase that is dropped from a skyscraper. It shatters on the pavement into a zillion pieces.

CRYING OUT

At this point in my life, I am crying out to God for my dream to come true. It's a simple dream. I am not sure why it has become so challenging. I desire to be in a relationship with a decent, spiritual woman. I am ready to place a woman above everything, except God and my health. If I am not healthy, I cannot take care of her and myself, and without God, nothing happens. She is the next-highest priority. This means we place each other above work, money, friends, and even our own extended families, when necessary. I know I am more content when I am in a relationship with a woman. I want to love and cherish a woman as she does me.

I spend most of that winter in Costa Rica actively seeking to find a relationship that I hope will lead to marriage. I have my share of dates with Costa Rican women, but there are lots of cultural differences. Other than my not speaking fluent Spanish, there are big challenges. It has led to some awkward moments. In Costa Rica, one's family is their tribe. If I find a Costa Rican wife, her whole family is welcome to come visit or live in our house whenever they want. I find that difficult to handle.

Before returning for the next season at Omega, I pray to God, "I am ready for a deep, meaningful relationship. Please send me the perfect woman whom I am meant to be with in this life! You know exactly what I need and you know who she is. I am praying that you will bring us together. I am waiting…still waiting…God are you listening?"

CHIEF THUNDER CLOUD

I visit Swan Song a year later. I tell her of my failed attempts at finding a wife in Costa Rica. I let her know I am still searching for the right woman. She listens and then whispers that she has something to tell me. She had not been in a relationship for the past year. With trepidation, I begin to wonder if she is finally about to reveal her affection for me.

She whispers her secret, "I have been dating Chief Thunder Cloud." I can see her excitement; becoming his partner includes an invitation to travel to foreign countries for spiritual-related work within different communities. He is one of our spiritual teachers whom I respect and consider a friend. I admire Chief Thunder Cloud. I consider him a role model. We have friends in the same circles at Omega and in Vermont. For a period, we both went to the same gym, which was my old high school. It's a small world. Over the years, I have given him several Native American token gifts to show him my appreciation. The last one was a cement, three-foot statue of an Indian with a bow and arrow.

Once, I had a strong vision of people from Chief Thunder Cloud's tribe becoming distressed by his actions. I did not know all the people in the vision, but nonetheless the feelings were intense. I felt I must tell him. I sat with him on a stone wall at Omega and shared with him my vision. He was a little alarmed that I knew all this information and confirmed that it had happened. I later learned that my vision had been a huge controversy in his life. Even though Chief Thunder Cloud had moved beyond it, I believe he was concerned about my prophetic insight prying into his past. I believe this vision was revealed to me for a few reasons; it helped me better understand the challenges he faced in his own life and how they led him to where he is today. It also let me know that a man will sometimes make choices that other people detest. These choices can alienate oneself and hurt other's feelings. A man must do what he feels is right. Pride can be a double-edged sword.

He ended our conversation by saying, "If you ever need to talk, consider me like your uncle or grandfather."

Swan Song and I do a ceremony that will bless their being together. If she is happy, then it brings me happiness. Clearly, for whatever reason, she is not comfortable with our being more than friends. I found a red-tailed hawk beside the road; it had been hit by a car. We use the tail feathers to bless their relationship. Swan Song travels and lives part of the season with Chief Thunder Cloud for the next four years.

HANDS ON HEALING

Althea is a meditation teacher at Omega Institute. She shares various techniques for personal spiritual growth through programs designed for the volunteers. She also offers one-on-one treatments. Althea has short, jet-black, wavy hair and grayish eyes. She has features like a Roman goddess and is grounded and firm like a marble statue. She is optimistic, with a large heart for helping others and will tell it like it is with a direct, no-nonsense approach. When Althea offers an invitation or says she will come visit you, she means it. She lives in Sarasota, Florida, but spends occasional weekends during the summer at Omega with her husband and their teenage kids.

One day, during that season, I go to Althea's staff program for volunteers. I am feeling sad and depressed about my past relationships. So far, it has been a disaster to date women in Costa Rica. In addition, I still feel a residue of pain from my marriage that ended fifteen years ago.

During Althea's class, I am given the opportunity to express my feelings surrounding my past relationships. At her suggestion, I lie flat on my back on the floor in the center of the group. They create a circle around me, lying on pillows and blankets, and they place their hands on my body. She instructs the class, "Just be present in your heart. Nobody needs to try to do anything."

God's healing presence arrives. Althea knows how to set the space for healing, when to get out of the way, and how to listen to guidance. If she had a personal agenda for this class, she threw it out the window, because caring for people requires living fully in the present moment.

God's healing spirit begins to work through all those in the room with their hands placed on my body. I start to feel a huge shift. In my vision, I see my fragmented second chakra drop from beneath my body, and a new, brightly-colored one replace it from above. One of the class participants, Terracotta, shifts to hold my head in her hands. After she does this, I visualize brightly-colored gemstones being placed in each of my seven charkas.

I begin letting go of my past relationships. Through the touch of these healers, I feel fully supported. I start to heal on different dimensions. I feel the sadness from my past relationships leave my body. From that moment on, I stop thinking about them, completely. Physically, I feel more solid in my core. Somehow, I am able to let go of the feminine traits I had been nurturing and feel more like a man. I am ready to rip down the silky, golden curtains in my home and go chop some firewood. The group lifts their hands off my body and slides back to form a larger circle again.

After the class is over, I walk out onto the campus at Omega. A friend, G. I. Joe, stops me on the walking path and enthusiastically squeals, "Man, something is different about you! I can't explain it! Something about your whole energy is different!" There has been a huge shift in my essence, and we both know it.

That evening, I go visit Swan Song in her tent. I ask with curiosity, "Do you notice anything different about me?" She lights up and says, "Yes, you are different, you have space for a relationship!" Her statement is welcome confirmation. I never knew why Swan Song was reluctant about our being more than friends. I had pretty much given up on her. I suppose she had her reasons. I never considered I was holding myself back because I had not yet let go of my past relationships. However, it makes sense. I would not hail a taxi if somebody was in it.

Why would she want to hail a new relationship if my heart was full with past relationships?

After this day, Swan Song and I spend more and more of our free time together. I am caught off-guard because she suddenly wants to be near me. She begins flirting and inviting me to her tent or she suddenly appears at mine. I get the hint. I was always fond of her, but now there is one big difference. She is allowing me to romantically pursue her, and she likes it. ■

CHAPTER 28

Song of Solomon

Sometimes on lazy summer afternoons, Swan Song and I lie together in a hammock by the lake. I especially enjoy napping and waking up next to her. Swan Song enjoys having me read aloud to her. One day, I begin to read Song of Solomon from the Bible. She just lies there with her eyes closed and a soft smile, relishing every word.

Beloved
 "Let him kiss me with the kisses of his mouth — for your love is more delightful than wine. Pleasing is the fragrance of your perfumes; your name is like perfume poured out. No wonder the young women love you! Take me away with you — let us hurry!
 Let the king bring me into his chambers."
(Song of Songs 1:2-4 NIV)

After I finish the first chapter, I stop reading. She sighs and says, "You can't stop there! Keep reading it." I say, "Okay," and continue on reading through the next chapter:

Beloved
 "I am a rose of Sharon, a lily of the valleys."
Lover
 "Like a lily among thorns is my darling among the young women.

Beloved
    "*Like an apple tree among the trees of the forest is my beloved among the young men. I delight to sit in his shade, and his fruit is sweet to my taste. Let him lead me to the banquet hall, and let his banner over me be love.*"

(Song of Songs 2:1-4 NIV)

Whenever I stop, she requests that I keep reading. This happens until it dawns on me that she will not be satisfied unless I read all eight chapters. Eventually, my reading of *Song of Solomon* and other poetry becomes a ritual that we both savor.

A cool summer breeze flows through the scattered trees. Today, Swan Song is sprawled out in a white lawn chair by the lake, receiving a foot massage from Althea. She has unusually small feet that crave to be endlessly caressed. She is relaxing deeply into the bliss — no need to talk to her; she probably will not respond. For her, being touched by another human is a basic necessity, like water or air. She has an uncanny ability to fully receive. She just closes her eyes and takes it all in.

From my perspective, Swan Song emanates love and light to all those around her. She loves being in nature. When given the option, she chooses to curl up in a tent and gaze at a campfire rather than stay in a fancy five-star hotel. She has never owned her own home and lives a nomadic existence, spending time seasonally in tents at Omega and the rest of the season with family, friends, and a few months in the winter living with her partner.

Each season at Omega, her tent is a lush and inviting palace. She has all the modern conveniences, with a hot-pot for tea, a dehumidifier, a large electric heater, and a fridge. One wall holds her hanging closet, with an array of dresses, and underneath it is a large basket filled with cozy, wool sweaters. There is a wooden bookshelf holding a small library of spiritual books, with her lamp and notepad on top. Her queen-size bed has layers of comforters. It is topped off with a star-design quilt and four plush pillows. On the flat headboard is her altar. There she places her candles, photos of spiritual teachers, and various gemstones and trinkets given by friends. The floor is covered with throw-rugs, and her drum and rattles are carefully hanging down in a corner. She jokes about having an entourage of men that come to help her set up and break down her tent, but it actually happens.

She smudges herself daily, usually with sweet-smelling sage from out west. But sometimes she uses sweet grass or palo santo. Years ago she sang in the church choir with her beautiful swan-like voice. She still sings at various gatherings. Women of all ages are drawn to her, and she has a large circle of delightful female companions. She nurtures them with loving hugs of support and provides them with spiritual counsel. Her cheerful disposition and sweet smile draw the attention of both men and women.

I come over and stand above Swan Song. Her dirty-blond, wavy hair is flowing down to her shoulders, and her blue eyes are softly shut. As I begin to softly speak with Althea, she motions for me to kiss Swan Song on her third eye. I hesitate, but it seems like a sweet thing to do, so I gently kiss her forehead. It was more than just a kiss. It was like I had a key and it unlocked the door to our hearts. I believe Althea knew all along that this would happen. I secretly blame her for setting us up to fall madly in love.

From that day forward, we become devoted to each other in an enchanted new way. We secretly enter each other's tents to leave cards, feathers, flowers, and cedar branches on the bed. We smile fondly when we find the gifts upon our return. Our regular gift-giving becomes a way to express how we feel about each other. Care and thought go into the fine details to make it a beautiful arrangement complete with ribbons and wrapping paper. Even the angle in the placement of the gift card is important. The right side needs to be lifted to a 30-

degree angle.

> *Beloved*
> "His arms are rods of gold set with chrysolite. His body is like polished ivory decorated with sapphires. His legs are pillars of marble set on bases of pure gold. His appearance is like Lebanon, choice as its cedars. His mouth is sweetness itself; he is altogether lovely."
> (Song of Songs 5:14-16 NIV)

> *Lover*
> "How beautiful your sandaled feet, O prince's daughter! Your graceful legs are like jewels, the work of a craftsman's hands. Your navel is a rounded goblet that never lacks blended wine. Your waist is a mound of wheat encircled by lilies."
> (Song of Songs 7:1-2 NIV)

At times, we both sense what the other is thinking. Our paths joyously crisscross throughout the day. When I see two red-tailed hawks circling overhead, I anticipate that we will soon be together. Once we are together, it's an eternal picnic of reading poetry, with flirtatious glances to fill in the pauses. We begin to spend most of our free time together in intimate ways. We give each other massages and take walks in the woods, but usually we end up in her tent. Once nobody can see us, our inner desires overflow. We both want to hold each other close. It feels as if a magnetic force is drawing our arms and legs to physically wrap around each other.

> *Beloved*
> "His left arm is under my head and his right arm embraces me. Daughters of Jerusalem, I charge you: Do not arouse or awake love until it so desires."
> (Song of Songs 8:3-4 NIV)

One brisk evening, she is preparing to leave for the weekend. I walk her down to her car. It is under the trees in the parking lot. The stars and moon shine brightly. She wears a big, cuddly sweater. I have on my jeans and a sweatshirt. Every moment I am with her, I feel life in every cell. Once we are at her car, I give her a gentle hug with both of my arms wrapped around her shoulders. She leans back against her car, and my weight presses firmly against her body. As I look at her, she looks back, and our eyes meet and hold. Then our lips melt together.

After she drives away, I float back up the hill to my tent. I can't stop thinking about her or wipe the soft smile off my face.

A few weeks later, she makes a confession: she says, "I am afraid I am falling in love with you." I smile back at her reassuringly. She says it's the same kind of feeling she had toward the man she married. She never thought she would have that feeling again. I believe that she *really is* afraid to fall in love. Later, I come to understand why.

KEEP IT HIDDEN

Chief Thunder Cloud and Swan Song are still involved in their relationship. She prefers calling him her partner. I am under the impression that she wants to tell "her partner" about our growing affection, but it doesn't happen. Over the next few months, they are together a few times. Each time, I expect she will tell him. But she doesn't do it…she keeps it hidden.

Usually we meet at night in her tent to cuddle. We have conversations about the events of the day. By now, we have spoken about everything under the sun. We have both shared about our past marriages, times at college, our families, and even our pets. She thinks I will get along well with her dad, who is a history buff.

One evening, I am feeling guilty about our being together. I sit up on the edge of her bed and say, "What we are doing does not feel right. We can't keep meeting like this. You need to tell Chief Thunder Cloud." I walk away from her tent in a melancholy mood. I assume she will speak to him, but if she doesn't, I am preparing myself to stay away from her. That's a hard thing for me to even consider. I am falling for her. The spell has been cast.

> *Beloved*
>
> *"All night long on my bed I looked for the one my heart loves; I looked for him but did not find him. I will get up now and go about the city, through its streets and squares; I will search for the one my heart loves. So I looked for him but did not find him. The watchmen found me as they made their rounds in the city. "Have you seen the one my heart loves?" Scarcely had I passed them when I found the one my heart loves. I held him and would not let him go till I had brought him to my mother's house, to the room of the one who conceived me."*
>
> *(Song of Songs 3:1-4 NIV)*

She finds me fifteen minutes later, and before I know it, we are dancing under the full moon. She loves to be twirled around. We are both all smiles as she leads me back to her tent. I am hopelessly, helplessly, and happily caught in her web.

> *"She threw her arms around him and kissed him, boldly took his arm and said, "I've got all the makings for a feast — today I made my offerings, my vows are all paid, So now I've come to find you, hoping to catch sight of your face — and here you are! I've spread fresh, clean sheets on my bed, colorful imported linens. My bed is aromatic with spices and exotic fragrances. Come, let's make love all night, spend the night in ecstatic lovemaking! My husband's not home; he's away*

on business, and he won't be back for a month."
(Proverbs 7:13-20 MSG)

Chief Thunder Cloud has a hunch that Swan Song is seeing another man. He asks her directly on the phone if she is seeing somebody else. Meanwhile, I am lying on her bed awaiting her arrival for the evening. She returns and does her ritual smudging with sage. Cleansing her space or our bodies with smudging clears away the emotional and psychic energy debris that tends to collect during the day. The effects of smudging can be surprisingly swift and dramatic. The rituals can help banish stress, attract love, soothe, and provide fresh energy.

By now it's engrained; whenever I smell sage I am instantly reminded of her. As usual, she begins to retell the events that happened during her day. I perk up when she mentions a phone call from Chief Thunder Cloud. She says, "He asked me if I was seeing another man." I give a sigh of relief. Finally, we can be together without any pretension or a guilty feeling buried in our conscience.

However, she nonchalantly explains, "I told him, 'No!' It just wasn't right to explain it over the phone." Perhaps in her mind, she did not think it was lying; just postponing the truth. I perceive it differently. I am shocked and concerned. This is serious. If she is willing to lie and justify excuses to her partner, then she will probably treat me the same. I am falling hard for Swan Song. I don't want to believe that she could be this deceptive. I want to believe that at least she is telling *me* the truth. I want to believe I am an exception to her lies. But deep down, I know that her persuasive words and smooth talk have started to taint the truth in ways that sound pleasing to both Chief Thunder Cloud and myself.

"Oh what a tangled web we weave, when first we practice to deceive!"
— *Sir Walter Scott*

There is the big fork in the road: I must cautiously make a decision at this junction. I can either abandon the possibility of our having a future relationship, or just keep traveling down this bumpy road. I assume that matters will only get worse if I am involved with a woman who desires to share herself with two men. It is not normal for me to date a woman who is already in a relationship. Yet these unexpected and delightful new circumstances with Swan Song are tossed into my lap in such a light-hearted way that it seems natural.

The journey towards love is passionately exciting, but in the distance a storm is brewing, and the clouds are dark. I begin to contemplate our situation. I know that a woman needs to connect with her partner on a physical, emotional, and spiritual level. Some of her needs, such as feeling secure, are being met by Chief Thunder Cloud. I believe a woman will not seek another relationship if her needs are being completely satisfied in her current relationship. She is trying to get her needs met through two different men. I sense that with me, she is craving to fulfil her needs for intimacy, playfulness, and touch. How long can this go on?

If I twist our scenario enough, I begin to believe it's ethically acceptable, because they are not married. I convince myself that it's okay to enjoy spending time with Swan Song. Besides, the whole scenario could shift instantly; all she needs to do is tell him about us. I really don't even mind her continuing to work with him. What it is about for me is some quality time when we can be together and sharing our hearts. We feel an insatiable passion for a reason.

It is gradually becoming apparent to me that Swan Song has exhibited a pattern of not leaving her current relationship until she is with a new man. Maybe it needs to happen that way. If that's the case, I recognize that I am willing to play her game.

I pause to consider what was left in the aftermath of her two prior relationships. They were both my friends. It was painful to watch their hearts being torn to shreds. It appeared to me that they were both emotionally traumatized for months.

A few weeks after their break-up, I had heard that My Native Brother had threatened to commit suicide. At one point, Swan Song believed his plan may have been to also hurt her. She was so fearful that she took refuge in a friend's trailer. She thought he had a gun. She hoped he wouldn't be able to find her there. It seemed to her that he was angry about losing her and didn't give a damn about what happened.

She confided that being in a temporary relationship with Lost Son was an easy way to break it off with My Native Brother. She said, "I told him up front: the reason I am with you is to end my last relationship." She said his response was to say, "Don't tell me that; I do not want to hear that." When I later shared this version with Lost Son, he said, "It is an off-based statement. What she had told me up front was that she was essentially on the rebound from the relationship with My Native Brother. She introduced this other perspective a few months after we had become intimate. I was pretty much emotionally involved and committed to a significant degree by that time. It was definitely not what I would consider up front."

LOST SON'S BREAK-UP (OR BREAKDOWN)

Late one afternoon, I stopped by to visit Swan Song after she had dissolved her relationship with Lost Son. Her disrespectful treatment had left him feeling like an expendable pawn. He was not taking it lightly. Swan Song was in her tent. Lost Son had stationed himself on a folding easy chair thirty feet away under a tree. He was badgering her through the walls of her tent with beer-enhanced slurs about their breakup. When I arrived at her tent, she was attempting to drown him out by playing music. She had a look of despair. I learned that his slanderous remarks, speckled with colorful obscenities, had been going on for a few hours. I felt compassion for Swan Song and Lost Son. Her chosen method to defuse the drama with My Native Brother by involving Lost Son had worked out to some degree, but in the process she had ruthlessly hurt Lost Son's feelings. His pain was erupting in spurts of anger.

After being disregarded, Lost Son attempted to drown his sorrow. After finishing his seventh beer, he was in a defiant, asskicking mood. As a friend, I felt I could resolve the situation by talking with him. Swan Song looked afraid. She was asking me for protection. I had never seen Lost Son this disheveled. I stepped out of her tent and began to walk toward him. He kicked a lawn chair in my direction. In my attempt to avoid it, I stumbled and bruised my shin on an iron tent stake. Before I could get next to him, he let loose a series of rapid-fire accusations about my involvement with Swan Song (all accentuated with vulgar profanities). My adrenalin began to rise. He was rude and out of control. I couldn't reason with him. He was inflamed and tumultuous. Definitely not the right moment for consoling. I was slightly afraid of what would happen next. I didn't want to provoke him. I turned and went back into her tent.

Swan Song and I discussed our options. We decided it was best to call upon Omega security. Two big men arrived in a golf cart. They took control and quickly persuaded Lost Son that it was in his best interest to leave the vicinity.

WARRANTED DANGER

How could a woman stir up such a violent reaction from two decent men? These guys are my friends whom I respect. Perhaps, there is warranted danger accompanied with mild deception. I will proceed with caution. Of course, I will not be emotionally incapacitated or deceived by her. I am solid and immune to this type of fate. At least, I am naive enough to believe that. In the end, it will all be worthwhile, once Swan Song and I are together.

"Say to wisdom, "You are my sister," and call understanding your intimate friend; that they may keep you from an adulteress, from the foreigner who flatters with

her words. For at the window of my house I looked out through my lattice, and I saw among the naive, and discerned among the youths a young man lacking sense, passing through the street near her corner; and he takes the way to her house, in the twilight, in the evening, in the middle of the night and in the darkness. And behold, a woman comes to meet him, dressed as a harlot and cunning of heart. She is boisterous and rebellious, her feet do not remain at home; she is now in the streets, now in the squares, and lurks by every corner."

(Proverbs 7:4-12 NASB)

CONCERNED

I must admit, I feel slightly uneasy when I look deeply into Swan Song's eyes. Sometimes they are cloudy and silted. Eyes are meant to be the gateway to the soul. When I gaze into her eyes, I do not feel she is fully able to trust me. But I will extend to her my trust. She needs to know that she can trust me. To my knowledge, I have never done anything to mislead or betray her, but maybe another man has. It doesn't feel like these issues revolving around trust are her natural state. I believe something traumatic happened.

Two thoughts continue to gnaw away. First of all, if Swan Song is not faithful and honest to Chief Thunder Cloud, why would she treat me any differently? Secondly, if being together and not telling him is deceptive, then it is not just on her part, but mine as well. This is compounded because Chief Thunder Cloud is my friend, too. This situation has the potential to get really nasty. It could even become explosive.

But alas, my heart sings a completely different song. The melody is sweet and her skin is soft whenever I am with her. Our lips drip with honey, and she is as smooth as oil. She has expressed that no harm exists in our being together. By now, the fragrance of love overrules anything that subtly resembles common sense.

Lover
"How beautiful you are, my darling! Oh, how beautiful! Your eyes behind your veil are doves. Your hair is like a flock of goats descending from the hills of Gilead. You are altogether beautiful, my darling; there is no flaw in you. You have stolen my heart, my sister, my bride; you have stolen my heart with one glance of your eyes, with one jewel of your necklace."
(Song of Songs 4:1,7,9 NIV)

On the few occasions when Chief Thunder Cloud comes to visit Omega, I am shuffled under the rug by Swan Song until he leaves. During these times, I find myself emotionally tormented. Once, the three of us ended up in the same room during ecstatic chant. It was worse than medieval torture. This woman, whom I consider my beloved, was being hugged and affectionately touched on her back by another man, in front of my very eyes. Inside, I was emotionally in shambles. It was like a burning hot rod was just shoved inside my heart. I wanted to shout out and cry in agony. Instead, I consoled myself with lies. I whispered to myself, *she is only pretending to want to be with him; she really loves me.*

Yet, I feel compassion for Chief Thunder Cloud. He is left in the dark. He will obviously be hurt if (or should I say when) he discovers we are lovers. It's awkward because I have no reason to conceal my love for her, not even from him, but she insists that everything must be kept hidden. I begin to feel shame in public. I am given no option; I must withhold showing affection toward the woman I love. Even our friends must not know.

Friends
"Who is this coming up from the wilderness leaning on her beloved?"
Beloved

> "Under the apple tree I roused you; there your mother conceived you, there she who was in labor gave you birth. Place me like a seal over your heart, like a seal on your arm; for love is as strong as death, its jealousy unyielding as the grave. It burns like blazing fire, like a mighty flame. Many waters cannot quench love; rivers cannot sweep it away. If one were to give all the wealth of one's house for love, it would be utterly scorned."
>
> *(Song of Songs 8:5-7 NIV)*

When others are near, it's inappropriate to give her long hugs or to send those loving glances. Instead, we whisper in the shadows of the night, behind-the-scene. Occasionally, I hold Swan Song and she cries. There is a lot going on inside both of us. I consider telling Chief Thunder Cloud myself, just to break it all wide open. Once, I sit down by the riverside to pray with my chanupa before I write him a letter that carefully explains our romantic involvement, but Swan Song pleads, "Don't send it!" Now, if I go against her wishes, I feel like I am betraying her, too. I know that eventually Chief Thunder Cloud will find out. I figure it's best to wait until she finds the courage to tell him herself. ■

CHAPTER 29

Available and Unattached

At the end of that season, I invite Swan Song to visit me in Costa Rica with one condition: she is *not* in a relationship with Chief Thunder Cloud.

She says, "I will not buy a plane ticket unless I am available and unattached."

I make my stand and don't look back. I feel good about myself. I am singing a new song filled with painful honesty, patience, and integrity.

I do a ceremony in Costa Rica to let myself know when Swan Song is ready to visit. On a pencil-thin tree branch on the far side of a brook, I tie a red piece of fabric. I request that when Swan Song and Chief Thunder Cloud both have clarity about her being, as she calls it, "available and unattached", the red fabric will fall down and float away in the brook. I learned from the experience with My Native Brother that it's not spiritually ethical to influence another's actions or thoughts in a relationship. This time, I will wait patiently.

Swan Song and I first speak seriously about her visiting in January. She is not yet "available and unattached." The red fabric still hangs over the brook. I look over and check it as we head into February. A heavy rainstorm washes away the log bridge that allowed me to easily cross over the brook. I can't see how well it is hanging on. Swan Song tells me she is close to having the conversation with Chief Thunder Cloud. I feel empathy for the unwelcome news he will receive. I decide to go over and check on the red fabric up close. Maybe I can sage it and he will receive some sort of comfort.

While having this thought, I take one step down the embankment, and my foot flies sky-high. I am thrown down hard in the mud as if slam-dunked flat on my back. The wind is knocked out of my lungs. I gasp for breath. My first thought is of the spirit of Chief Thunder Cloud. He must have kicked me in the ass. It comes with the spiritual reminder: as a man, he does not need nor desire any comfort from me. I stand up covered in mud. I can hear his spirit laughing. I also begin to laugh out loud. He got me good that time!

While in Costa Rica, I buy a female Rhodesian Ridgeback dog named Thunder. During my early morning walks with her, I watch a lone hawk. Near the end of February, it has found a mate. The two are together. I know it's a sign that Swan Song and I will soon be together. There is a great spot to swim in the river behind the home I am renting. It's set amongst the rainforest with slabs of gray clay layered in the side bank. While swimming, I sense the presence of Swan Song's spirit in the water. She does love the water. Time is a thin veil, like a weathered leaf, with no past or present. Her spirit has arrived slightly before her body. I can sense her swimming nearby in the water. I write down all these prophetic signs as a poem. I send it to Swan Song prior to her arrival.

Lying under the Buffalo Robe

When a red-tailed hawk soars above me,
I know your spirit is on the way.
From the heart of the universe we heal and pray.
Lying under a pine tree,
I feel the earth.

When two red-tailed hawks soar in a circle,
I know our spirits are together.

From the heart of the universe, our love is born.
Lying under the buffalo robe,
we share our love.

When the red-tailed hawks migrate by the hundreds,
I know our spirits have united.
From the heart of the universe, our dreams come to life.
Lying under the stars,
we give thanks.

Hurray! Hurray! Swan Song tells me she has purchased a ticket for three and a half weeks in Costa Rica starting in March.

She says, "I am now available and unattached."

This is a powerful step that she has taken of her own free will. I am overwhelmed. She is consciously and deliberately making a decision to leave Chief Thunder Cloud to be with me.

Lover
"My dove in the cleft of the rock, in the hiding places on the mountain side, show me your face, let me hear your voice; for your voice is sweet, and your face is lovely. Catch for us the foxes, the little foxes that ruin the vineyards, our vineyards that are in bloom."
Beloved
"My lover is mine and I am his; he browses among the lilies. Until the day breaks and the shadows flee, turn, my lover, and be like the gazelle or like a young stag on the rugged hills."
(Song of Songs 2:14-17 NIV)

She does not tell me any of the details about her final conversation with Chief Thunder Cloud, but her whole choice of words (or lack of words) seems a bit out of character. She ended a major relationship with one of our friends and does not want to share the details of how it went? That's not like her. Maybe it is deeply personal. I'm sure it was not easy. Given the situation, I am not going to pry. I am thankful she honored my request. What is more important is that she and I have newborn integrity. Her decision will have a huge impact on the lives of all three of us.

I am filled with joy as I anticipate our time together. My current role is as a facilitator in the Cristo Morpho Volunteer Program. I explain to the volunteers that I want to take a week to be with Swan Song. We desire to travel to Bocas del Toro in Panama to celebrate her birthday. We discuss the situation. I express how important it is for me to have this time with Swan Song, but I don't want to falter in my commitment. The volunteers boost the ante. They desire the full month of March to explore Costa Rica. They want to take that time to travel to the Envision Festival, explore the Pacific Coast, travel with friends, and visit other spiritual communities.

SWAN SONG ARRIVES IN COSTA RICA

I am standing outside the airport among a crowd of dark-skinned Latinos and overzealous taxi drivers, when Swan Song walks out from the glass doorway. I have a soft smile as I watch her emerge from the crowd. She has a big sun hat and wears a bright, flowered, knee-length dress. Swan Song travels with more baggage than most women, but in her case I welcome it all. She looks around trying to find her bearings amongst the crowd. I am standing silently fifteen feet away, admiring her. She starts to walk in my direction, but has not yet noticed me. When she is a few feet in front of me, she begins to teeter back and forth awkwardly, as one does to avoid bumping into a stranger. Suddenly she recognizes me. She catches herself in midair, smiles, and transforms her stumble into a fling, landing in my open arms. Our adventure has begun!

On the bus, she stares out the open window, mesmerized

by the rainforest as we wind up paved roads through the steep mountains of Braulio Carrillo National Park. It rains regularly in these high mountain passes. Waterfalls spill out from high, canyon-size walls carpeted with large green tropical leaves that shimmer in the misty fresh air.

One month earlier, I went to a roadside gift shop and bargained with a short Latino woman to purchase a batik-style, orange and black-striped hammock made to hold three people. This hammock is reserved for Swan Song and me. I kept it hidden away from the volunteers until her arrival. I place two hammock hooks between coconut trees on the far bank overlooking the river. The cool, steady breeze makes it an ideal place. Here we shall cuddle, take lazy naps, read books, and share our hearts.

> *Beloved*
> *"Come, my lover, let us go to the countryside, let us spend the night in the villages. Let us go early to the vineyards to see if the vines have budded, if the blossoms have opened, and if the pomegranates are in bloom — there I will give you my love."*
> (Song of Songs 7:11-12 NIV)
>
> *Lover*
> *"I have come into my garden, my sister, my bride; I have gathered my myrrh and my spice. I have eaten my honeycomb and my honey; I have drunk my wine and my milk."*
> *Friends say*
> *"Eat, O friends, and drink; drink your fill of lover."*
> (Song of Songs 5:1 NIV)

Upon her arrival, we prepare to recline in the king-size, batik hammock. Swan Song has her own way of doing things. Sometimes it's better, but it is different from how I would normally do it. She explains, "The most comfortable way to sit in a hammock is diagonal with your head on one end and mine on the other." I admit it is pretty comfortable. Plus, I get her cute bare feet to play with.

Another way Swan Song and I are different is the rate that we make decisions and act upon them. It will take her a month to make a major decision and another few weeks to act, whereas it will take me an hour to decide and it will be done later that day. Symbolically, she is a turtle and I am a rabbit.

Sometimes when I am waiting for her, I often think, but seldom say, "What is taking you so long?" At other times, she will look absolutely puzzled and exclaim, "You made that decision and did it already!"

When we come together as a team to make decisions, it's a learning process: I slow down and she speeds up. It's all part of the universal plan to find harmony between a man and a woman. Together, we teach each other to respect our differences.

Today Swan Song and I are sitting crossed-legged in the hammock facing each other. This way we can be fully present and gaze into each other's eyes. This is our first deep conversation. She starts by saying, "You need to listen and understand: I am here as a friend. I am here to be free. I don't want to place any limits on us."

I do listen, but in my book, we have been more than friends already. We have been sleeping next to each other for months. I understand she needs some space and perhaps to take a step back before we can take a step forward. As a woman, she is unpredictable. I gave up trying to figure out or anticipate what she wants or will do next. All I can do is enjoy being with her.

I prepared the women's volunteer room for her to stay in during her visit. After the first night, she drags her bags into my room. She wants to sleep next to me on my full-size bed. It's a peculiar friendship she desires. At first, I instinctively hesitate to let her sleep with me. Of course, we both want to cuddle up, and that is nothing new, but I am concerned about the moments when my passion and hers start to rise.

LET'S TALK ABOUT SEX

Prior to now, she has never been available and unattached. If she wants to sleep together now, we better talk about sex. I request that if we are to have sex for the first time, we discuss it and both comply. As a safety net, I suggest we wait 24-hours after we both agree. This way we won't slip and go there during the height of passion. She doesn't understand why there needs to be a 24-hour window.

I recall a conversation we had about sex in her tent while cuddling in her bed at Omega. It shocked me when she said, "I will not marry a man unless we first have sex." I stare at her, wide-eyed, "Are you serious?" She replies, "What if the sex is lousy?" That set me back. I tell her, "It is my intention to wait for sex until after I am married." I did not always have this belief. In my past I had sex before marriage and after my marriage ended.

Let's discuss this issue. It is an important one, especially for young adults. Some believe it's biblical to wait until marriage before sex. The Bible does not use the phrase "premarital sex." But what the Bible does talk about is sexual immorality.

> *"Flee from sexual immorality. All other sins a person commits are outside the body, but whoever sins sexually, sins against their own body."*
>
> *(1 Corinthians 6:18 NIV)*

"Sexual immorality" is the English translation of the Greek word porneia, which means "fornication." Fornication means "voluntary sexual intercourse between two unmarried persons."

Following the Bible is an excellent reason, but I have other reasons. I want to get to know the woman and love her as my best friend before we get married. I desire a mutual commitment for better or worse, regardless of our sex being great or lousy. I also feel that waiting somehow sanctifies the marriage. There is a purity exhibited, even if they both had prior sex. It shows discipline. Their actions honor sex as sacred, both before and after the marriage. Lastly, I want to feel self-respect and respect for my partner and her beliefs. Sex is important, but love and respect go hand-in-hand as the foundation for a sound marriage.

Swan Song, having been raised in a Christian home, has shared that she used to believe in marriage before sex. But she was not able to keep her quintessential values. She eventually gave in to peer pressure. She went to parties and was part of the popular crowd. She sadly confesses, "I had sex before marriage. After that I felt soiled." I feel empathetic. She continues, "After I did it once, there was no reason to not have sex with other men."

CHAPTER 30

Swan Song in Costa Rica

Together, we create our own little tropical paradise. She often reads or takes a lazy afternoon nap in the hammock. As I live with Swan Song, I begin to learn her ways, but she still whips out surprises. At first, all she wants to eat is fruit. I make rice, chicken, and vegetables for dinner and all she wants is watermelon. Her diet consists of watermelon, pineapples, melons, papaya, and mangos for the first five days. I begin to wonder if I am living with a woman or an orangutan. She proclaims, "The fruit here is fresh and yummy!"

Friends
"Where has your beloved gone, most beautiful of women? Which way did your beloved turn, that we may look for him with you?"
Lover
"My beloved has gone down to his garden, to the beds of spices, to browse in the gardens and to gather lilies. I am my beloved's and my beloved is mine; he browses among the lilies."
(Song of Songs 6:1-3 NIV)

Beloved
"Your plants are an orchard of pomegranates with choice fruits, with henna and nard, nard and saffron, calamus and cinnamon, with every kind of incense tree, with myrrh and aloes and all the finest spices. You are

a garden fountain, a well of flowing water streaming down from Lebanon.
Lover
   "Awake, north wind, and come, south wind! Blow on my garden, that its fragrance may spread everywhere. Let my beloved come into his garden and taste its choice fruits."

(Song of Songs 4:13-16 NIV)

Eventually, she starts to eat warm food and salads. We take turns making meals. When she makes a salad, both hands dive into the bowl to mix it up, which I find rather cute. I don't know how I have survived all these years without squeezing lemons and pouring large quantities of salt on all my meals. It must have been mandatory in her home.

I am surprised to find out that she likes to play board games. We enjoy playing chess, and for being fairly new at it, she is better than I expected. Each chess game is a ritual battle of teasing. I let her grab a piece or two of mine before we begin, just to make it fair. I come prepared with hot tea and coconut chunks to dip in peanut butter. She has popcorn and half a bar of chocolate for when the battle gets tough.

Before we start, I smile and ask, "Are you ready to lose… again?" She will respond by ruthlessly kicking my butt and playfully say, "I won again."

CAHUITA NATIONAL PARK

In this area, the rainforest comes down to meet the beach. Nearby, there is Cahuita National Park and the Gandoca Manzanillo Reserve. We hike through Cahuita National Park, which follows the Caribbean coastline for a seven km trail. It holds the claim as the largest living coral reef in Costa Rica, with 35 species of coral and over 400 different types of fish. In the early morning, on occasion, I have seen dolphins leaping up as they travel down the coast. This park has abundant wildlife, and as a photographer, I am excited to take close-up photos of howler and white-faced monkeys, iguanas, the yellow viper, and the slow-moving three-toed sloth.

There had been a big storm which scattered coral and shells along the beach. I have a surreal sense that I need to find the perfect conch shell. I keep searching, but find only broken ones. I am caught up in fondling all the shells, like a five-year-old child. I gather a collection of shells in a sack. Swan Song chooses a few shells with exceptional beauty. I excuse myself to go behind a tree with some toilet paper. As I squat down and peer under my butt, there it is…the perfect conch shell. It's smooth, bleach-white, and artistically designed with rose-pink swirls and curves on the inner caverns. It's the one I came to find!

DON CANDIDO MORALES, INDIGENOUS PLANT MEDICINE

One of my indigenous friends is Don Candido Morales. He operates an indigenous cultural center called Tururuwak in the small village of Patino. He offers indigenous plant medicine treatments and has knowledge of 1,500 plants. He learned about the rainforest plant medicine from his mother, and it has been passed down through the generations for over 5,000 years.

Swan Song and I visit Don Candido. He utilizes various methods to diagnose a patient, but he often starts by pressing points on their feet. The areas that are sensitive indicate a specific system or organs that need attention. They are his top priorities. He was a savior by removing copper from my liver, and gave me a rainforest remedy for dengue fever that brought my blood count back to normal in two days. It left all the doctors baffled.

Swan Song receives a diagnosis and treatment with rainforest plant medicine. He keeps calling Swan Song my wife, as does Maria at the internet café. I quietly smile about it and don't bother correcting them anymore. When we are together, we anticipate each other's actions. We find ways to provide each other with simple pleasures. Our rituals for greeting and saying goodbye are filled with hugs and soft glances of affection. Once a friend couldn't understand why I was so crazy about her, until he saw a picture of Swan Song and me. Then he understood; we were meant to be together.

Don Candido invites us to come over in the evening to join him and his sons in a fire ceremony designed for friends. Fresh fruit is offered at his gatherings as a way to make sure everybody has a sweet disposition. He makes a fire using pago wood on a square, indoor, stone fire hearth. We stand at the sides to represent each of the four directions. In their tradition, they honor the north as the eagle, the east as the dolphin, the south as the jaguar, and the west as the bear. We circle around the fire to each get a chance to represent all four directions.

Don Candido places dried plants on the flames. When Swan Song is standing in the south, the smoke wafts around her. He speaks in Spanish, and his son, Enrique, translates: "The smoke goes in the direction of the person who is in need of that type of energy or healing."

BIRTHDAY MONTH

Swan Song makes a big deal of birthdays. She calls March her birthday month, and it grants her special attention for 31 days. For her actual birthday, we visit Bocas del Toro in Panama for five days. There are a few areas where one can commonly spot dolphins. Swan Song has swum with dolphins before, and they allowed her to touch them. It was a moving experience. It's my hope that she can get close to them on her birthday.

Unfortunately, we don't spot any dolphins. However, in the middle of a downpour, we seek shelter at the fancy Dolphin Hotel.

For her birthday treat, she buys chips and a beer to consume while we play our ritual chess game on the balcony overlooking the sea. We depart the next day for a daylong boat tour. We snorkel in the turquoise Caribbean Ocean near gigantic, orange sponge coral with starfish the size of hubcaps, black eels, and an underwater parade of angel and parrotfish.

It feels great after swimming to lie on the beach completely wet and bake in the hot sun next to Swan Song. And we take long walks holding hands on the stunningly beautiful, wide, sandy beaches. Whenever we are together, there is a divine spark in our eyes. Finding each other is a gift. I am grateful for every moment we are together. In reality, we never know how long it will last.

I have engrained precious memories of being on the beach in Maine during a vacation with my past wife, Forevermore. During a memorable walk on the beach, I had taken a photo of our names drawn in the sand, encompassed within a heart symbol. I cherished it and had a photograph enlarged for our wedding guests to sign with a glitter pen.

Now, while being on the beach, memories of Forevermore and Swan Song are beginning to merge. A similar, strong feeling of love is surfacing. As we stop to sit on the beach, I confess to Swan Song that I am feeling love for her, as if she were my wife. I turn to her and say, "I never thought I would feel this kind of love for a woman again." She quietly responds, "I understand. It's okay to have those feelings. Other guys have felt that way about me."

We make it a complete birthday vacation by dining out overlooking the ocean. We fill our evenings by playing pool and ping-pong on the hostel veranda. She plays a viciously fun game of ping-pong, but her pool skills are pathetic. The next day, she insists on paying for both of us to go on the zip line adventure. It is under the guise that it's her birthday week. We each strap on a harness and glide over a series of cables from one rainforest treetop to another.

THE CHOCOLATE MASSAGE

On our return, I stop to pick up paint for my three-bedroom home in Buena Vista. The volunteers will soon be returning, and it will be our project to paint the house. I pick up a five-gallon bucket of cream-colored paint because it costs a lot less in Panama than in Costa Rica. But I must carry it a quarter mile across the bridge that connects the two countries.

We return for her last week at the rental house. We are feeling relaxed as one does during a lazy beach vacation. Prior to her arrival, I had a few dreams about making love with Swan Song. They felt prophetic, which is much different than a fantasy. A prophetic dream has great significance. I am sent this message for a reason. I know that we will make love. Remember Swan Song gave me one of her prerequisites for being married: she must have sex first. One doesn't casually toss this kind of information out to anybody. I contemplate it.

At this point in my life, if I marry someone, I want it to be her. I truly believe that if we don't have sex, I can't even be considered a potential marriage partner. We have had an intimate friendship for several years. We have gotten to know each other. We love and respect each other. Now that she is available and unattached, it seems natural that sex will soon be on the table. (no pun intended) Of course, I would enjoy making love to her, but it means I will compromise my values regarding sex only after marriage. It causes some inner conflict. I can't keep my standard and meet her prerequisite.

One evening while lying in bed, we revisit the discussion about having sex. We both give consent. I would be a liar if I said the only reason I wanted sex was to meet her prerequisite. The first time we make love we are impulsive and the 24-hour window is disregarded. Making love is always a sacred act. I am not going to describe our lovemaking scenes. What I will share is that we treat each other with tenderness, and with her, I am always in my heart.

The next day, we take turns giving each other massages. She bought some chocolate designed for massage. We are playing around and having some fun with it. As I lick some chocolate off her shoulder, I think I have figured out what she meant by saying, "being free without placing any limits."

NO VISIT TO BUENA VISTA

Even though Swan Song badly wants to visit my land in Buena Vista, I get strong guidance that we should not go there. I know there must be a good reason why. I have always been guided with precision about if and when people should come visit my land in Buena Vista. I often share with volunteers the exact day I feel they are guided to arrive and I usually know the day they will depart. There are poisonous snakes, spiders, and scorpions, but in ten years nobody has been bothered by them. I feel God's protection while we are on our land, but I must obey His given guidance.

> *"I have given you authority to trample on snakes and scorpions and to overcome all the power of the enemy; nothing will harm you."* (Luke 10:19 NIV)

However, she continually persists. She exclaims, "I came all this way expecting to see your land!" Tomorrow is the last full day before she starts her journey to leave Costa Rica. Finally, I give in. I reluctantly reply, "Okay, we can go visit my land in Buena Vista tomorrow."

In the morning, we sit down on the back porch to discuss the plans. As we start talking, it becomes apparent to me that I am going against God's desire for the sake of pleasing the woman I love. I feel strongly that I can't allow this to happen. In her presence, I break down and cry out with tears, "Please God, forgive me for whatever will happen! I know that we are acting against your will."

Swan Song finds compassion for me. I am relieved to

know she is willing to compromise when she sees how upset I am. We settle instead for a day on the beach in Cahuita. We have a picnic lunch. There is a steady breeze as we hold each other close, lying in the sand. We throw her sarong over our heads to close out the world. We share our deepest thoughts in whispers. I can still smell the sea and her warm, sandy skin next to mine. Our time together has come to an end. The next day, I escort her on the bus back to the airport.

The volunteers and I live the next few weeks in Buena Vista. We plant another phase of fruit trees: one that includes mangosteen, jack fruit, guanabana, and some edible greens like pacific spinach. As a group project, we paint the house inside and out. Afterwards, we take time to explore a part of our rainforest land. We start by following a brook; along the way, we observe red and green poison dart frogs and wild yellow plums. Hundreds of them have dropped into the brook and gathered bobbing in a pool.

When I find time to send Swan Song a few emails, I write enthusiastically about how I can't wait to be together again. Our time together had a natural flow that was easy-going and filled with delightful moments. Our relationship reached a whole new level of intimacy. I tell her I am excited that our relationship is deepening. I think to myself...*Finally, the two of us can be together in public. There will be no more façade. The wall she built to keep our love affair concealed from her partner can now be dismantled.*

A week later, she responds with an email that resounds in my mind like an echo shouted out from the top of the Grand Canyon.

"I am Not...not...not available
for a Relationship...relationship...relationship.
How does this make you Feel...feel...feel?"

CHAPTER 31

Sacrum Meltdown

I return to Vermont in May after the Cristo Morpho Volunteer Program ends. I have a grueling trip back with heavy luggage. I ride a Mountain bike with a backpack down the mountain and then 24 kilometers into town to catch the bus. Then I end up sleeping on the floor in the airport terminal during my layover in Austin, Texas.

Upon my return, I attempt to email and call Swan Song, but there is no response. I am floundering in disbelief after I learn that Swan Song left for Europe with Chief Thunder Cloud. In the last email I had received, she vaguely explained, "I will not be available to communicate with you while I am away." Swan Song is obviously no longer "available or unattached." I have been deceived.

She had asked, "How do I feel?" I am thoroughly confused! The rough return trip put some strain on my back, and I am struck with a feeling of being emotionally abandoned. I experience what I call a full-blown sacrum meltdown. Basically, my core muscles lose control and forget how to function. I am in shock. My sacrum has gone numb. It is unable or unwilling to feel nor comprehend what Swan Song has done. And it's not alone; my heart and mind are equally lost.

Chief Thunder Cloud is a man of integrity. I can't say I have always been that way. But now I am upholding integrity to the best of my ability. From my perspective, I made my stand for integrity and Swan Song used it as a platform for her deception.

For the next thirty days, I place my full effort into reeducating my core muscles so they know how to function. I go to physical therapy, massage, Pilates, and chiropractic treatments. This regimen slowly strengthens my core muscles. Eventually, I regain most of my normal physical muscle functions. I feel like I am recovering from a near-fatal car accident. When I tell people my condition was caused by a relationship, they raise their eyebrows.

I get no response from Swan Song for the next month. I am coming undone and start to lose it. I conjure up all sorts of horrid conclusions about her, none of which include me in the scenario. In a moment of desperation, I call Lost Son and share my dilemma. I feel better after talking to him. We have both been gravely wounded by Swan Song, and he can relate to my suffering.

I force myself to start doing serious meditation as a way to control the torrents of *self*-destructive thoughts. It's like my mind is being attacked by Japanese kamikaze pilots. Their target is my self-worth, my self-esteem, and my self-respect. Finally, a month later, Swan Song returns from Europe. Upon her return, we speak on the phone. I am comforted by her voice and my sacrum rapidly recovers another few fractions. We need to meet face-to-face for a heart-to-heart conversation.

DEVIL'S ROCK

We meet twice in Vermont. Our first encounter is at Lake Willoughby. Being at this lake with its deep, cold waters is comfortably significant. It is a sunny afternoon. I bring bikes and we ride them along the paved road following the shoreline until we come to Devil's Rock. This is where young men, like myself and friends, would test our bravery by plunging thirty feet off the rock cliff into icy cold water.

Swan Song and I sit on Devil's Rock watching the wind push the waves from the north shore as we soak in the sun.

We both know that we desperately need to talk about what transpired, carefully. We sit still in silence for several minutes to get in touch with our feelings. We both need to find the right words. Swan Song is oblivious to how much I have suffered. I am feeling vulnerable. I gave her my heart and soul in Costa Rica.

I delicately explain how I felt frustrated about not being able to communicate with her for a month and about my sacrum meltdown. It had been overwhelming. I continue to tell her all the challenges I am facing during my recovery. She admits that not communicating for a month was not a good idea. She apologizes. It caused problems for herself and others. Omega Institute had also attempted to contact her regarding her work schedule and was unable to reach her. It almost placed her job in jeopardy.

While she is talking, I unravel that Swan Song *never* told Chief Thunder Cloud that she was going to spend time with *me* in Costa Rica. She says she told him she was going to Costa Rica for a vacation. It was a far cry from ending her relationship with him. She returned directly from Costa Rica to live in his home, and then they travelled to Europe together. It is obvious they are still partners. We do not even discuss her deception. It is somehow deflected and diffused. I can't yet comprehend it. My emotions have frozen. They are not willing to accept that she lied to me. It might mean I would forfeit what I cherish more than life…her.

Upon their return from Europe, he insisted firmly that she tell him whom she had spent time with in Costa Rica. It was then she finally broke down and told him. She gave him my name. She suggested that I avoid any form of contact with him in the future. She says, "Just stay away from him." My sense from what she says is that he is fuming with indignation toward me for my actions, while Swan Song is above reproach. I wonder if Chief Thunder Cloud knows how badly we have *both* been deceived.

She has mastered the art of not revealing pertinent information. Trust is the foundation for an intimate relationship. Trust means full disclosure. Little things like where she is going next and with whom are pretty damn relevant to him and to me. With carefully chosen words, she skirts the real issues. I had assumed by misleading hints in our conversations that she was going to stay with her parents after leaving Costa Rica. She never came out and said it, but it was implied. All along, she had the intention of returning to Chief Thunder Cloud.

CHEWING GUM NUMB

I was not angry when the deception first occurred. Actually, I felt some relief in knowing that Chief Thunder Cloud had finally coaxed the truth out of her. Afterwards, my whole world began to crumble. Not just because she deceived me — it is true, what she did was inconceivable to my mind and heart. She built up my trust and self-esteem. I thought she was standing by my side. I was trying to live with honor. She took it all away. She destroyed that beautiful piece of artwork called integrity. She took an ice pick and began marring it. Then she handed it back, worthless.

It took me a few more years before I could process it all and get in touch with my real feelings. Around that time, I have a conversation with a woman from the prior community where Swan Song lived for several years before Omega. Our topic is deception in relationships. Out of the blue, she describes a pretty woman, with wavy blond hair and blue eyes, who left their community to go to Omega. She said, "This woman deceived and hurt a lot of men. She would use her beauty and charm to get away with it." I perked up. She may not have known it, but she was referring to Swan Song.

Only then did I realize that Swan Song has been deceiving men for decades. It seems that deception became her standard method of operating with men. I feel empathy for her situation. I love her regardless. She might even be doing it all subconsciously. I don't think she is aware of how deceptive she is with men or how much her lies batter a man's soul.

> *"With persuasive words she led him astray; she seduced him with her smooth talk. All at once he followed her like an ox going to the slaughter, like a deer stepping into a noose till an arrow pierces his liver, like a bird darting into a snare, little knowing it will cost him his life. Now then, my sons, listen to me; pay attention to what I say. Do not let your heart turn to her ways or stray into her paths. Many are the victims she has brought down; her slain are a mighty throng. Her house is a highway to the grave, leading down to the chambers of death."*
> (Proverbs 7:21-27 NIV)

CARING FOR THE HEART

We all have our issues. I am in no way an exception. But one's mate can witness their partner's issues more clearly than they can. Swan Song is great at pointing out mine: I change my plans, make fast decisions, and sometimes I am judgmental. Sometimes it's damn annoying, but overall I am grateful to know. I truly hope, more than I can express, that Swan Song can find healing for her deeper issues. I know I can't change her or heal her. I love her and accept her as she is. But I want her to be a woman of integrity, even if she is not my partner. I want what is best for her. I will eternally support her in this way.

While in Vermont, I make an appointment with a couple who are the New England Caring for the Heart counselors. I hope that Swan Song and I can attend some joint sessions. The appointment happens by fate to fall on one of the only other days that we could be together. Swan Song agrees to accompany me to a preliminary conversation with the counselors.

A week after our rendezvous at Devil's Rock, we meet with the counselors. Their advice is that Swan Song should, as the first step, receive individual counseling for her deeper issues. I am surprised when Swan Song agrees to come back for three days of counseling later in the fall. I have faith in this form of Christ-based counseling. I know it's possible for Jesus to heal her past traumas, including whatever happened in her first marriage. I have experienced it. I am excited for her. She is willing to work on her own stuff. It's a vital component of any conscious relationship. I await her counseling sessions enthusiastically.

BACK AT OMEGA

I volunteer the next summer season at Omega. Swan Song and I continue to spend time together intimately, but we have new challenges. A pattern begins to emerge. She defines us as being friends again. But really, whenever we are together, we grow more and more intimate. I believe that after we have been apart for a spell, Swan Song feels remorse. It's a vicious cycle. I feel drawn in close and pushed away like a yoyo. My heart and mind are sent mixed messages. In reality, she doesn't want to acknowledge our love and affection as a relationship. My existence within her world feels unstable and ungrounded.

As an individual, Chief Thunder Cloud has power and a certain amount of charisma. I dare believe that she might be more in love with what he offers her: his image of power, the type of spiritual work she revels in, access to a community of like-minded friends, the security of a man and his home, and travel to foreign countries. She certainly wants the world to acknowledge her as Chief Thunder Cloud's partner.

> "This above all: to thine own self be true, And it must follow, as the night the day, Thou canst not then be false to any man."
> — William Shakespeare, *Polonius*

In some ways, my desire to be with her has turned into a blind obsession. I can't bring myself to terminate our affair.

In part, because she gave me her heart, then her body, accompanied by her soul. With the gift of her body, our spirits did merge and I have had a taste of her soul. That bond cannot be easily retracted or shaken off. Besides, she savors being together and continues to furnish hope.

It leads me to set an intention to be a loving friend who will understand and serve her. Now, I have made it my business to get to know her deepest desires, the subtle nuances in her facial expressions and body language, and the simple pleasures that she enjoys. I become her humble servant. I get to know her routines. She tells me she is grateful to have a friend that cares. During my errands, I pick up chocolate and iced coffee for her. I actually enjoy doing little things, like turning on the light in her tent before she comes home. I don't want her to fumble around in the dark. To my surprise, it has become a satisfying way to express how I care.

We talk about our commitment as friends. We agree to communicate openly, be intimate, and touch, but neither of us wants to be sexual while at Omega. We continue to have fun by spending time playing games like chess and ping-pong. But the most cherished part of our friendship is the time we set aside for healing. This includes giving each other massages and encouragement by praying together.

Once she grabbed me as I came out of the dining hall and pulled me into the bushes. She said, "I really like praying with you. I want to pray right now." We often prayed together in the mornings but had not today. She likes it. We both know that there is power in our prayers. They manifest easily because our hearts are wide-open and in unison. We hold so much love for each other. I wonder, has she ever considered our being a perpetual couple? I know she would experience immense spiritual growth, warm-hearted intimacy, and her soul would rest securely. She will never know these things if she dares not to wade out into the deep water where love flows.

I meet with the councilors available for staff at Omega. I

am still seeking to make sense of the whole triangle relationship. It's not happening. My counselor points out that the man Swan Song is living with has been her and my spiritual teacher. This creates a whole new complicated dynamic. Generally, in a student and teacher relationship, the student attempts to seek approval and desires to please the teacher. If it carries over into a personal relationship, it becomes codependency. I don't want to speculate about their relationship. It's all getting more perplexing. I believe that Swan Song has, in many ways, found some spiritual growth from her time with Chief Thunder Cloud.

CHAPTER 32

The Buildup to the Showdown

Evelyn Lim, Intuitive Consultant of Singapore, shares the following information about the Akashic records.

"The Akashic Records refer to a database of every word, thought or action that is stored energetically and encoded in a non-physical plane of existence. They are said to contain the information of every Soul or Being in the cosmos. The Records are continually updated, with each new thought, word or action that every Soul or entity makes. The Akashic Records therefore contain the energetic prints about the origination and journey of every Soul through its lifetimes. They are embedded with information about your previous lifetimes, your Soul Origination, current life lessons and your purpose. You will meet with lessons that will be provided again and again, until you have gained mastery.

"The records are accessed through being in a deep state of relaxation or meditation. Anyone can have the same access to the Akashic Records. It's like having an internet access to the same database of information. In reality, no special powers or abilities are needed to get into the Akashic Records. The same records are accessible by the subconscious mind, through dreams, intuitive and esoteric exercises. However, a cluttered mind, ego, little connection with one's Higher Self and *a lack of trust in one's divine power are hindrances that an Akashic Record reader needs to overcome first. It's only when there is complete harmony between the conscious, subconscious or superconscious that Truth from the Akashic Records can be determined.*

"*One of the most famous of Akashic Record readers is the late American psychic Edgar Cayce (1877-1945). He has been called the "sleeping prophet," the "father of holistic medicine," and is about the most documented psychic of the 20th century. He has done readings on more than 10,000 topics. Other famous personalities who have accessed the Akashic Records include Nostradamus, Rudolph Steiner, Mary Baker Eddy and Emmanuel Swedenbord.*" [22]

There is one spiritual intuitive who works at Omega and offers Akashic readings for clients. Her name is Krystal Baal. She has glistening, blond, shoulder-length hair and a smile that covers her face. Her skin emanates softness. She is all about having fun. I am also able to view past lives through the Akashic records. I am self-taught in retrieving and interpreting them. I offer Krystal and another spiritual intuitive a session. Afterwards, they confirm that I am receiving and interpreting authentically.

Just for fun, Krystal reads my past lives. She is one of the few people who know of my affection for Swan Song. She says, "I have never seen so many past lives intersect. You and she go way back." I am excited about being together with her for so many lifetimes. Then as a friend, she says. "I suggest that you end it with Swan Song." I feel disappointed. That is not what I want to hear. But she is probably right. I am sitting on a powder keg, playing with matches.

PAST LIVES

When I journey to the Akashic Records, I start by diving into the ocean. There is a big white shark, my protective guardian, which swims around me. I dive to the bottom of the ocean. There I see a large, wooden chest that contains some significant item, like a gemstone, a key, or a star. I swim to the shore and come out of the water. I walk down a street of Roman courthouse structures with tall, white columns. There are seven different buildings all having to do with past, present, or future lives.

I go up the white stone steps of the Akashic Record Library and inside. Behind the counter are two Egyptian-looking attendants. One has the body of a woman with the head of a fox. I offer them a basket of fruit. They love peaches and watermelons. With their permission, I request a book from my past life or that of another person. They escort me to the appropriate aisle. I find the book I am seeking. I will often request to see where one life intercepts with another. When I open the book, symbols appear such as a pine tree, a sled, and two children. I interpret the symbols and in my mind's eye it creates a visual story. In nearly every past life Swan Song and I have lived, we found each other. And there are hundreds of books. It is true!

In one of our more recent past lives, we were brother and sister around ages eight and ten, living in India. A landslide covered the schoolhouse we were in. We were both trapped down low, but could move around among the rubble to be near each other. We held hands in the darkness. Although we both succumbed to starvation, we found comfort in each other that took away the fear of death. Now, in our present lives, we both keep a food stash, even when meals are provided. With this insight into our past life, we can better understand, and if we choose, change our behavior in this life. Maybe we don't need to hoard apples, almonds, and chocolate.

Swan Song vividly recalls a past life when we were sorcerers. When she talks about it, I feel it's during the medieval period in England. As in this life, we both have the power to heal and wield magic. She recalls the time I cast a horrendous spell. Most likely, I had used my power in an attempt to win her over. Whatever it was I did, it left such a deep impression that she has not forgotten it in this life.

PAST WIVES

I request to be shown books relevant to Swan Song and my lives intersecting. I am shown three of our past lives where we were involved in a relationship. In the first past life, I read the symbols of a rabbit, coyote, moon, stars, and a cooking pot. Each symbol represents an important part of our past life. One by one, I focus on the symbols. Then the life vision it represents appears.

This is not the first life in which Chief Thunder Cloud and I have encountered each other with Swan Song's love and affection being the central conflict. In this one, Swan Song is living in a Native American village with Chief Thunder Cloud. He is a husband of good standing, and together they have many kids. They multiply like...ah...*rabbits*. I live in another Native tribe and meet her at a trade gathering. At first sight, our hearts are drawn toward each other. I secretly travel to visit her village at dusk. We make passionate love in the *moonlight* in the woods behind the canyon edge. When she returns to her husband, her face reveals instantly her betrayal. As I am running back towards my village, there are beautiful sparkling *stars* filling the night sky. It's a feeling of being young as my heart beats madly, overflowing with the joy of being alive and in love. Then the *coyotes* start to howl, just as they did in this life when I was forced away from her tent. It's the cry of our hearts for each other. We both hear it and know it.

Now Chief Thunder Cloud has a dilemma: he could ask her to leave or stay; it's his right to decide. He chooses to have her stay and deal with the hardship surrounding the situation. He wants Swan Song to continue her role for the sake of his family and the tribe. He needs a wife to keep the *cooking pot* full of stew. A year later, we spot each other again at the trade gathering. This time Chief Thunder Cloud keeps her close. We have no more physical interactions, just a glance, a memory, and a longing.

After viewing this first past life, I close the book and leave the hall of records. I walk back to the shore, preparing to swim back. Before I touch a foot to the water, something unheard of in this spirit realm happens. Chief Thunder Cloud comes out of the water. He is rather upset and yells, "You have stolen her from me in three different lives!"

Needless to say, there has been tension between Chief Thunder Cloud and me regarding Swan Song for a few past lives. Clearly, it's still not resolved. Once he cooled down, Chief Thunder Cloud and I actually had a discussion about her. True to his nature, he even suggested a few pointers about how to get along with Swan Song. He says, "When she gets upset, just be silent." Perhaps, somewhere deep in his soul, Chief Thunder Cloud knows that Swan Song and I have a special bond of love that has endured through many lifetimes.

I return to the Akashic records to read our second past life together. Swan Song is married again but to a different man. We meet during a heavy snowstorm in a Scandinavian town. She is sniffling with a cold, so I offer to bring her home with my horse and sleigh. I bring her back to my home, not hers. I make a warm fire. Perhaps from this past life, she has taken with her a romantic affection for fires. She does not make it back to her home until the next morning. Upon her return, her husband uses a horsewhip to punish her. Once again she is punished for being with me.

The third life encounter goes way back to when we were living in caves. She is out gathering food and is attacked and eaten by a saber-toothed tiger. I watch it from a distance, but it's too late and there is nothing I can do. It's devastating for me. My unrestrained primitive heart wails out in agony for her. This may explain why from early on, it has been hard for me to be away from her for long. It seems we have left each other with an unexpected death, mine with the bear and hers with the saber-toothed tiger.

THE BUILDUP

Once while walking to a yoga class at Omega, Swan Song asks me out of the blue, "Will you protect me?" I reply, "Yes." But I ask myself. *Why is she scared? What do I need to protect her from?*

She actually is safe, but for her to *feel* safe means something completely different. I believe she wants to know that she can fully relax and feel secure in my presence. Obviously, she will not be physically hurt while she is with me. But women have a variety of ways that allow them to feel psychologically and emotionally safe. I know the true nature of my beloved. Being held or touched brings her the most comfort, along with cozy blankets and pillows, praying together, being with friends, or sipping a hot cup of tea.

Early one morning, Swan Song slips into my tent in her pajamas and crawls under the covers beside me. We both know that Chief Thunder Cloud will arrive at Omega later that day. Why do we meet at such a precarious moment?

"Those who restrain desire do so because theirs is weak enough to be restrained."
— William Blake, The Marriage of Heaven and Hell

Since being back, we have discussed the topic of our lovemaking in Costa Rica. Initially, she said, "It worked for me." It led me to believe that she enjoyed our lovemaking. But today when it comes up in our conversation, she refers to it as "a mistake." I can't believe she considers our lovemaking a mistake. It hurts my pride to even consider our making love as a mistake. The most I will admit is that maybe she is right, and maybe I am wrong. But in all honesty, I don't regret it. There have been so few lovers in my life with whom I was capable of expressing my love in a healthy, wholesome way. Oh Lord, allow me to keep one shred of pride. *No!* I hear you. We both made a mistake.

It feels awful when she leaves my warm bed to go pack her bags to stay with Chief Thunder Cloud in his cabin. Whenever he comes to Omega, it is her ritual to go and spend her nights in a cabin with him. When it is time to depart, she becomes instantly cold. The sudden leaping from my bed to his feels nasty. I want to retain integrity if I am to be with her. Now I am sucked back into being a part of this devious affair. Our being together is once again taking place behind his back. We are being as sneaky as we were before Costa Rica.

During the times Chief Thunder Cloud visits, I no longer exist in Swan Song's world. When he is present, she suddenly becomes his humble and devoted servant. This is the chameleon side of her I have never met. As soon as he drives away, I reappear and my beloved changes back into the woman I know and love.

On one rare occasion, while Chief Thunder Cloud is on the campus, she breaks through this barrier to show affection towards me. I am staying in her tent and she comes under the guise of needing a pillow and fetching toothpaste for him. We embrace each other while lying in her bed for what seems like an hour. It is clear to me that she needs to be held. Although she ensures me that he would not visit her tent, the thought of him making a sudden appearance makes me nervous. I feel that uncomfortable, on-edge feeling. I imagine it is emotionally draining for her to hold space for two men on the same campus. There are other nights when Swan Song feels haunted by the possibility that Chief Thunder Cloud will suddenly appear and find us together in her tent. For this reason, she is most at ease when we are at our camping spot a short drive away from Omega.

OUR CAMPING SPOT

Tucked into the woods off the hiking trail around a quaint pond, is a three-sided lean-to made of large, pine logs. There is a stone fire pit directly in front of it and a weathered picnic table off to the side. There are pine planks on the floor and it all smells like pine inside. Someone had used a knife to carve, in old English script, five of the seven deadly sins. On the three surrounding walls are the words GREED, WRATH, and ENVY. PRIDE hangs overhead. LUST finds its place on the floor directly in front of our tent opening. How appropriate a reminder. (If you're racking your brain, gluttony and sloth are the two missing deadly sins.)

The opening faces toward the pond, which is no more than 25 feet away. In the late afternoon, the ducks come in for a landing as a marmalade sunset engulfs the horizon. At night the frogs near the shore create a chorus of peeps and chirps with the exceptional, resounding, deep croak from a bullfrog.

When I am here by myself or awaiting Swan Song, I always find peace looking at the reflections in the pond. There are tall grasshopper-green grasses and gnarly tree limbs half submerged in the water. They make an ideal place for the turtles to rest while bathing in the last glistening rays. If I move suddenly or a hiker passes on the trail, the turtles plop back into the water. A moment later, a head slowly appears and stretches out before its cautious return.

During our first autumn together, we claim this site as our camping spot. We stick a red prayer flag filled with tobacco high in a tree overhanging the pond directly in front of our camping spot. When we return the next summer, we are glad to see it still hanging, though it has faded. There is an old John-Deere-green hand pump not far away. It provides our drinking water. We take turns pumping the handle as the other rinses the dishes or takes a quick shower.

From near the hand pump, we can watch the smoke from

our fire and look down the length of the pond. We gather firewood together before dark. Swan Song loves to sit and stare into the fire. On the cold, fall nights, we are cozy and sleep deeply as we hold each other beneath my buffalo robe. She always sleeps on her left side. I spoon her. If I'm not close enough, she wiggles herself backwards to fill in the crevice. My right arm rests comfortably upon her waist. My hand cups her small, soft fingers. The nostalgic smell of smoke mixes with the smell of the buffalo leather and the scent of our skin. At night when we first bed down, a silhouette from the flames dances on the side of our tent. Later we hear the crackling and popping of the fire as it peters down to form red-hot coals.

We both cherish our favorite camping spot. In the fall, we wear jeans and cuddly, wool sweaters. I savor the comfort of her leaning her head onto my chest while we lie on a woven blanket in the sun. It's as much about the warm, glowing feelings of being together in nature, as being in love.

The timelessness of the breeze gently blows the leaves. I gaze at her watching the clouds. She notices and smiles, returning my glance.

THE MEDICINE WHEEL

"Native American traditions were not based on a fixed set of beliefs or on an interpretation of sacred writings, but on the knowledge of the rhythm of life which they received through the observation of Nature. All of Nature expresses itself in circular patterns. This can be seen in something as small and simple as a bird's nest as well as in things much greater such as the cycle of the seasons or the cycle of life (birth, death, rebirth). And therefore, to Native American peoples, the circle or wheel represents Wakan-Tanka ("the Great Everything" or Universe) and also one's own personal space or personal universe.

> *"In Native American belief, the cardinal directions are linked to great Powers, or intelligent forces, whose energy (or Medicine) can be harnessed. The directions can be charted on a circular map, the Medicine Wheel, which can enable one to come into alignment with these spiritual powers and absorb something of them.*
>
> *"Each direction on the Wheel constitutes a path of self-realization and self-initiation into the mysteries of life which can lead you to the very core of your being where you can make contact with your own High Self. Each path can help you to acquire the knowledge to work changes that will put meaning and purpose into your life, bringing enlightenment and fulfillment."* [23]

During our second season together, we build a Native American medicine wheel on the moss a few feet away from the pond. We use slate rocks to create a circular border. The circle represents the sacred outer boundary of the earth, often referred to as the sacred hoop. Then we create horizontal and vertical lines through the circle's center to divide it into four quarters. They represent the four directions and all the other correlating components from the circle of life.

The National Library of Medicine states,

> *"Different tribes interpret the Medicine Wheel differently. Each of the Four Directions (East, South, West, and North) is typically represented by a distinctive color, such as black, red, yellow, and white. The directions can also represent:*
> - *Stages of life: birth, youth, adult (or elder), death*
> - *Seasons of the year: spring, summer, winter, fall*
> - *Aspects of life: spiritual, emotional, intellectual, physical*
> - *Elements of nature: fire (or sun), air, water, and earth*

- *Animals: Eagle, Bear, Wolf, Buffalo and many others*
- *Ceremonial plants: tobacco, sweet grass, sage, cedar"* [24]

We are always barefoot when within the medicine wheel. We walk in a clockwise, or "sun-wise" direction. In the center, we keep sage and a few white eagle feathers, standing upright. The eagle feather is a sign of the power our Creator has over everything.

It's the way we made the medicine wheel together with love, that stirs up my sentimental feelings. There is more power in the harmony that exists between a man and a woman then we tend to acknowledge. Of course, there is power in the Native Medicine, but love multiplies it exponentially. I brought Althea's husband, Huck Finn, whom I truly respect, to visit the medicine wheel while we were on a biking expedition. Huck just sat barefoot on a log in front of it and meditated. He could feel the love, the power, and the magic inherent in it. Then he was catapulted into an intoxicated state of bliss. I know what he felt; it was our love. The love that my beloved and I share is not of this world.

THE CONFLICTS

One Friday, Swan Song suggests that I go during the day to place my tent on our camping spot to ensure we reserve it before the weekend. She says, "I have a feeling you had better go set up your tent so we get our spot." I am reluctant. She says, "Chief Thunder Cloud listens and follows my intuition." Her statement was a low jab. I feel resentment, but begrudgingly go and set up my tent. When I return in the evening, my tent has been stolen.

She has a spare tent that we use. The stolen tent is not a big deal. What is more important is that she now knows not to treat me or expect me to react and operate in a manner similar to Chief Thunder Cloud. It is normal to draw from our past relationship experiences, but it can also be misleading.

Swan Song and I experience inner growth when we are being vulnerable with one another. I never want to repress what she says and have always encouraged her to be open. No doubt her claim to be available and unattached before her visit to Costa Rica should have made me wary, but somehow her charm and beauty override it. In general, she is honest with me. While we are discussing a couple's relationship retreat at Omega, she exclaims, "This is the kind of relationship work I want to be doing with Chief Thunder Cloud!"

I say, "You mean what we are already doing?"

She responds, "Yes!"

The rawness of her being *that* honest wears on me. She has no hesitation to speak about a future with Chief Thunder Cloud in my presence. Once she even said, "It doesn't really matter which man I choose as long as I keep working on a relationship."

Eventually, Swan Song finds compassion, and says, "I know my actions have hurt you. I don't want to keep hurting you."

I respond, "Well, one thing you *can* do is stop talking about Chief Thunder Cloud when we are together."

Swan Song clearly begins to shut me out during these intense emotional moments when Chief Thunder Cloud is around. Once while he is on campus, I return to Omega and see her on the path by the café. She looks around and gives me a quick, nervous hug. I begin to walk with her along the path. Her fear that Chief Thunder Cloud will appear erupts. In anger, she shouts, "Go away! I can't have you near me."

Around this time, our stress had reached a pinnacle. Later on, I realize our trust has grown solid enough to withstand expressing real emotions like anger without holding back. Studies show that women who deal with anger indirectly or attempt to suppress it are more likely to experience depression, anxiety, and physical complaints than women who are more direct. There is freedom in being able to express a full array of emotions. We have always been able to forgive each other after a spat because our love allows it.

After Chief Thunder Cloud departs, I immediately go to her tent. She is physically and emotionally exhausted, but that does not matter. It is my turn to express my exasperation at being diminished. I go into her tent and fall upon my knees. I tell her, and express with tears streaming down my cheeks, how humiliated she made me feel. I do not deserve to be cast aside like a piece of trash when Chief Thunder Cloud is present.

Afterwards, whenever possible, I make arrangements to leave the Omega campus when Chief Thunder Cloud comes for his visits. But Omega is a small campus and eventually we meet, face to face.

THE SHOWDOWN AT OMEGA CORRAL

When first revealed, the truth does not always make life easier. After it has been withheld for months, the impact is compounded. Chief Thunder Cloud knows about Swan Song and me being together in Costa Rica. Even though I am glad the cat is out of the bag, so to speak, it makes my next encounter with him intensely uncomfortable and downright despicable.

The Omega dining hall is filled with 300 - 400 people that are a combination of volunteers, retreat participants, and spiritual teachers. For those who live and breathe in this community, the dining hall is a sensitive and energetic place where you must stay grounded so as not to wash away in the energetic flow of chatter. One has to step mindfully down the main aisle as the kitchen volunteers, in blue aprons with handkerchiefs on their heads, bustle back and forth, carrying silver trays loaded with organic veggies, through swinging, saloon-style doors.

In the main corridor are two food lines that converge into

a giant T-shaped formation. Each branch flows into a station on the left and right with four milk dispensers hanging down like the teats on a cow. There are coffee dispensers at chest level, with red handles that extend out resembling slot machines. Against the wall is an assortment of fruit with a display of layered rocks stacked behind it. If this were a town in the Wild West, the innocent bystanders would have ducked behind the rocks when the shots started firing. On the countertops, bouquets of tall, wild grasses hide innocent-looking flowers that sit prettily as they watch the flurry of commotion below. The participants, carrying white plates and bowls filled with salads and chickpea gumbo, meander down both sides of the food line and overflow into the center arrangement like tumbleweeds in a dust storm. They bounce against the back wall or gather in small clusters before sliding over to fetch a drink at one of the stations.

It's high noon when I enter the back door of the dining hall after eating outside. I know without glancing up that Chief Thunder Cloud is in the room. The air is thick. We are about to have our first uncomfortable encounter since he uncovered our forbidden secret. The fact that I now know that he knows makes it even worse. I step out into the clearing at one end of the dining hall. The room becomes deadly silent. The floor clears of all its participants, as if they know there will be a showdown. One lone participant looks up from filling a glass of milk and scurries nervously away. In my left hand I have my dirty plate, and a fork and a knife in my right trigger-finger hand. I peer down the long, striped lines on the wooden floor that lead directly to the far end of hall where Chief Thunder Cloud stands. He has just dropped off his dirty dishes at the counter. He turns his boots to face in my direction.

I take a breath and tell myself, *Stand tall. Stay strong. Wait until you see the whites of his eyes. Let him react first.*

A participant in the corner strums an eerie twang on his guitar. The showdown has begun. Chief Thunder Cloud starts to walk towards me and I towards him. There is no turning back or changing our paths. This is not a time to waver or show weakness. I feel every breath. My heartbeat pounds in my eardrums. We walk as if in slow motion. As he passes a bowl of oranges, crazy thoughts enter my mind: *If he grabs an orange and pegs it at me, can I deflect it with my plate? If he takes a swing at me, should I duck or block it?*

We both have our arms dangling at our sides, ready to draw our pistols, as the timeless spiritual showdown over Swan Song begins. Fifty feet away now. No backing down. Our paths are going to cross. Twenty feet away now. In slow motion, the details become clear. I can see the whites of his eyes. I lift my eyebrows in a gesture of acknowledgement to this man, who was once my friend and spiritual teacher. He stares straight ahead with a cold, rattlesnake stare. I hold ground anxiously, as if I were the prey standing before the rattlesnake with its head raised, ready to strike. I hold my breath; this is the inevitable moment I have been waiting for and wanting to avoid. We pass each other like two giant cargo ships that pass so close they scrape the paint off the metal with a screech. Both of us are left shaken but still standing.

I stumble and stagger away towards Eric the Viking, who in that moment had swooped in for a plateful of chocolate chip cookies. He says, "How are you doing, man?" Maybe he sensed my desolate pain. He gives me a long hug. He was a refuge for me in this battle-scarred, barren land.

He says, "Wow, I really needed that hug!"

He has no idea what just happened, but he held my soul for a moment, when I could no longer bear it. Our hug welds back together the cracks that formed in my heart. I attempt to express my gratitude to him for being there in that moment, but fall short.

He laughs and says, "I gain my emotional nurturing from eating a mountain of chocolate chip cookies."

CHAPTER 33

Sacrum Meltdown II

I sit alone in Swan Song's tent. It will be the last time I am in her tent this season. I absorb the unwanted fact that I will be leaving her soon. We have spent most of our free time together as if we were inseparable. During our moments together, time nearly stopped. But then again, two months passed as quickly as a wink. I look at the blankets and pillows on her neatly-made bed. We spent precious time lounging on top of them, sharing the mundane and outlandish details from our days. She bubbled up when she retold her interactions. I enjoyed listening. It became a self-indulgent treat.

When we are physically together, our intimacy grows. When we are apart, it's never the same. We agree to communicate once a week, or was it once a month? I forget. It felt like a tedious negotiation. It doesn't really matter on some level. Regardless, once I leave, our level of intimacy will fade. I fear our inevitable parting. There are deeper emotional and psychological implications and I don't pretend to understand them all. I just don't want to be away from her. It's unsettling. Her soothing smile and her internal rhythm are like a cozy blanket on a chilly night. And it's about to be yanked away.

When I slowly walk away from her tent, my sacrum begins to tremble and quake. I place my right hand on my pelvis and my left hand on the sacrum region of my back. There is no holding it back! The internal earthquake begins to erupt. I am going into a full-blown relapse: my second sacrum meltdown.

I drop my bags at my side and stare straight ahead. Instantaneously, the harness of muscles around my sacrum starts to wind as tightly as a winch with steel cables. *It is out of control. I can't turn it off.* Red lights flash. I attempt to hit the emergency button. No success. My response is to hunch over and curl up. My skeletal structure *cracks* and *pops* as it dislocates my spine, sacrum, and ribs. Then it creaks to a cringing halt.

At this point, I am messed up, but when I am with Swan Song, I feel completely loved. She is the one I want beside me when I am suffering. Even the thought of death is not so bad, if she is holding my hand. But the tragic thought of not being with her is enough to mess up my fragile world. I can barely walk and I am in no condition to drive away. *Have I become a co-dependent marshmallow?*

At Omega, when you are in a bind, somebody just appears at the perfect moment. My fairy-like friend, Blossom, instantly vaporizes from a cloud of magic dust. I hobble down with her to a cabin by the lake, where there is a massage table. She brings some relief to my muscles through her soothing touch. Nonetheless, my sacrum and ribs remain dislocated.

Blossom compassionately explains, "This healing crisis stems from your emotions. It's all about Swan Song."

I don't want to admit it, but I know she is right. I am shocked that my emotions have the power to instantaneously incapacitate my body. During the tremor, my mind left my body. It's standing on the breakdown lane on the interstate in L.A. watching rush-hour traffic zoom past. Meanwhile, my body is crying out to be touched by Swan Song. Something deep inside, beyond my awareness, is afraid to leave her.

Suddenly, Swan Song appears with a smile. Beside the lake, she carefully sets out a blanket in the sun. I slowly lie down on it. She starts by softly massaging my tight legs and back muscles. Then I hobble back to the massage table in the cabin for the remainder of her massage. When she is done, she lightly holds my feet for a moment. I am lying face up on the massage table. She skips to the left side of the table and swings her leg up and over like she is getting on a horse. Instead, she lies down with her full body in contact with mine. She ends with a big, long hug on top of me. I utter out...*Awhhhh!* This is not what I expected, but it's what I needed. What I desired more than anything was to have her full body and heart close to mine. My body may still be in pain, but my emotions and spirit are being nurtured.

During my dinners at Omega, friends listen and support me with hugs. I recover enough after three days to drive to my friend's home in Pennsylvania. I call him Cowboy, for a good reason. He used to work at Miracle Mountain Ranch. That is probably where he learned to crack whips. He has been the main attraction at a few western events. It sounds like a gunshot when cracked properly. It actually breaks the sound barrier.

Cowboy rented a room in the same house while we both went to Liberty University. One of the first nights, he charged into my room wearing tights and a jester's hat, wielding a long, moon-shaped sword. I burst out laughing! We are the best of friends. I stay with him a few weeks as my sacrum heals. We often share what is happening in our relationships. He listens patiently to my agonizing trials with Swan Song.

SPIRITUAL WARFARE

During my drive down, I listened to a recording of Freud. He explained how sexual dysfunction is caused by our emotions getting tangled up in our sexuality. His remedy is to do non-sexual regressive work to express anxiety, aggression, and other emotions related to sexually traumatic events.

Caring for the Heart counseling uses a similar technique of regressing to the original trauma through visualization, and then Jesus comes to heal the trauma. My emotions are entangled in my sacrum area. It feels like a ball of cold spaghetti tied up in knots. My issues could be more sexually related than I realize. I am beginning to understand how my sexual addiction is an intimacy and attachment disorder. I can't continue to aggravate this unhealthy pattern with Swan Song. I need to heal it.

As a counselor trained in Caring for the Heart techniques, I begin to work on myself. I use them as a weapon to break apart the spiritual bindings of my past traumatic sexual entanglements. I arm myself with prayers, a Bible, and worship music before charging into battle. It lasts for seven days. I address the sex I had with any women other than my wife and all my deviant sexual acts: pornography, strip clubs, and sexual fantasies. I repent these acts. I call back parts of my soul that were stuck clinging to past sexual partners.

My first battle was when I was 13 years old. I had my first sexual encounter when a so-called friend molested me. During this session, I pray to be shown the visual effects it had on my heart. In my heart, I see a pitted, black crater. I go back and relive what I felt during that encounter. It's a mixture of pleasure and fear. Then, my insides lock up. During this session, Jesus comforts my 13-year-old self.

I ask Jesus, "Why were you not able to stop it?"

Jesus replies, "Men have free will and Satan was given authority to rule over certain aspects on the earth. I have the authority to heal what has been damaged by him."

Jesus sits a foot away from me in a chair. He says, "Give Me your pain."

It's my choice to hold on to the pain or give it to Him. The pain is not serving me. I start by giving Him a flake of the pain from my pocket. Then I begin to pull out my pitted, black-crater heart and hand it all over to Him.

As I am doing this, I yell, "It hurts! It hurts! It hurts!"

I worry that Jesus or somebody else will receive this horrible pain.

He says, "The pain will not be given to Me or anybody else."

He places my pitted, black-crater heart in a plastic beach pail and kicks it far out into the white light. Then, I give Him a red-hot metal bar that is in my spine and a collar that is around my throat.

I was told by my perpetrator to keep it all a secret.

Jesus explains, "What this man did to you was wrong."

Jesus gives me a new heart. I can feel the warmth inside me. It's a bright pink heart that is bouncy and flexible.

Jesus says, "I love you."

I now know that even if you are molested, the perpetrator can never touch that part inside of you that is Holy.

JESUS WALKS BESIDE ME

Jesus then reveals a past experience from when I was eight years old, to show an example of how He is different from my father. At that age, I would run and play for hours without end. While at camp, The Lion would, on occasion, go into the woodshed and come back disguised as a monster. His costume consisted of removing his toupee and brushing his remaining hair on either side straight up. He would become a scary hunchback by placing a pillow under his shirt on his upper back. He wore a set of plastic fangs over his teeth and would walk with a deformed limp in his right leg. Growling and snarling, he chased my siblings and me in circles around the kitchen table.

In his way, he was being affectionate, and we all had fun. Even though he was playing, this game was about our being afraid of the monster my father had become.

Jesus says, "I will walk beside you. If you run, I will run next to you. I will always be with you. I offer healing to the people that come to Me."

In my experience, healing occurs when the receiver is ripe. It requires an intervention from God, but the actual format that the healing manifests is of lesser importance. God has many channels and people who act as His instruments.

At the end of my session, Jesus sends a beam of white light that shines on my sacrum. It melts some of the tightness. Healing occurs though subtle shifts. I acknowledge the forward step I have made. ■

CHAPTER 34

Finding a Hero

I stay in a cabin in Virginia near Yogaville for the next few months. I focus on getting stronger and dedicate my energy towards rebuilding my body. I receive regular chiropractic appointments to adjust my ribs and sacrum back into their proper locations. I get a weekly massage, attend Integral Yoga and Zumba dance classes, swim, hang on an inversion table, and start to lift weights twice a week to build up my strength.

I feel the urge to write more of my book, but when I take the time to listen deep inside, it's not the right time to write. I need to relax and allow my back and neck muscles time to heal before I attempt to sit and write. I don't write one word of my book during my time at the cabin. The fastest way for me to heal is in silence. It allows me to quickly get in touch. I pray for guidance on how to deal with the complex issues surrounding my topsy-turvy relationship with Swan Song.

I am silent for ten days. It feeds my spirit and soul. I set the intention to find the hero inside myself. At a yard sale, I buy a series of 1960s movies with Hercules and an array of heroes from *The Odyssey*. In each movie, there is always a villain, usually a battle with man or monster, a defining moment to prove the hero's character, and a beautiful damsel whom instantly falls head-over-heels in love with the hero. Hercules, to my surprise, likes to take naps and lounge around and relax. I think I could handle being a hero in that regard! I can't swing trees around to knock men off their horses like Hercules, but I can find inspiration in the hero's character, strength, and courage.

FOUR QUESTIONS FROM JESUS

Jesus is also my hero. During my silent 10-day retreat, I feel Jesus ask me four questions. They are regarding our relationship and my obedience towards him.

1) Jesus asks, "Do you choose to follow me above all other forms of God?"

I answer, "Yes, but why can't I follow all forms of God?"

Jesus replies, "I want you to choose all of me or none of me!"

In that case, "Yes, I want to choose you, Jesus!"

2) Jesus asks, "If I ask you to read the Bible each day, would you do it?"

I reply, "Yes, I give my highest authority to you. I want to be obedient to your requests."

3) Jesus asks, "Will you live in a community filled with corny people that are devoted to me?"

Many of my friends are Christians. They are decent people, whom I love and respect. Once I get to know them, they aren't that corny.

I say, "Yes, I would live in a community of corny people devoted to you."

4) His last question is the toughest. Jesus asks, "If I asked you to let go of Swan Song, would you do that for me?"

I start to cry and yell out, "NO! That is a mean question. I will not give up the woman I love for you."

Jesus says, "Now that you are being real, we can start a relationship."

I begin to contemplate the last question. If God has a sovereign plan that determines everything that happens in this universe, then being with Swan Song is out of my control. I believe that God has an individual, detailed plan for my life.

After a few days, I surrender. I let Jesus know, "Yes, if you ask me to let go of Swan Song, then I will do it."

I know that Jesus will not request something of me that is not in my best interest. Mind you, Jesus did not actually make any of those requests. He was checking the state of my heart. He may, in fact, make such requests at a later date, or I might find out that His request is my only option.

SITTING TO MEDITATE ON THE LOG

I ask myself what a hero would do in my situation with Swan Song. I walk out into the woods and sit in the sun on a log to contemplate. How do I feel about Swan Song deep down inside? There is no doubt… I love her. In a relationship I need to feel sparks. Like two magnets placed near each other, they either repel or attract. Swan Song and I certainly feel divine sparks when we are together. I reflect on the closeness we have developed and those actions that strengthen our bond.

She once gave me a bookmark that shows a walking path in the forest. It read, "It doesn't matter where you go in life… It's who you have beside you." Her written words like these and her actions lead me to believe she wants us to be together. I think I know how she feels about me, but her actions and words are often contradictory.

Our health and beauty diminish as we get older. But in my eyes, Swan Song gets more beautiful each day. Consider her bizarre sleeping rituals. She likes the bed tucked in, with lots of covers, and each morning she meticulously makes her bed. While sleeping, she puts in earplugs, places a scarf over her face, inserts a knee pillow, and cuddles with a dagger-size stone of selenium. She says it emits healing vibrations. That's not the worst part. Lately, she has begun a strange new ritual. She sleeps with duct tape over her mouth. This way she is forced to breathe through her nose. How would I kiss such a horrid creature good night? Should I remove the duct tape or just kiss it? My point is that her inner beauty is what matters; her external, daytime beauty is a bonus.

During this last season at Omega, Swan Song has grown to have more integrity in her relationships. I believe the primary reason is that she has to teach other women about relationships and it has forced her to look at herself. This was an area of concern, but now it's a reason to find her more appealing. I know that neither of us is perfect; we both have our "stuff" that comes up. When it does, we take time to sit down face to face. We really listen and share from our hearts. I actually look forward to our arguments because I know we will resolve our problems with kindness. It draws us closer. Together, we find spiritual growth and expand to become the best versions of ourselves. As part of this process, I get to understand more about her needs, interests, fears, goals, dreams, and what brings her joy and sadness. I want her to live in a way that will bring her happiness, whether we are together or apart.

What we are experiencing in essence is a "conscious relationship." That means we came together with the intention to find emotional and spiritual growth as individuals and a couple. We allow the other space to fully express and feel. Even if at times those feelings trigger something within the other. We focus more on embodying love and being vulnerable than the outcome of our relationship. We certainly have experienced more growth together than we could have alone. But at this point, I can't continue with Swan Song unless there is a shift to allow integrity to be at the core of our relationship.

In the past, I have prayed very specifically for the qualities I sought in a wife. She needs to communicate openly and honestly, and be dedicated to the relationship even when times get tough. This means being kind, compassionate, understanding, and forgiving, even when it's hard to do. She should have her own life and friends. She should not take life too seriously, because I like to laugh with my mate. It's best if we are both on the same spiritual path or aligned with similar values.

Once, after I prayed for a wife, God whispered, "You will find this woman. She is going to be far more magnificent than you can ever imagine!" It could be Swan Song. I am not sure.

While sitting on that log, I get in touch with my heart. There is a strong desire in my heart to be with Swan Song. We are soul mates. We were inexplicably drawn together. In her presence, I feel a sense of peace, calmness, and joy. She fills my heart. When I think of her, it begins to melt and burn. She has told me that she has had similar feelings. When I am near her, I feel divine light shine from within her, and it makes me glow.

A hero will express how he feels to the woman he loves. He will take action. I do not want to let Swan Song, whom I adore, slip out of my life. My heart needs to express to Swan Song how I feel about her. There is no way to capture all the love I feel in words. I must find a symbolic way to let her know. It's time for my heart to override my mind. I am ready to make a hero's stand.

I decide, sitting on that log, that the best way I can show Swan Song how much I love her is to ask her to marry me. In a bizarre way, it makes sense, given our crazy situation. This step would allow us to break away completely from the web of deception. Swan Song has had the past twenty months to make a decision about which man she wants in her life. Her choice has been to use both men to fulfill different needs. But now, all three of us are caught like buzzing flies in a sticky web. We are just waiting for the spider — the spider that has already begun to devour me from the inside out.

If I propose marriage, then Swan Song will *need* to make a decision. I take into consideration that she has told me she is not available for a relationship. But maybe that is on a superficial layer, because she considers herself spoken for. Deep down I believe she loves me, to the depths of the sea. Marriage has a way of bringing love to a whole new level. I want her to experience marriage with a man who will treat her with kindness, love, and respect. She never received that in her first marriage. She deserves it. This could be a second chance for us both. If she chooses to marry me, she will be endorsing our love in front of our friends and family. This way, all three of us can retain our respect and dignity.

Swan Song has three days of Caring for the Heart counseling sessions scheduled for the fall. I have faith that the counselors, with the help of Jesus, can heal her broken heart. I eagerly await the results. This could give her a whole new perspective on marriage and some of the deeper issues that have surfaced. I decide it's best to place my faith in Jesus. If Swan Song is ready, Jesus can resolve her past marriage issues in three days. I have placed her in the best hands I know. I decide that I will pray for Swan Song each day for two weeks prior to her counseling and all during the actual sessions.

SWAN SONG'S FIRST MARRIAGE

Swan Song had been raised in a Christian household. I believe her father was a pastor. They upheld traditional family values. In her early twenties, she was engaged. Both she and her mother thought her fiancé, Michael, was a real honest-to-goodness angel. She wanted a simple, small wedding. Her mother instead insisted on a large, formal wedding. Her mom, in part, took control of Swan Song's wedding plans. She allowed her mother to do so, even though it was not exactly what she wanted.

On the wedding day, a few hours before the ceremony, her husband-to-be changed his mind. Michael confessed to Swan Song that he did not want to marry her. He wanted to call it all off. The pastor was a family friend. When he found out, he took Michael aside and they had a stern talk.

The pastor told him, in no uncertain terms, "Swan Song is a quality woman. It will be a big mistake if you back out of the wedding now." Under mounting pressure, the groom complied. But he still confided to the pastor that deep down, he did not want to marry her. They went forward with the ceremony. The crowd was waiting, and the ceremony would temporarily evade shame for Swan Song and her family. However, the pastor never even sent in the official wedding certificate. Their marriage never became legal. Michael had become a fallen angel.

To say that Swan Song was devastated after this experience is an understatement. I assume she felt abandoned and disgraced by her incomplete and short-lived marriage. I don't know if I can even call it a marriage. Swan Song was left in a state of miserable disarray. Her husband was like an actor in a Shakespearean tragedy. Her first love had passed her a bottle filled with a poisonous concoction of confusion and deception regarding love and marriage. She had no option but to drink it. The whole audience watched, but only she and a few others knew of the underlying deception. The ceremony ended before it began. A few weeks later, Michael left the scene and boarded a plane to Japan. But the ramifications for Swan Song were deep scars. It is understandable why she has a fear of marriage. She confided in me that she never processed her marriage. I believe many of the issues that stemmed from her first marriage still exist today.

There was nothing any man could ever do that was worse than what had already happened to her. I know that the initial trauma damaged her in some deep ways, and I am truly concerned. I am not a psychoanalyst. But I did focus intently on their scenario and asked God to reveal what He may. What I present is a theory: Swan Song was hurt so deeply that she stopped trusting men. Is it possible that Swan Song's future method of coping with men after the "Fallen Angel" incident was to become deceptive with them? Maybe it's completely subconscious on her part. It seems normal to try to avoid being hurt again after the torment and heartache that Michael inflicted. Even if it meant stretching the truth. In some way, it makes sense that she would treat future men in the same manner that she was treated by Michael. He deceived her. She learned to deceive them. My theory explains why, when I gaze into her eyes, I sense a lack of trust: *It's hard for her to trust a man.*

I hope it will bring some comfort to Swan Song (and others) to know that she is not alone. We have all been rejected, abandoned, or let down. I recognize her situation was a severe calamity, but you can't expect a relationship to exist without its eventually causing some pain in one way or another.

After one is hurt in a relationship, they may attempt to protect themselves by not extending trust. Perhaps a better approach is to extend trust and give people the freedom to make a mistake. The good news is we can all make a conscious decision, starting right now, to trust people again. Trusting people feels better for everyone involved. But we need to accept the fact: *sometimes we will get hurt.*

Recently Swan Song found information on the internet about Michael. He was still living in Japan, apparently happily married, with two kids. Swan Song and her mother wept together when they found out. Swan Song still thought that Michael was meant to be her husband. She was secretly waiting to be his wife. For the past twenty years, she had hoped that her first love would return. Now, it was clearly no longer possible.

TALKING ABOUT MARRIAGE

In her past, Swan Song wanted to honor the sacred bond of marriage. I talk to the Caring for the Heart counselors and they suggest that we discuss marriage in depth before I propose to her. Through my prayers, I had been guided *not* to talk about the possibility of our future together until after her counseling sessions. It would probably bring up her stuff prematurely. Over the past year, we talked about marriage to a limited degree, but never in depth. Because of her past marriage trauma, I consciously make a commitment, deep within my cells, to never abandon her if we do get married. With her, divorce is not an option.

Since we have been apart, I have sent her half a dozen cards that include big references about marriage. These are big hints. She sends me back nice cards, but her prevailing theme is that we are friends, again. But her actions and affection tell me we are more than friends. In her unspoken words she tells me she loves me, over and over. At the very least, after I propose, I will know exactly where she stands. I guess I really don't know. It's still hard to fully accept that she was capable of deceiving me, just like she did all the other men. I still want to feel special; I want to be the exception, so there are places I fear to go. If I dig deeper within myself, I find a layer of denial. I don't dare believe that she doesn't love me as much as I love her. In my own naive way, I believe that if we both make an honorable stand for love and marriage, all the lying demons will be chased away.

She is staying at Omega until the end of October. I attempt to visit her as I pass by on my way back to Vermont. This time could be our moment to talk more in depth about marriage. But she has made plans to go away that weekend.

REALITY CHECK

Before I leap forward, I figure I had better check in with a few wise female friends. This is my reality check. I call my friend Sunshine, whom I greatly respect, and ask what she thinks about my proposal. She tells me, "Follow your heart." Okay.

On my way back to Vermont, I spend a night at Omega. I enter Swan Song's tent and make an elaborate decorative display on her bed with feathers, leaves, and cards. While I am there, Blossom stops by to return a book. I tell her that I plan to propose to Swan Song. I ask for her advice. She says, "Five guys have proposed to me. I knew right away if I wanted to marry them or not. There were a few guys who never proposed, but if they had, I would have said, 'Yes!'"

I feel some encouragement. Blossom suggests that I give Swan Song all the time she needs to make the decision after the proposal. It generally takes her a long time to make big decisions, so I am planning to give her a month or two for this one.

On the bright side, Swan Song and I set a date a month in advance to meet and go on a hike the afternoon after her final counseling session in Vermont. It will be the first time we have been together in a few months. The day after that, she will travel south for over a month to fulfill other commitments, and then she will go to spend Christmas with her parents. This is the *only* time we can be together in the foreseeable future, so this is when I feel I *must* ask her to marry me.

CHAPTER 35

The Desert Oasis

Before I propose to Swan Song, I want to make absolutely sure this is all God's will. I ask God for definite confirmation. I have two things that need to happen. First, I need to find the perfect wedding ring for Swan Song. Second, I need the money to buy it. The property taxes on my home in Vermont are due each October. After paying them, I barely have enough gas money to make it back to Vermont from Virginia. My prayer to God for the money to buy this ring is asking for a small miracle.

I want to buy a wedding ring that represents the quality of life I want to share with her. Therefore, it needs to be a brand-new ring. Swan Song is particular about her jewelry. I am searching for a diamond with turquoise stones on either side. Swan Song loves turquoise and wears it often. My heart will know the perfect ring when I see it. At the moment, I am poor financially, but rich with the overflowing joy of love. The possibility of money presenting itself so I can purchase an expensive wedding ring is crazy. But with God and love, anything is possible!

Turquoise is more popular in the Southwest. During my initial search I can't find any diamond rings with it. While travelling up the east coast I visit numerous jewelers, with no success. Then, out of the blue, I find Kokopelli Jewelers in southern New Hampshire. They sell high-quality diamond rings with turquoise, made by Kabana Jewelers in Albuquerque, New Mexico. The owner is a man from Greece named Stavros Eleftheriou. In 1977, he bought a historical missionary church, saying that it had "a good feeling and a blessing inside." It was there that Stavros set up shop and founded his jewelry business. As a tribute to the church's bell tower, he named his company, *Kabana*, which means "bell" in Greek.

I note one ring called the Desert Oasis, with turquoise on either side. Kabana puts in the extra effort, time, and expense to ensure each piece conforms to the highest standards of excellence. Kabana jewelry contains more gold per piece than most jewelry on the market. Thicker pieces result in more durability and safety for the stone inlay. All pieces are hand-polished to ensure a flawless result. I also like this place because each piece is completely manufactured in the U.S.A., while many jewelry manufacturers outsource parts of production to areas such as Southeast Asia. The Desert Oasis has 58 facets. Those are the planed surfaces. This is a high-quality diamond. Holy smokes! Swan Song will love it, but it's damned expensive.

Kabana says they can custom design this engagement ring in the size I need to fit her finger. The first part of my confirmation has been answered. I have found the perfect ring! If I give her this ring, it will show her how I truly feel about her better than words. (Forgive me if I am starting to sound like a diamond ring advertisement.) The next big question is: Can I come up with the money to buy it?

It will take sixteen days for the whole custom process and shipping from New Mexico. They request a thirty percent down payment to place the order. If I can come up with the deposit and the remaining payment a few weeks later, the ring can be in my hand the day before Swan Song and I plan to rendezvous.

I return to Vermont for the next few weeks before our date. The Lamb has been accepted into a senior housing apartment complex. I want to be there to help her move in. I show The Lamb a picture of the Desert Oasis wedding ring and ask if she will loan me the money to put down the deposit. It's practically impossible for her to say "No" when she sees how happy I am. She will gladly embrace Swan Song as her new daughter-in-law. They have met on a few occasions when Swan Song came to visit me at our brick home.

If I sell my junky, ten-year-old car and use all of next month's income, I will have just enough money to buy the Desert Oasis. I spend my remaining time happily staying with family and friends, even though I must sleep on the floor with cushions for a bed. After ten days, my car sells! There is no sacrifice too big. God has fulfilled the second part of the confirmation. Now I have the money I need to buy the Desert Oasis. I am filled with so much joy that I can't stop singing!

DEER CAMP

As a 46 years old, life is a dream. I am a grown man. It has long been a tradition in our family for the men to go to hunting camp during deer season, even if they no longer hunt deer or drink booze. But one does need a doctor's note or a pretty bad hangover to be excused from drinking. As a teenager, it was sort of a rite of passage to go to hunting camp with the men. It was a big deal to get outfitted as a hunter. It's not just about getting a decent hunting rifle with a 3-8x scope and a license. You need to sight in your gun and scope out your hunting ground before the season starts. Some hunters even spread out apples or buy a salt lick. It's illegal. (I never did it, but some of my nameless friends did.) One needs a belt for your bullets and a nice buck knife. You need to carry a rope to drag the deer out, and a compass, even if you don't know how to use it. You need the proper attire: a red wool jacket, an orange cap, long johns, wool socks, and boots rated for 20 degrees below zero. I like a red Styrofoam pillow to sit on for warmth. You have to bring some snacks, like a bag of peanuts and raisins. Part of the fun as a kid was just getting all decked out.

Once I started going to hunting camp, I found there was a

lot of jesting. It's okay to call somebody a dumb ass. Your really don't need a reason. You just make one up. Sometimes it is done just to get a reaction. There are a lot of obscene words being tossed around. I guess it makes us feel more like men. It is good for men to hang out. When there's work to be done, like hauling firewood, we all pitch in. It sure feels nice to stand near a wood fire, especially after traipsing around in the cold. Everybody brings some groceries. The wives often make a roast, baked beans or a pie. My Grandfather, Buck used to say, "Always pay a little more than your share so nobody will think you're cheap."

Our hunting camp is a bit more elaborate than others. During the first week of deer season, we provide a few gourmet meals like steak, shrimp, or lobster. In Buck's day, they even hired a Dixieland band for opening weekend. But we can still count on my Dad, The Lion to belt out some old songs like "Sweet Gypsy Rose" and "Mack the Knife" on the piano. Those more adept at cooking usually take that role, while others do the dishes. There's usually a chance to target practice or shoot a bow and arrow. And there is the occasional cribbage or poker game with a few guys smoking cigars. If you wake up at 4 a.m. to go hunting or stay up until 2 a.m. drinking, then the afternoon nap time is pretty essential.

It has been several years since I have gone to camp during hunting season. The men-only tradition has been abandoned this year. The Lion, his girlfriend, their daughter, and three married couples his age are all spending opening weekend at the hunting camp. Hunting is low on their agenda. They are scouting out martinis and Bloody Marys. There is no shortage of time to drink and converse.

Gadget, my brother, has parked his RV camper on the lawn nearby to ensure he has privacy and a good night's sleep. He will be one of the few who are serious about hunting. He has shot a few big bucks...most of them were even legal. This year he douses himself with buck scent before heading out to his tree stand with wrap-around camouflage netting. Gadget hilariously describes this year's hunting camp as "senior citizens daycare." One woman has Alzheimer's disease. She intermittently breaks out in a song. She has not forgotten them. Her husband will patiently ask her to be quiet. During dinner she asks for the pepper. She does not use the pepper but places it in front of her plate.

I ask her, "Why did you want the pepper?"

She explains, "I find comfort in having it near me."

She also finds comfort in having her husband nearby. In the middle of the night, she yells out his name repeatedly until he wakes up and responds. He yells back, "I am right here! Be quiet and go back to sleep!"

The Lion has A.D.H.D. and sleeps with a radio tuned into a nostalgic country station that plays songs by Johnny Cash and Patsy Cline all night long. It's one reason that I sleep on the couch downstairs; besides, the bedroom loft is filled with a slew of drunken chatter, bodily noises, and a chorus of moans and groans. The Lion wakes up at around 3 a.m. and bangs around for an hour rearranging the living room furniture before he starts cooking breakfast.

I vow to be positive when I am around The Lion. As a son, I want to support him and spend time with him. But each day I need some time alone in the woods to keep my own peace of mind. I have not hunted deer for several years. I sold all my guns, but the thought of fresh venison on the table changes my mind. I purchase a license at the local convenience store and borrow my Grandfather Buck's rifle. I am going to go deer hunting this year.

COYOTE CRY NO MORE

It's unusually mild weather for November. The weather has been odd, and the apple trees did not bear this year. The deer are seeking alternative food, such as acorns. Early in the first morning of deer season, I climb up and sit in a tree stand.

I have a nice view of the deer run coming from the maple clearing into a thick clump of pine trees on my right. After five minutes, a huge whitetail deer waves its flaggy tail and bounds out from the thick pine trees. I barely have time to swing my rifle in that direction. I can't tell if it is a buck or a doe. Now it has vanished up the mountain to safer terrain. But it gets my adrenalin pumping.

It's nice to just sit in the woods. I watch the chickadees sing, the squirrels scurrying about, and a woodpecker drumming on a dead log. I drink my ginger and licorice tea. Occasionally, I lift my gun to point it at tree trunks to make sure I can move quickly and quietly to shoot in all directions.

By mid-morning I prepare to leave. Suddenly, a young male coyote trots into the clearing near two bare apple trees. It's not aware that I am sitting so high above it in a tree. I raise my gun to look at it through the scope. I have spotted coyotes before while hunting nearby. I enjoy watching them with curiosity. I am not sure why I do it, but I take aim and pull the trigger. He is hit in the midsection. The coyote whimpers and cries out for a minute, scratching in the dirt with involuntary nerve impulses. I climb down the tree and walk over slowly with a feeling of great remorse. He takes his last breath beside a small pine tree. I start to cry as I pet his beautiful coat. I say to him, "I am sorry, you are so beautiful. I don't know why I shot you."

For me to kill this coyote is not normal. Perhaps I had a little buck fever and became trigger-happy. Being at camp and listening to hunters telling their deer stories might have brought it out. The coyote had always been a welcomed messenger. Swan Song even bought me a Native American necklace with a coyote howling. When coyotes howl, it reminds my heart of how Swan Song and I long to be together. They have a strong symbolic meaning to us. But coyotes are also known as tricksters. They deceive and mislead. That is certainly not what I desire before a potential union with Swan Song. Perhaps

I felt this coyote was carrying a message that was unpleasant: something I did not want to hear. Whatever the coyote's message was, his death reminds me that life is fragile. This coyote will howl no more.

RETRIEVING THE RING

The senior citizens daycare and The Lion are set to leave on Monday. I stay alone at the camp for another day. The next day, I find a dead partridge mysteriously lying in the front yard. It is still warm. I pull the nicest tail feathers off and place the body in the woods for wild animals to eat.

Swan Song begins her Caring for the Heart counseling sessions today. I put a few logs in the box stove and settle in to pray during her sessions. I sing a few songs to set the mood. Then I pray aloud for her. I pray about the abandonment issues from her first marriage when her husband backed out on their wedding day. She often forgoes retelling the details. The short and sweet version she tells acquaintances is, "He left me standing at the altar."

I pray about her fear of authority figures and her desire to please other people. This probably relates back to her childhood. I can feel the Holy Spirit working with her to release some of the trauma she has experienced. Our hearts are so connected that I can sense her emotions. I can feel her pain. She has slight apprehension, but she is being brave. I hope that my prayers help create a safer space for her heart to heal.

The day before Swan Song and I plan to meet, I receive a message that UPS had made an attempt to deliver the package with the Desert Oasis engagement ring to my sister's home. Nobody was there to receive it.

I leave camp and urgently go to the UPS office. I ask, "Is there any way I can get my package today?"

They say, "The driver is in such a remote area that he can't get cell phone reception. But we can give you a few addresses close to your sister's home where the driver will deliver packages later this evening. You can intercept him en route and pick up your package."

I say, "Okay, let's do it!"

I hold my breath. Dusk is settling in. I wait patiently on the side of the road, near the driveway, at the appointed time. The UPS driver comes briskly up the road in his big brown truck. He stops in the road by the driveway, and hands the precious package to me. I feel a weight lift off my shoulders. I am so grateful. It all worked out. This must be God's plan. All along I had faith that it would. But I was not expecting it to be at the very last minute.

All week long I am filled with joy at the thought of proposing to my dearest beloved, Swan Song. We plan to meet tomorrow and then take a jaunt up to the rock ledge overlook at the top of Devil's Hill. It is here, at my favorite spot, where the view looks out towards Peacham Pond, Owl's Nest, and the rolling mountains in Peacham that I will propose to Swan Song.

CHAPTER 36

The Proposal

Around noon, I meet Swan Song at the church. She has just completed her final Caring for the Heart counseling session.

I tenderly ask her, "How are you doing?"

She softly says, "I feel vulnerable."

"Are you up for a picnic?"

"Okay"

We drive down to Harvey's Lake to have a picnic lunch. Our conversation is kept light. It's nice to be with her again, especially on a gorgeous, sunny, fall day. After our picnic, I take a stick and write our names in the sand and place a heart above them. I am rather taken aback when she takes her foot and crosses out her name. It's not a good omen.

As we start to hike up the forest path, I bring up the topic of what a hero is. I start by saying, "A hero will express how he feels. It's an attitude. Like when I lift weights, I dig deeply because I want to be strong for myself and others."

I ask her, "What about you? How do you find your inspiration?"

She is breathing hard as she replies, "I am inspired by Kundalini Yoga. And I keep a disciplined diet."

She talks about an eleven-minute, forty-day journal practice that she created. She states, "My journal allows me to express my feelings in a continuous free-flowing style. At the end of the week, I read it and contemplate."

I notice that her foot is wrapped in medical tape.

Concerned, I ask, "Are you hurt?"

She says, "Nope. I'm good. It's a way to keep my feet in proper alignment. The medical tape keeps the bones in my feet from popping out."

I jokingly say, "Are you saying your body is held together with tape?"

She laughs and replies, "Yes, now that I'm older, tape basically holds me together."

We reach the summit, and I lead her to a small flat plateau area at the top of the rock ledges. The trees are mostly bare; the colorful fall maple leaves have all blown off. We look down upon the bare treetops. An island of pine trees distinctively stands out. I spread out a woven Mexican blanket. We take off our hiking boots and socks. It is a brisk fall day. We are grateful to feel the warmth of the sun in November. It shines upon us as we slowly smudge each other with sage.

I say, "I would like to put up some prayer flags for the four directions. Do you want to join me in saying prayers?"

She quietly replies, "Okay, but I want to say my prayers silently."

I unpack four long, cloth strips in the colors of red, yellow, black, and white. We make traditional Native American prayer flags by placing a quarter cup of tobacco on one end of the fabric. We pray as we wrap the end of each flag into a bundle. I say my prayers out loud. After each, she says hers quietly to herself.

I start my prayers, "Red is to honor a fresh beginning. Yellow is to bring healing. Black is to allow freedom and be grounded like a mountain. White represents purity, like the snow."

I ask her, "Will you sing that song to honor the directions, where you call in the grandmothers?"

She replies, "Sure." I love to hear her sing, as does almost everybody. With her beautiful, swan-like voice, she sings a Native melody that calls to the grandmothers from each direction.

It asks them to come and be with us and give us their blessing. She kneels down to sit on her half of the blanket.

I creep barefoot along the rocks to tie four prayer flags on four surrounding pine trees. From where we sit, we can see the four strips of cloth hanging from each limb. Each is two-feet long with each color corresponding to its proper direction. White represents the north, red is for the east, yellow for the south, and black symbolizes the west.

I read two cards from a deck of affirmations by Louise Hay. The first says, "I am worth loving. I am willing to let love in. It's safe to let love in." The other says, "I release the past with ease and I trust the process of life. I do not use yesterday's mental garbage to create tomorrow's experiences. I create fresh new thoughts and a fresh new life." These seem promising!

Then I hand her two letters with cards inside. She had sent them to me in Virginia during the past few months. In one she had suggested that we go for a hike together in Vermont.

I enthusiastically say, "See, now we are doing it." In the other card is a picture of Krishna and Radha, the divine couple. Krishna is standing behind Radha in the garden, holding her as he plays the flute. Radha wears an orange, flowing veil, with glitter and jewels glued to the front of the card as her jewelry.

Swan Song had written in this card, "Thank you from my heart for holding me in all the ways that you do."

I awkwardly start into my daring proposal, "One of my dreams is to share my life with a woman who communicates openly, has her own life and friends, and is willing to work on herself." Swan Song listens intently.

I continue, "And it's you who has answered this prayer." I compliment her on how much work she has done on herself, during this last season at Omega.

I playfully say, "Swan Song, close your eyes."

She replies, "Why?"

I tell her, "I have a gift that will express how I feel about you. But I need a minute to get it ready." She enjoys this kind of fun and squeezes her eyes shut. I have the large, white conch shell that I found when we were together on the beach in Costa Rica. It's bundled in a soft, yellow towel that is wrapped tightly with red fabric strips and topped with a huge, fancy, white bow.

I say, "No peeking, I am not ready yet."

She smiles and says, "I am keeping my eyes closed."

When her eyes are closed, I place the 18 partridge feathers I found at hunting camp in a circle around the huge white bow. They fan out to make a beautiful display with black and white zebra-striped feathers.

I softly say, "Now hold out your hands."

She holds out her hands. I gently place the wrapped bundle, with the feathers sticking out of the bow, in her hands. She opens her eyes and is delighted by the feathers. She smiles cheerfully like a child. She fumbles in her bag for her cell phone and takes a picture of it.

She carefully pulls out the feathers and with kindness asks, "Do you want to keep some?"

I wasn't expecting her to give any feathers back, so I say, "It's a gift for you, but if you insist, I will take three feathers."

She says, "I want to share them with you."

I pick out three feathers and she keeps the rest. Then she unwraps the red fabric strips from around the soft, yellow towel to reveal the conch shell. She knows how much I love it. She initially hesitates to take it.

She sighs and says, "I know how much this conch shell means to you."

I smile and tell her, "I want you to have it."

She says, "Okay."

She accepts it and begins to unwind a spiraling web of baby blue ribbon that surrounds the conch shell. Tucked inside the conch shell opening is a two-inch square, thin, wooden box the size of a zippo lighter. It has the word LOVE carved on the center of one side of the box and a small heart inlaid in one corner on the opposite side. On the front of the box there is a secret sliding panel. Inside is the Desert Oasis engagement ring. It is placed gently on a piece of soft, yellow fabric.

She takes her time unwrapping the shell and holds the wooden box. As part of our gift-giving ritual, we flirtatiously take our time and embellish these moments.

I softly explain, "The box has a secret door."

I slide my finger on the box and edge open the sliding door. She continues to slide it open, and the Desert Oasis engagement ring is revealed.

She stares at it. She doesn't look at me but stares straight ahead. She becomes distant and her eyes glaze over. She is showing mild signs of shock. She is far away. It seems like she is catapulted back to the misery and grief from her past marriage. When I look at her face, I see only heartache, disgrace, and disappointment. This is not good. Her eyes proclaim, "Why is this happening to me?"

Still numb and disorientated, she slowly recovers to the present moment and vaguely says, "What kind of stone is this on the ring?"

It's pretty obvious what it is, but I say, "It's a diamond." Her mind is piecing it together. It seems like a part of her wants to deny what is actually happening. I feel some sadness about her reaction.

I look at her and softly say, "I am inviting you to share our lives together. Please take this ring and take all the time you need to make a decision about marrying me." I take a deep breath and exhale. I expect it's going to take her a few months to decide.

Held Up by Love

Rare it is to hear pure Love tapping at my door.
I did not seek or invite it, but let us explore.
Could it be this love so pure chooses when and where to
  implore?

I peek through the eyehole and wonder who it could be.
I really must decide; do I dare open this door?
If I open the door, love will come in like a flood,
sweeping me off my feet, unpredictable, relentless,
barely giving time to breathe,
as I am turned and tossed in the waves.
Yet, in this slushy lushy love,
each moment is a present wrapped with a glistening bow and ribbon.
A gift offered to bring me closer to my own divinity.
What fool passes up such a gift?
Such a fool am I.
I dare not open that door.
Neigh, I did it once before,
the torrent of deceptive love,
smashed me against the shore.
But could it be this is a different man, a different time, and a different door?

NOT A LITTLE SURPRISE, BUT A BIG ONE

I don't expect an immediate decision. I am shocked when Swan Song turns to me sniveling and says, "I don't want to keep this ring. It's too valuable; you must keep it."

She turns and looks at me with tear-filled eyes and loudly says, "No. No. No. I am not ready to marry you."

I am too shocked to react. I am too numb to feel.

She pauses and says, "One of my worst fears is being asked to marry before we fully discuss it."

I apologetically say, "Given the situation, it did not seem appropriate; besides, I wanted to surprise you."

I hesitate and then ask, "Would you consider marrying me in the future?"

She pauses and says, "I don't want to say no, but I don't want to say yes because this may lead you to having false hope."

She continues, "I am not even ready to date you yet."

I am somewhat confused by her statement. When we were last at Omega, we spent most of our free time together. Sometimes we went to the movies or out for dinner. We have been on dozens of dates. We usually slept together in her tent. She came and spent three and a half weeks with me in Costa Rica. And now she is not ready to date me?

There is a long pause. We both look at each other and then out at the rolling mountains and the lakes.

I quietly say, "I will probably go to Costa Rica for the next year. It might be best if we have some time apart. I can visit you when I return."

She says, "I may be ready to date you in a year. We can go to the movies."

I perk up and say, "So there is some hope for us?"

She says, "I said I *may* date you; it's not definite."

I can't fully feel in this moment. I am not yet in touch with my emotions around her response. We spend time holding each other and more intense emotions surface. She cries again. I join her this time with tears streaming down my cheeks.

I softly ask her, "Are you a little surprised?"

She opens her eyes wide and says, "This is not a little surprise, it's a great big one!"

I remind her, "It will take me a few days before I can really get in touch with my feelings."

It's starting to get colder, and darkness descends as we walk back down the forest trail. She stops to admire layers of mushrooms growing sideways out of a tree.

I pop my head around the tree next to the fungi and, trying to lighten the mood, say, "Do you prefer this fungi to this fun guy?" We laugh. At least we can be ourselves even after being so emotionally vulnerable moments earlier. She gets cold and we stop. I rub my hands rapidly over her legs and arms to warm her. She warmly accepts my touch, as always. We laugh about how I move too fast in life, like a rabbit, and how she moves too slowly, like a turtle.

As we are walking down the trail, I say, "I am ready to live with you for the rest of my life, and you are ready to date me in a year!"

She reminds me, "I *may* be ready for a date in a year."

We start to drive back to her car. I hold her hand knowing it may be the last time we are together for a year. There is an awkward silence lurking in the air.

She says quietly, "I feel empty." There is nothing I can say. It seems like she is caught in a cold, dark place. I wish I could help her.

I stop driving and pull over to hold her for a moment. Then we continue. We pull into the parking lot where she left her car. On the car stereo, I play the song she had picked out as our song that summer. It's called, "I Won't Give Up On Us" by Jayson Mraz

At her car, she gives me a large poster of Krishna and Radha. It is a scene with the timeless lovers kneeling on a plush couch courting each other in the jungle. We hold each other and look up at the stars. I let her know that we can always look up and we will see the same stars. In this way, we can still be with each other. As she sits in her car, the streetlight mingles with the shadows on her face, and her silhouette reveals a gorgeous smile. This is what I choose to remember as we part. ■

CHAPTER 37

The Aftermath

I am lost in a fog for the next few days. I continue to sleep on The Lamb's floor on sofa cushions, but it no longer feels like I am making a grand sacrifice. I feel like a dog curling up with my wounded self-esteem. I try to get in touch with my feelings. My friend, Sunshine, suggests that I breathe into my heart and just feel, but this is too much for me to handle. I am afraid of feeling all the pain that will accompany Swan Song's rejection. I am free falling in a tailspin, surrounded by dark, dismal clouds.

In Vermont, I visit a beautiful, stone Catholic church that one would expect to find tucked away in France. It sits atop a hill, amidst rolling fields, surrounded by gorgeous views of the green mountains. Swan Song and I once met here for a picnic in the flower gardens. I recall our lazy afternoon. We both sprawled comfortably on a blanket. My head rested in her lap. We had read Rumi poems to each other as we ate chunks of cheese and fresh strawberries. Now this is all in the past. I load my chanupa with kinnikinnick and securely set it in the Y of a tree branch.

Nearby is the Stepping Stone Spa. I walk over to take a sauna. During this same time, Swan Song is far away, participating in a sweat lodge ceremony. I sage myself and enter the sauna. In my mind, this will be my sweat lodge ceremony. I bring in my drum to chant and sing Native American songs. I do four rounds in the sauna. I raise the heat until it is unbearably hot. My heart and spirit are torn. I welcome the physical pain as relief. I better understand how My Native Brother felt during his eagle hang at the sun dance ceremony. I pray that Swan Song's heart will continue to be open and filled with love. I pray for my own healing. When I go into my heart, I do not feel pain; I feel only love towards Swan Song. I have a burning desire to be with her, as always. But I know it's not going to be that way for a long time. I console myself to keep going forward.

When I am finished in the sauna, I go back to retrieve the chanupa from the tree branch. The late afternoon sun is shining down as I walk through the grassy field by the stone church. The view through the valley looks out towards Willoughby Gap. I find comfort in gazing out at the two mountaintops. As a child, I imagined they were like two scoops of ice cream. They are no longer scoops of ice cream, but two mountains. We both grew up. I have fond memories of being with friends on the beach, hiking up the surrounding mountains, and biking along the shore.

As I stand surveying the view, my mind is drawn back to the last time I was there. It was with Swan Song just after she returned from Europe. We had our big talk on Devil's Rock. After that day, something shifted. I was never really the same. Before the deception, I had trusted her fully and completely. But on that day, I felt like she wanted to pull me into that dark, obscure place with her — into her deceptive web, with all her honey-coated lies. She has the power to rip apart my soul because I have given her the key to my heart.

It feels wrong. I love Swan Song and she loves me. She is far away with Chief Thunder Cloud — the man she told me she was leaving. It doesn't make sense. Why did she tell me she was available and unattached? Why did she come to Costa Rica? Why did we make love? Could it be she is afraid to let herself take the free fall that is required to really fall in love again after her heart has been broken. All I know for sure is that when we're together, we are both vibrantly alive. I also know Swan Song will not be in my life for the next year.

A refreshing breeze moves the grass in ripples across the field. I observe it dance and swirl. I let my sadness float away with the wind. After the sauna, I feel pure and ready to pray with the chanupa. I locate a spot at the breach of a hill and settle down on a woven blanket to gaze out at Willoughby Gap. Here I find the tranquility to say my prayers.

There is a life-size, snow-white statue of Jesus with both hands raised up toward heaven in front of the church. I go up and blow smoke from the chanupa on the statue of Jesus. After returning to my car, I notice that a quarter-size Australian opal containing lightning rainbow streaks has fallen off the stem of my chanupa pipe. It's starting to get dark. Somewhat distressed, I retrace my footsteps from the tree to the field where I sat, but I don't find the stone there. Then I walk to the statue of Jesus. I find the stone lying at his feet. I am so happy to find it that I hug the statue of Jesus.

During my overflowing joy, I whisper my deepest prayer to Him, "Jesus, please bring Swan Song back into my life."

I know I must go on. I must be a man about it. My thoughts are fuzzy and my whole purpose in life is unclear. My world has been shaken. I felt somewhere deep in Swan Song's heart, she wanted to be with me. I am the man she loves. We had an immediate connection the first moment we met. As our connection grew, I began to doubt if I ever truly loved anyone prior to her. Swan Song and I understand and connect with each other on so many levels. I sadly accept that she is not ready to join me.

Now I am much more aware of the harshness in the world. Before, I would notice the beauty; now I am drawn to the lack of beauty — the cold despair and desolation of being forsaken. It feels like I have been cast onto the dark side of the moon.

The best therapy I can find is scraping and salting the coyote skin behind The Lamb's senior housing apartment. When

I am preparing the skin, somewhere in my mind I can hear the coyotes howling. At that moment, even a longing from our past is better than the empty, hollow feelings that reside in my heart.

I needed to know to what degree Swan Song was willing to stand up for our love. I have her answer. I must respect her decision, even though it's not what I want. Given her situation, the odds were probably not in my favor. I need not take her rejection as a personal attack on my self-esteem. I am still a worthy person. There is no need for me to get depressed or angry. She is not ready for marriage. She is not available for that kind of a relationship. She chose the most appropriate action to bring her what she felt would be the most happiness in her future.

If my actions were purely to meet my own needs, then I would be devastated. For me, the next level was to provide Swan Song with the beautiful experience of marriage — the way it's intended. If I expect Swan Song to try to please me or act in a certain way, I am constricting our relationship. I want us both to be free, even if that means we are not together.

An orange tree will naturally blossom and offer fruit. We may think this is our fruit tree and that it's intended to serve us. But if the fruit is not picked or lies on the ground uneaten, it's an offering gladly accepted by animals, birds, worms, ants, and the earth. My offering to share my life with Swan Song is not in vain. The orange tree is not attached to or trying to control the results. If I can learn to give like the orange tree, then I will be at peace.

RETURNING THE DESERT OASIS

My reality is that I am holding in my hand a very expensive engagement ring. I no longer have a car, and I have scraped the bottom of the barrel for cash. I humbly stay another few days with family and friends. I call and explain to Shellie, at Kokopelli Jewelers, the sad situation.

She empathetically says, "I can't believe she said no."

She knows I am in an emotionally tender place.

I reluctantly ask her, "Is returning the ring an option?"

By now, we have had numerous conversations. I remind her of a friend in Boston. Shellie speaks to the owner and he grants permission for my custom ring to be returned, minus 10% for their service and the shipping costs.

When I consider returning the ring, I start to cry. I went through so much to get it for Swan Song.

I tell Shelly, "I need time to make sure this is what I want to do." The ring captured what I wanted to express from my heart but could not with words. I am having trouble letting it go.

I call Swan Song and say, "I am considering returning the engagement ring. I need your help to make this decision. If there is any chance that one day you will wear this ring, then I need to know it now." Instead of answering on the phone, she writes me a letter.

Swan Song's Letter

The ceremony you created, the setting, the ring — all of it so beautiful and from the heart. Here now, I need to share my truth with you. Please hear my heart. The custom of surprising a woman with a ring is beautiful, romantic, and fabulous. But for me it's not complete if it comes before there has been in-depth discussions and agreement about a lifetime commitment together — that beautiful work of going into this consciously and together — every step of the way. In this way I have not understood this custom.

Working things through, together, in decisions that concern us both is vital for me. Coming to a decision of marriage, for me, needs to take time and lots of life experience and talking and working through issues around things together. I just want your heart to be safe and cared for through this, since you went into such a vulnerable place with me. Even given everything I've been telling you, I need to be just friends with you right now.

You are so precious. You know what you mean to me, how I love you. This is really not about you at all. I want you to know how deeply you touched me. How amazing it was to be with you on that mountaintop, prayer flags waving, conch shell, love box, ring, and feathers. What devastates me is that it came at a time when I couldn't answer with a 'YES!' But yes is not the authentic response I can give in my situation. How devastating, not only to you, but to me. I hear you needed to do it for you. You wanted to let me know. For me: I am sorry this couldn't have come in a conversation and, if our lives moved us in this direction ever again, a big proposal would have come when we were both sure we were saying yes on every level.

Her responding letter did not remove all my reasonable doubt about returning the ring. Is she saying at a different time she might say yes? I need clarity before I make this big decision. Then I receive a text from her.

It reads, "If you need the money, then return the ring."

Her text has provided me with thirty minutes worth of courage. It is enough time to repack the ring and mail it back. I don't hesitate. There is a park in the center of my quaint Vermont town, with a bandstand in the center, surrounded by old maple trees. I somberly walk to the post office that is stationed at one corner of the park. I stand in front of the chest-high, gray counter surrounded by red and blue priority mailer envelopes. I gently place the glimmering, gold Desert Oasis diamond ring with the turquoise stones on either side, back into its original hard, ring case. I work slowly and mindfully, attempting to observe my movements.

My real feelings stay outside the post office. They hide somewhere behind a maple tree. The top and bottom of the ring case are perfectly covered on the inside with cream-colored silk cloth. I close it and place the case in a small cardboard box and seal it with packing tape. I surround this box with bubble wrap and place it, along with the appraisal letter declaring the value of the diamond, into a toaster-size box. I insure it and mail it back to the Kokopelli Jewelers. There is no need for rush delivery. Soon it will be cast back into the jewelry store case with all the other engagement rings. The ring is being given back, like a mother dropping off her unwanted baby at the adoption agency, with underlying hopes that somebody will give it the love and care it deserves.

I leave the post office and walk to the opposite side of the park where there is a quaint, old library. I am out of minutes on my cell phone and borrow The Lamb's cell to make another call to Shellie at Kokopelli Jewelers.

I stand in the middle of the park and say, "I have made my decision to return the ring." I spot my feelings peeking out from behind a maple tree. I motion with my finger for them to come get back inside my body. Like a disobedient child, they shake their heads and duck behind the tree. They listen in the distance like a child eavesdropping on a fearful grown-up conversation.

Not knowing the torment I have gone through to make my decision, Shellie asks, "Are you sure you want to return the ring? A woman can change her mind, you know!"

I speak slowly in a low growl, "Shelly, take the ring back."

Later, I receive a sympathy card from Shelly at Kokopelli along with a refund check for the ring.

She writes, "Words can't say how sorry I am to hear she said no. But hopefully sometime in the future she will change her mind and say yes!"

It seems my luck is running out along with my mom's cell phone minutes. The library is only open every other day. Today is one of those sunny but cold fall days, and it's just my luck that the library is closed. I balance my laptop on a wooden book-return box and use the library WiFi to make a Skype call to my Omega life coach, Nora Queesting.

She receives my call and says, "I am at the airport, waiting for my plane. We can talk until they start to board."

I bring her up to speed.

"I proposed to Swan Song and she said No... No... No... I just mailed the engagement ring back to the jewelry store."

She says, "Take a few breaths and feel what is going on inside your heart."

My feelings start to sneak around the corner of the library and they take a running leap and dive back into my body.

I quietly say, "I feel hurt and disconnected. I am a mess, completely undone. I want to cry, but it's too hard to do."

She acknowledges, "You took bold and courageous steps by expressing your feelings to Swan Song."

I rapidly say, "Swan Song said she is not ready for marriage. She said maybe she will *date* me in a year. We are still communicating, but she has left the state."

Nora gives me worthy advice, "Right now you need to focus on yourself and what you need. It's not productive to get caught up in thoughts about Swan Song."

I say, "Okay, I will try to take care of myself."

She asks, "What is it that you need right now?"

After a moment to get in touch, I say, "I find myself desperately wishing I could hug my dog, Thunder, in Costa Rica. That is what I need." ∎

CHAPTER 38

Faith, Hope, and Love

With the ring refund, I purchase a one-way ticket for Costa Rica and leave the next Saturday morning. I rent an apartment in Heredia near where Thunder is located in a kennel. I need to settle down for a spell and pull myself together. I focus on improving my Spanish and getting in some quality walks, hugs, and play time with Thunder. I start to get in touch with what I really need. I join a local gym and regularly attend yoga, spinning, and Zumba classes. I need to stay grounded and remain flexible and strong in my body and mind. I lift weights a few times a week. Exercise helps clear my mind, and the Latino women in this gym are tough and beautiful distractions. To pass the time, I watch them do pushups and side planks. They lift one arm toward the sky in between rounds. I have no desire to be in a relationship, even with the gorgeous Latino women that surround me. There is currently no room for any other woman in my heart.

I push myself at the gym to physically and mentally get beyond what has happened between Swan Song and me. I try to keep myself busy. Being far away in a foreign country, my senses are hyper-alert, because I need to combat my loneliness. My feelings oscillate between extreme highs and extreme lows, with long, stable periods of the in-between. During all these times, I am nurturing a relationship with myself. But Swan Song captured my heart. I place her framed picture on a decorated corner stand in the kitchen. Beside it, I keep a fresh red rose in a cup.

We agree to take a month without communicating to let ourselves process the marriage proposal. We call each other a few days before Christmas. I have let her know how I feel by proposing to her. I suggest that she initiates the conversations as we go forward, so it will be at her slow, turtle pace.

After two weeks, she wants to discuss the marriage proposal. I listen to her intently, then share my side. Every situation we go through is a process. Often we create false assumptions and don't understand each other's perspective or motivation until we talk about it afterwards.

She begins with an emotional waver in her voice, "A woman should not accept an engagement ring unless it's her intention to marry the man. I needed to make my decision on the spot!"

I say, "It seems contrary to your nature to make a rapid, on-the-spot decision about something as important as marriage. I can understand your reasoning, but I was counting on its being a process."

I sense that her emotions are somewhat frozen, but she has the genuine desire to work through it. She says, "I told you in the past I need to discuss marriage before it happens."

It did happen, but not to the degree she needed. I guess that is my fault. I was unaware that my marriage proposal would push her buttons.

I say, "Would you like me to explain the reasons why I proposed to you?"

She enthusiastically says, "Yes!"

I say, "It was the best way I could express how much I love you. I assumed that your Caring for the Heart counseling session would heal your past marriage issues. I was wrong."

She compassionately says, "We did work on my past marriage and abandonment issues. But I need more sessions to resolve them completely."

Through our process, I learn to be more sensitive toward

Swan Song. Through our conversations, I continue to listen and support what she needs to heal. Meanwhile, I continue to figure out what I need to do to take care of myself. I thought my future with Swan Song would be resolved and I would either marry her or my life would take a drastic turn without her. Neither has happened yet.

As a way to express my locked-up emotions, I create a one-hour video that guides me to laugh, cry, meditate, and worship. Through it, I am able to release many of my hurt and confused feelings. But I am still hanging onto a thread of hope, waiting to find out what will happen with Swan Song. She did say, "I *may* be ready to date you in a year."

FAITH, HOPE, AND LOVE

Around this time, the coyote skin I had nailed to the rafters to dry in a shed at Helen Keller's camp in Vermont has somehow wriggled back to life, jumped down, and run back into the woods. Before the proposal, it was my intention to send it to Swan Song, but now it feels awkward to offer her any gift after she has rejected the most precious one I could offer her: our life together. The coyote pelt vanished, like her affection, without leaving a track in the snow. I don't expect either will return.

Everything happens for a reason. I don't understand it all, but I do have faith in love. I want to write about love, yet Paul from the Bible has covered it rather elegantly. All we need to do is read it. The Bible guides me through the most intimate parts of my life.

> "And now these three remain: faith, hope, and love. But the greatest of these is love."   *(1 Corinthians 13:13 NIV)*

And we all know how Paul defines love?

> "Love is patient. Love is kind. It does not want what

belongs to others. It does not brag. It's not proud. It's not rude. It does not look out for its own interests. It does not easily become angry. It does not keep track of other people's wrongs. Love is not happy with evil. But it's full of joy when the truth is spoken. It always protects. It always trusts. It always hopes. It never gives up."

(1 Corinthians 13: 4-7 NIV)

This is amazing. My experience with Swan Song has led me down a long, winding spiritual path to discover the truth about love. Paul and I have learned much about love from Jesus. We both are sharing it in our own way. I am starting to understand… God is love. Love is in Jesus. Jesus is in me. I am love. Therefore, God and I are connected by love. God loves me and I love God.

This passage on love is worth reading twice. For fun I have included the Message version, which I slightly modified by adding the word (Love). If you want an additional perspective, after you read it once, replace the word "love" with "Jesus."

"So, no matter what I say, what I believe, and what I do, I'm bankrupt without love.
Love never gives up.
Love cares more for others than for self.
Love doesn't want what it doesn't have.
Love doesn't strut,
(Love) Doesn't have a swelled head,
(Love) Doesn't force itself on others,
(Love) Isn't always 'me first,'
(Love) Doesn't fly off the handle,
(Love) Doesn't keep score of the sins of others,
(Love) Doesn't revel when others grovel,
(Love) Takes pleasure in the flowering of truth,
(Love) Puts up with anything,

(Love) Trusts God always,
(Love) Always looks for the best,
(Love) Never looks back,
  but keeps going to the end."
(1 Corinthians 13:4-7 MSG)

I recall my last interaction with my life coach, Nora Queesting, at Omega. We decided to take a canoe from the beach back to her cottage. We talked casually about the situation with Swan Song. As we were pulling up to the shore, I desperately exclaimed, "I can't wait forever for her!"

Nora hopped out of the front of the boat and stood on the shore with her hands on her hips. I was still in the boat. She quickly refuted it by saying, "One of your options is you can wait forever!"

I paused, having never considered it before.

I took a deep breath and sighed. Then I said, "Yeah, you're right. One of my options is I can wait forever."

ONE YEAR LATER

This season I am a volunteer at the Abode of the Message, a Sufi community about one hour north of Omega. At the Abode there are no turtles near the pond, which I find unusual, but there are scores of rabbits. Swan Song and her turtle energy are nowhere to be found here. She makes plans to come visit one weekend a few weeks after my arrival, but changes her plans.

One month later, I go to our favorite camping site, which has a view of a marshy pond. There are four turtles sitting on a log. It might sound crazy, but to me it indicates that here is where Swan Song will appear. I make a campfire and fix my dinner. I call to let Swan Song know where I am and invite her to join me. She stops by that evening. We don't discuss any serious topics, but instead simply enjoy being together again as we sit in front of the fire. When it gets late, she drives back to Omega.

It has been almost a year since my marriage proposal. I recall her saying, "I *may* date you in a year." It is time to find out if she was serious about it.

I ask her, "Do you want to go out for dinner and a movie on my birthday?"

She replies enthusiastically, "Yes! I would love to." I am delighted and rather surprised that she said "Yes!"

The next day, she reads a prior email I sent her. I had written with a request that she tell Chief Thunder Cloud if we are going to be together, especially as a date. She texts me stating she has changed her mind. She no longer wants to go on a date. In her rollercoaster fashion, I get her answer.

SACRUM MELTDOWN III

I am not sure if my body can recover from a third sacrum meltdown. It has taken three to six months to recover after the first two, and the symptoms never completely go away. The first meltdown occurred when Swan Song ceased communication with me for the month after Costa Rica; the second was a year ago, after I left her at Omega.

A few weeks later, Swan Song and I plan to rendezvous again, for a second time, during a three-day weekend at our favorite camping spot. I have some anxiety about being together because, this time, I know we will have time to share our deeper feelings. Just prior to our meeting, Swan Song informs me that Chief Thunder Cloud and she are still partners, and her desire is for us to stay friends. I am still in love with Swan Song. This might be our final goodbye.

The day before our second meeting, I am working in an awkward position to drain the gas from the lawnmower at the Abode and pull the muscles in my lower back. One possibility is that these muscles are more vulnerable, but I know what is happening; my sacrum is having its third meltdown. I am anticipating our last goodbye. Initially, it's not as crippling as it was in the past. At least it didn't dislocate my sacrum and ribs this time. I tell Swan Song I won't be able to make it this weekend because I need time to heal my back.

That day I stay at the Abode in a retreat cabin doing stretches and breathing exercises for my back. I make an attempt to contact a friend, Izabella, to hang out, but I can't stop thinking about Swan Song. I can't even bring myself to take the steps to call Izabella, and I abort the attempt after a few tries.

LOVE VERSUS FEAR

I know my emotional attachment to Swan Song is unhealthy. I text Swan Song and ask if I can call in healing for us. She grants her permission. I pray to Jesus to come and heal our hearts. My heart is filled with frustration and resentment. I feel upset because my heart's desire is to be with her, but as long as the situation with Chief Thunder Cloud and her remains the same, I am in the same stale predicament.

That evening, I do a Caring for the Heart counseling session. I see a vision of my heart covered with snakes. Jesus comes and picks off the snakes to reveal a bright luminous heart. I can feel it burning and glowing. Then, he visits Swan Song's heart. I see a black, greasy sludge surrounding her heart. It's fear. I ask Jesus to provide her with some healing.

Love has no obligations nor expectations. With fear, we are expected to do things, and when our expectations are not met, it hurts. We may even blame others. If at a given moment one is living with more fear than love in their heart, then it's hard to respect anything, including yourself.

Jesus takes a fire hose and sprays the sludge off Swan Song's heart. It reveals a bright, glowing heart filled with love.

After my counseling session, I feel a shift. I am now able to call up Izabella. I leave a message inviting her to come visit me at the retreat cabin on the mountaintop at the Abode. This is a strong indication of a breakthrough.

Swan Song had once given me a quarter-size, red, transparent stone heart, which I carry in my medicine bag. I take it out and I take off the amber ring I first bought for myself when I arrived in Costa Rica. Buying the ring comforted me after being rejected from the marriage proposal. To symbolize letting go of any attachment to the situation with Swan Song, I take both items and toss them over the edge of a suspended wooden bridge that is known at the Abode as The Bridge to Nowhere. In the distance there are fireworks. It's a celebration. I am no longer as emotionally attached. I know it. I feel it. The best confirmation is when I return to my cabin. Izabella is sitting on the porch of the cabin. We chat while drinking tea and play a few songs from our cell phones. It is a comfortably pleasant evening. ■

CHAPTER 39

The Final Cut

DEFINING INTEGRITY

Late the next morning, Swan Song sends me a text. She writes, "I am at our camping spot starting a fire." I can't believe it. She still went there without me. I tell her, "My back is slightly better. I am coming."

Beloved
   "I slept but my heart was awake. Listen! My beloved is knocking:"
Lover
   "Open to me, my sister, my darling, my dove, my flawless one. My head is drenched with dew, my hair with the dampness of the night."
Beloved
   "I have taken off my robe — must I put it on again? I have washed my feet — must I soil them again? My beloved thrust his hand through the latch-opening; my heart began to pound for him. I arose to open for my beloved, and my hands dripped with myrrh, my fingers with flowing myrrh, on the handles of the bolt. I opened for my beloved, but my beloved had left; he was gone. My heart sank at his departure. I looked for him but did not find him. I called him but he did not answer. The watchmen found me as they made their rounds in the city. They beat me, they bruised me; they

took away my cloak, those watchmen of the walls! Daughters of Jerusalem, I charge you — if you find my beloved, what will you tell him? Tell him I am faint with love."

(Song of Songs 5:2-8 NIV)

I make the hour drive and meet Swan Song at our camping spot beside the pond. I arrive late in the afternoon and find her sitting cross-legged in front of the fire. She is wearing dark mala beads around her neck. She is in what she calls "stillness" and requests that I don't talk too much. She has just finished a weekend program immersed in shamanic teachings.

She enthusiastically tells me a little about it, "We, as humans, are evolving consciously at a rapid rate."

Eventually our discussion winds back to talking about our being friends. We both know we need clarity around what that means. I am not sure if I can handle being just friends. I am still feeling too much "in love" with her. Whenever we are together in private, we end up clinging together in an embrace. It provides boundless comfort. I am not sure if either of us wants to or has the ability to restrain that desire.

Suddenly, our conversation takes a feverish turn.

She confidently explains, "I am clear about my decision to continue in a partnership with Chief Thunder Cloud."

She repeats the word "integrity" again and again. It begins to feel like an argument.

She sighs and says, "I was in love with Chief Thunder Cloud in the beginning."

I cautiously ask, "Are you in love with him now?

She says quietly, "I would rather not answer that question."

She explains, "My decision to be in a relationship does not require being in love. My decision takes into consideration what will most benefit those in our community."

I cannot fathom being in a relationship for any reason other than love. She has a right to be in a relationship with whomever she chooses, for her own reasons. I will respect her decision, even though it breaks my heart.

We apologize for what felt like the start of an argument. She is sitting on a rock near a tree, watching the fire. I bend down on my knees next to her and bring my head close to hers. I understand her. In her list of life's priorities, our love is near the bottom. Our love is being washed away as no more than a forlorn illusion. I relinquish my dream of our being together. My hope has vanished. I feel dismal.

I lie down on a blanket by the fire. She massages my back, which is in pain from the drive and hauling all my gear to our campsite. Afterwards I massage her feet and hands. She loves to have her itty-bitty feet massaged.

She says, "I can't stay all night."

I quietly reply, "I understand."

Now, it's all about parting in a delicate way.

We cling together in my tent as we have always done, holding each other for the next three hours. I feel her restraining herself, trying to turn and pull away, not wanting to let her passion rise. Underneath, a part of her heart wants nothing more than to surrender to the moment. After a while, she falls asleep in my arms. I lie wide awake, holding her in the still of the night. I can feel her heartbeat near mine. I am aware that any sudden movement could nudge her awake and cause her to flee like a deer back into the darkness of the woods.

Being together feels different after nearly one year apart. My heart and hers have had some time to process and heal. We restrain from kissing. My lips were always elated to be near hers. They don't understand why hers are suddenly off-limits. This is where she has drawn her line. It is how she defines integrity. But I know the sad truth; *for integrity to truly exist, we must cease being together.* Lips or not, I am still drawn to her magnetically, but after tonight, I am no longer satisfied being physically intimate unless Swan Song is willing to tell Chief Thunder Cloud. I will no longer compromise the love and respect that I deserve. Nonetheless, my soul breathes a sigh. I have waited a year for this moment. All I have wanted in my heart was to hold her close again.

Part of me is relishing every moment and another part is regretting our inevitable parting. She softly stirs and awakes in my arms. Swan Song discreetly pulls herself away from our embrace and slips out of the tent. She stands by the fire, somber and sleepy. Her hair is disheveled. She vanishes silently into the darkness. She's not coming back. No matter how it happens, the final goodbye is always a dark night for the soul.

(This is the place in the story where I cry!)

Dark Night of the Soul

On a dark night, kindled in love with yearnings, – oh, happy chance! I went forth without being observed, my house being now at rest. In darkness and secure, by the secret ladder, disguised –oh happy chance!

In darkness and in concealment, my house being now at rest. In the happy night, in secret, when none saw me, nor I beheld aught, without light or guide, save that which burned in my heart. This light guided me more surely than the light of noonday. To the place where he (well I knew who!) was awaiting me –

A place where none appeared. Oh, night that guided me, Oh night more lovely than the dawn, Oh, night that joined Beloved and Lover, Lover transformed in the Beloved!

Upon my flowery breast, kept for himself alone, there he stayed sleeping, and I caressed him. And the fanning of the cedars made a breeze. The breeze blew from the turret as I parted his locks; with his gentle hand he wounded my neck. And caused all my senses to be suspended.

I remained, lost in oblivion; my face reclined on

the Beloved. All ceased and I abandoned myself, leaving my cares forgotten among the lilies.

— *Saint John of the Cross*

THE CAFÉ IN RED HOOK

We plan to meet briefly the next morning at JJ's café in Red Hook. I wait for her at a corner table by a window with my chamomile tea and a blueberry muffin. That morning, I had walked around in the forest for hours, recapping what she said the night before and all she has told me over the past three years. I am trying to fit together all the pieces in my mind. Perhaps my mind can comfort my heart, which is at a loss in this matter of love. I want to get closure and clarity for myself. I feel it will aid me to explain what I understand to be the current situation regarding her past marriage, her relationship with Chief Thunder Cloud and with me.

Swan Song arrives, but tells me she can only stay for fifteen minutes before she has to zip off to work. With this time limit in mind, I need to get to the point.

I rapidly say, "I want to tell you everything the way I see it, and if I am wrong about anything, please interject and correct me."

While I am talking, she stops me short to explain that our commitment as friends has changed. She explains the new deal: "We will now heal ourselves and forget about sharing any of the messy emotional processes you go through." I am taken aback; our commitment as friends changed drastically. I am starting to feel a sudden chill. When did she decide this?

She adds, "And don't pray for me anymore." Ouch, that hurt!

I continue to quickly recap what I believe are the facts Swan Song has told me. I say, "Chief Thunder Cloud is your partner, but he has no desire to ever marry you."

She says, slightly irritated, "That is not true. There is a

possibility that he could ask me to marry him. It has not happened, but it's possible."

I am flabbergasted. This is a big deal! I probably would not have proposed to Swan Song if I thought there was a chance that Chief Thunder Cloud had an inclination to marry her.

Swan Song stands up from the table and starts to shake her whole body up and down in jittery movements, like she is having a seizure. She couldn't care less about what anybody in the café is thinking.

She says in a jittery voice, "I need to release some energy."

She is getting anxious over our conversation, and her fifteen-minute time limit has nearly expired. I shorten our conversation to briefly touch upon the essential points.

Afterwards, she concludes with a breeze of a remark, "Your perspective of my life is a pinpoint of my reality." Then she gives me a slight smile, spins around, and departs. I watch her step out the door and walk down the street. Her wavy, dirty-blond hair is floating up and down. My eyes are soft. They still desire to savor her walking away.

FULL CIRCLE

I have come full circle. I am sitting in the café in Red Hook. It is the town where I first arrived to meet Pandora. My journey with Swan Song feels like it's nearing completion.

I begin to question Jesus, but He stops me in my tracks.

I am reminded of when Jesus asked, "If I asked, would you let go of Swan Song?"

After much turmoil I said, "Yes"

There is a higher purpose to all that has happened. It is surely beyond my own understanding.

I turn to the book *Jesus Calling* by Sarah Young. It reads,

> *"Trust me enough to let things happen without striving to predict and control. Relax and refresh yourself in the light of my everlasting love."*

My faith in Jesus is restored. He loves me and wants what is best for me.

After all I experienced around the marriage proposal, I came away with more integrity and higher standards for being in a relationship. Foremost, I know now how important it is to love and respect myself. If I allow our escapade to continue, then I am not doing so. I recognize and accept that her ways and mine were deceptive and disrespectful to Chief Thunder Cloud.

I have been told to never apologize for what I write. I need to break that rule. Chief Thunder Cloud was my friend. I apologize for how I deceived him. I am sorry for the pain and discomfort I caused due to my entanglement with Swan Song.

BURGER HILL

I leave the café and drive to Burger Hill. I return to the place I used to go with Swan Song. It seems like a lifetime ago when I kidnapped her to drum and sing, another time when we had healing ceremonies around her relationships, and again, a third time, as part of her woman's rites of passage.

It's a sunny fall day, and I stare out at the mountains to contemplate and absorb all that has occurred between Swan Song and me. I write a letter to Swan Song. I let her know our time together is complete. We have come full circle. I thank her for all her love, our fond memories, her sweet cards and gifts with pine branches on top, her smile, and the precious moments that we held each other close. Our connection is too precious and meaningful to erase my memories. I want to cherish them, so for now, I will continue to fondly wear the trade-bead necklace she gave me. I let her know that our spirits will meet again in another life, as we have done so many times before.

I roll the letter up as a scroll. When I returned the Desert Oasis ring, I also returned the small wooden box with the word "Love" carved in it, which I had purchased from a local jewelry store. There were too many emotions wrapped up in that box to keep it, but I did hold on to the small piece of soft, yellow fabric, which my mother had tenderly cut to wrap up the ring. I could handle keeping this small yellow piece, and I have carried it for the last year in my medicine bag, close to my heart. I take out the piece of soft, yellow fabric and use it to wrap around the center of her scroll to hold it tightly in place. I place the letter to rest in a protected hole in the heart of a big, old maple tree.

I am standing at the top of the knoll surrounded with rolling grassy fields with tall, bare, scraggly trees along the outer edge. It reminds me of a European landscape with trees formed by an artist's thin paintbrush. I am here to find my stillness. As I peer up, a bald eagle soars thirty feet overhead in the direction of the Hudson River. I can clearly see the details in the individual snowy white feathers that circle the neck and its tail feathers. I watch in awe, accepting this eagle as my confirmation to pray with the chanupa for Swan Song and Chief Thunder Cloud. I blessed them when their relationship began. I shall continue to send my blessing to Swan Song and the man she has chosen to be her partner: Chief Thunder Cloud.

The first time I saw a bald eagle in this area, I was on my way to the sweat lodge with Swan Song and My Native Brother, seven years ago. This eagle is another sign that we have come full circle. I step up on a flat granite stone with the surrounding mountaintops carved upon it and press the chanupa stem into my heart. I step in clockwise circles, chanting in a Native American language toward the surrounding valleys and mountains.

I feel tingling all over my body. It's the medicine man, Wichahcala, who Swan Song prayed to in her prior life as Wicahpi Ska (White Star) to be reunited with Cetan Luta (Red Hawk). He appears to me in a spiritual vision. Yes! It feels like I have come full circle. During this life, Swan Song and I were united in a way that brought us both healing. I hope the spirits of Wicahpi Ska and Cetan Luta are together. I am not sure. It feels like something is still keeping them apart.

He concludes by saying, "Iyuskinyan Wancinyankelo, Cetan Ohitika," which translates, "I am happy to have known you, Brave Hawk." "Toksha ake wacinyanktin ktelo, I shall see you again."

I text Swan Song about the scroll and send a message, "I am at Burger Hill. A bald eagle just flew overhead. I am sending a blessing for you and Chief Thunder Cloud. I send you my endless love."

She responds kindly, "And my love eternal. I see you. You are ready to soar like that eagle. Be unfettered in every regard and spread your beautiful wings wide! You are a blessing in my life. I treasure the work we have done and are doing in this and other lifetimes. Thank you for the gift of you. May we always have each other's highest good a priority. I love you."

CHAPTER 40

The Shaman: Charcoal

EVICTION FROM THE HEART

Once a relationship ends, it's not really over. It takes time to get over the heartache. I will always feel love for Swan Song. Sometimes I get sucked back into believing that maybe, just maybe, our relationship could work out. This might be caused by soul ties that need to be energetically broken.

Thinking of her is less of an issue when I am busy in Costa Rica, but now after another winter, I have returned to the United States, and it feels like she is living inside my heart again. Lately I think of Swan Song when I am in a dreamy state, often before sleeping or upon awakening. Sometimes I feel like I am her. I like the feeling of light that radiates from her heart. When you get that close, your spirits merge. But I can't go on in this way forever.

If Swan Song lives in my heart, then she has a comfortable abode. I don't know if my heart really wants her to leave or if I can undo my cellular structure, which has relinquished itself to be devoted solely to her. It was a prerequisite I imposed upon myself prior to proposing marriage, given her past circumstances.

It's unclear if we can ever be just friends, but I am willing to try. I call up Althea, who led the healing class at Omega that cleared out all my past relationships. I am wondering if she can help me resolve this current one. I want to know if Swan

Song and I can be friends; if not, I need help to remove her from my heart.

I tell her my situation. She says, "You need to call Swan Song and find out if she wants to be your friend: yes or no. Then ask her if she is open to the possibility of being in a relationship in the future. You need clarity, without a wishy-washy answer, to know how to proceed."

I say, "She is pretty good at being unclear with me because she does not want to hurt my feelings."

She says, "If she is unsure, then find out what it will take to give you a solid yes or no answer."

I say, "The last time we spoke, she told me that she is not available for a relationship and that Chief Thunder Cloud is her partner."

She retorts, "Swan Song is not in a *real* relationship with Chief Thunder Cloud. They just work together."

I say, "Yeah, I know."

She says, "You call Swan Song, find out the answers, then call me back."

My stomach starts to churn. Althea is direct and I need to know where I stand. I feel reluctant about calling Swan Song. When we texted a few days ago, she told me she was not wanting to communicate for two weeks.

I go for a walk up by the cornfield and stand under a shelter. It's raining lightly. Then it starts to come down in hard pellets. I am practicing what I want to say. Maybe I can just leave a message. Lightning strikes with a crack in the cornfield, followed by a huge *boom* of thunder.

I think back to my marriage day with Forevermore and how thunder spoke on that day. God's got my attention! He may be trying to say no matter what I do, Swan Song is a no go.

Then my cell rings. Hopefully it's God calling to explain. Nope! It's God using Althea to explain.

She says, "I only have a minute, I just spoke with Swan Song. I told her that you were planning to call her and she became furious. I asked her if there was a possibility for a future relationship with you. She said no. I asked her if she wanted to be your friend and she said she had already explained her answer. It's no."

I say, "So it's clear. There is no possibility of a future relationship. She does not even want to be friends. Thank you. I know now what I need to do. I will evict her from my heart."

She says, "Did you say *evict*?"

I reply, "Yes I will *evict* her from my heart." Evict is the word that fits. It means force somebody to leave where they are staying when they are not willing to pay what is due.

I know what I must do. I need to make the final cut.

To seek some physical relief, I go to a local sports massage therapist. My muscles can barely budge. They are starting to become rigid and hard. I know the root cause is emotional. The massage therapist tells me about a shaman, Charcoal, and how she helped him. But, he says, he does not believe all the past-life stuff she told him. She said he was a murderer. He smirks with an evil grimace and says, "My massage is going to hurt you, but you will thank me for it later."

CHARCOAL: THE INVOCATION

I make an appointment with Charcoal. I am ready to have Swan Song removed from my heart. I buy Charcoal a gift at a garden store. It's a large, golden, clay sun with one eye that appears to be winking. There are gemstones in a circle around the outer edge. I have a strong feeling that Charcoal will remove Swan Song from my heart. My intuition says she can do it. Surely, this will warrant a nice gift.

I am led through a back room and up a set of stairs by a spry 71-year-old woman, no taller than my chest. She proudly lets me know that she just returned from hiking in the Sedona Mountains. It's renowned as a highly-spiritual place. I am glad she is feeling elevated. She will need to call forth some powerful energy to successfully perform this open-heart, spiritual surgery.

We enter her dimly-lit room. The smell of incense hangs thickly in the air. There is one huge altar table with a large, white porcelain statue of Buddha cupping a blue glass marble in folded hands that rest upon his lap. I am glad to see a glittering card of Jesus standing at the front of her altar near the pillar candles. The whole room is carefully decorated with an array of spiritual paraphernalia. I am sure many were personal gifts from other clients. Each one, like my gift, has a meaning that is relevant to her.

She sits me down in a swiveling, banana-shaped chair covered with a sheet, and places a pillow behind my neck.

I look surprised and ask, "Is this where I will be when you perform my treatment?"

She asks, "Are you here for a reflexology session?"

I sigh and reply "No! I am not sure you can help me."

I explain the trauma in my sacrum that was caused by my last relationship.

I softly say, "She is still in my heart. I want her removed."

She confidently says, "I can do a Reiki session from head to toe, but it's God who will do the healing. The Arch Angel Michael will come with his blue sword of light and slash away."

I enthusiastically say, "Now, that is why I am here."

She has the kind look in her eyes of a grandmother; behind her spectacles is a small, square face framed by her shoulder-length, bark-colored hair. She directs me from the banana chair to sit down in a large armchair.

She takes sage oil and pours some on my palms.

She instructs, "Rub this oil around in a circle and then inhale it deeply three times. Then I will rub a little frankincense oil on your back."

Afterwards, she sits down in a chair beside me. She says, "We will start with a meditation. Let's begin with three

Om's."

She leads by saying "Om" and I follow, but fail in my attempt to match her tone. During the second Om, I start off low but adjust to synchronize with her. On the third Om, she changes the tone in the middle and brings it up to hit an extremely high note. I join her in the tone shift. It feels like we just went down a slide on the playground.

I am sitting there meditating with my eyes closed while she starts her invocation.

She says with vigor, "I call on the Arch Angel Michael with his blue sword of light and a band of one thousand angels, Jesus and the Holy Spirit, Mother Mary, Father Sky, Mother Earth, the directions of the north, south, east, and west..."

When she is done with her rather lengthy invocation, she invites me to sit on the edge of the massage table.

She refers back to the toning, "Now wasn't that Om fun?" It was fun, but I am acting rather somber because I am here for a serious spiritual removal.

She says, "You had fun doing it. Don't you dare tell me you did not!"

I lighten up some. She lights sage and smudges me with a long turkey feather.

She says, "This sage came from South Dakota, and I only use the purest oils."

Of course, the scent of sage immediately reminds me of Swan Song and the way she would smudge herself every evening upon returning to her tent. I am feeling more comfortable. I lie on my back on her massage table as she covers me with a sheet and places a handkerchief over my eyes.

THE REIKI TREATMENT

She places an amethyst stone beneath the massage table under my crown chakra, a rose quartz stone under my heart, and a smoky quartz stone under my feet. I feel the channels in my head and feet open with a tingling sensation.

She says, "The sages and saints, healers and prophets that are working for the divine light of God are here in this room."

I can sense Althea in the room, or at the very least, her intentions and prayers for my healing are present.

Charcoal places her hands on my forehead, and I feel the heat coming through. I was not a big believer in Reiki because I never had great results with it. But today, the time is ripe. God uses Reiki as His chosen channel for my healing. It's the laying-on of hands. Thoughts of Swan Song start flashing through my mind. They are being pulled out and away in long strands. I feel the space where the grooves of her thoughts existed being filled and smoothed over with light.

I tell Charcoal, "They are working on my thoughts."

She says, "Be open to it. Twitching and yawning are signs that you are releasing. Do what you need to release the energy. Don't hold back."

Once she is done by my head, she claps her hands together, then moves on to the next spot by my neck. In my vision, I see Swan Song standing in my heart.

I ask Charcoal, "Do you want to know the name of the woman?"

She replies, "Oh Yes! What is her name?"

I feel emotions swell up as I speak, "It is…Swan Song."

Swan Song has set up camp in my heart. It's somewhat like her tent. She has made herself comfortable along with all her belongings. I need not evict her; she knows that she must go. There is no sense of urgency in her actions; she calmly starts to pack her bags. There are boxes of books, clothes, and bedding. It all goes into baskets or containers, as if she were leaving Omega at the end of the season. I often assisted her in the real world by carrying her bags and baskets to the parking lot during her weekend escapades.

In my vision, she says, "I need help carrying my bags."

I say, "I cannot help you today. There are lots of angel and light workers around; why don't you ask if they can help move your bags?"

She smiles and they willingly comply.

Lastly, her tent and bed are dismantled and hauled away. Swan Song is just standing on the empty tent platform.

I am reliving the moment along with her. We take time to absorb and release our seasons of fond memories. It's as if our past times together are being played backwards, like a movie on rewind. I twitch as I view my proposal to her on the top of Devil's Hill. Then our favorite camp spot by the pond. How we cherished our time beside that campfire. The way I held her body close to mine under my buffalo robe. Then our endless encounters at Omega. Dancing in the moonlight, her smile, the joy she radiates, the way I felt so fresh and alive in her presence. The days we spent on Burger Hill drumming and singing. And earlier when I was with her, Lost Son, and Feather Maker in her big tent. Then our first visit at my retreat space with Pandora, but instead of her coming in and giving me flowers, I hand them back to her, and she walks out the door backwards. My memories and the feelings I relate to Swan Song are being drawn out and flushed away.

She stands there on the platform alone, no regrets. She is pure and divine in her beauty, fully acknowledging and appreciating our love and friendship for all of its goodness. Charcoal claps her hands to signify that she has finished on my neck. As she begins to lower her hands down towards my heart, Swan Song fades away and disappears. I am fully present for it.

PAST LIFE KARMA

My vision of the healing does not end with Swan Song's departure, but it moves on to our past lives. The first is when we were children, as a brother and sister, trapped under a school building in India. The feelings become overwhelming. There is a part of my karma that I must release. It's dark; Swan Song and I are both trapped down low but able to crawl around. We touch each other's hands. She is the first to die. I cannot bear to go on living without her. With her death, all my hope diminishes. What I want more than life is to be with her. I choose death over life without her. This is my karmic burden. I burst out in uncontrollable tears on the table. Charcoal senses my feeling of being crushed and gives encouragement.

She says, "Keep open. Let it release. Breathe through it."

I am feeling huge shifts in my torso and continue to twitch and release. Charcoal finishes at my heart and claps. She is doing a lot of blowing and whishing away. As she progresses down my body, there is a flow of relaxation in the muscles in my chest and shoulders. When she proceeds below my heart, in my intestinal area, it feels like the corpse of a dead animal is being pulled out from my insides. As Charcoal moves toward my sacrum area, I sense we are approaching the past life we shared as Cetan Luta (Red Hawk) and Wicahpi Ska (White Star).

I politely make a request to Charcoal, "Can you smudge with sage near my sacrum?" She quickly lights up more sage and smudges my backside.

During this past life, I only see blurry glimpses in my vision, but I feel intense emotions. My past lives are still in reverse. She creates a cloud of smoke that hovers above my body as the sage is poured on thickly. Wicahpi Ska is having to console our kids about my death. I feel her anguish. She wants to be a strong mother, but she, herself, is torn up inside. I know the next thing I am going to feel is the grizzly bear's claws like a knife jabbing into my back. I am bawling like a baby on the table. It's overwhelming! The tears are running down the sides of my face. I feel the moisture of the tears gather in my left ear. I can't fully see what is happening other than a swirl of sunlight and green branches. I'm in a seamless place. Time continues to travel backwards in slow motion. Cetan Luta and Wicahpi Ska are together before he died.

At that precise moment, Charcoal yells out, "Call back your soul! You need to get your soul to come back! Do it now!

Call back your soul!"

There is a lot going on. I don't think Charcoal understands everything that is happening. And this is not the right time to explain. It's not my soul that is reuniting; it's theirs. Somehow their souls were still kept apart, even after all we have been through. Maybe this is how it all had to happen. But I know at this moment, without any doubt, their souls are reunited.

Charcoal says, "Roll over on your stomach."

She continues near my sacrum, as if the other half of the corpse of that dead animal in my intestine is now being tugged out my tailbone. I hug a pillow under my chest and continue to cry face down. But I am no longer crying over the intense emotions from the bear attack or Wicahpi Ska's sadness. Now my tears are feeling ecstatic joy for Cetan Luta and Wicahpi Ska being together.

Charcoal says, "Just keep letting it go."

The world I know is clashing around; my mind is frantically trying to figure it all out. I thought I was Cetan Luta in my past life. Yes! I had just felt the bear's claws. Our spirits are definitely separate now, and he has just reunited somewhere in the Spirit World with Wicahpi Ska. This must mean that Swan Song's spirit is also separate from Wicahpi Ska. But didn't we both live as them? I feel my soul is fully back in my body. But it is, or was, him, or a part of him. His spirit worked through me in this life to fulfill what it needed to do in the spirit realm.

Now they are together in the Spirit World, but Swan Song and I are apart in this physical world. I believe we came together as them in this physical plane because they couldn't do it in the spiritual one. That part makes sense, but I still feel confused. Why can't Swan Song and I be together? It's simply complex.

WICAHCALA'S BLESSING

Charcoal places her palms on the bottom of my feet, and my body fills with golden light. She stands up near my head and starts to chant in a Native language. I just listen to the words and let them do what they need to do. This is no normal Reiki session. It feels like Charcoal's chanting is channeling through to the medicine man, Wicahcala, who just slipped in the backdoor.

He is present to give us all his final blessing. Now that the spirits of Cetan Luta and Wicahpi Ska are reunited, his commitment to Wicahpi Ska is complete. The circle is full. Maybe he knew I could not bear to live with Swan Song in my heart. The guidance and shamanic healing provided by Charcoal and Althea and the medicine man, Wicahcala, were all orchestrated with precision. It removed Swan Song from my heart, cut our primary past karmic bonds and reunited their spirits. We are all connected to the circle: past lives, and present lives, spirits and those in the flesh. We are here to help each other. Sometimes we get to receive; other times we must give. In my case, I had to give up and let go of Swan Song completely.

After the session, Charcoal admits, "Yes, it turned into a shamanic healing, but most people around here are not open to that."

I say, "I am fine with it."

She confesses, "More entities came out of your body than anyone I have ever worked on."

Charcoal leaves me alone in the room for ten minutes. When she returns, she cuts the energy cords to close our session. It feels, after this session, that Swan Song and I have severed our soul ties. I am free at last.

For now, I stand alone. Swan Song is neither by my side nor living in my heart. I feel as whole and complete as I can. Swan Song is on her own journey. She is always a reminder that there are still a few remnants of magic left in this world. ■

"When a man or woman on a spiritual path faces adversities, they will not seek refuge in a friend who provides comfort by encouraging their fruitless ways. How much better to find a friend who will unwaveringly aid them to courageously endure their suffering and pass through it. When repeatedly exposed to such vulnerability, the psyche will eventually dissolve, revealing their indestructible divine inner glow."

The Final Guided Meditation

In the beginning of the book, I asked you to set an intention as you read the book. If you have read every page, now is the moment for you to receive a word of wisdom, a vision, or healing. Words have the power to heal, but combined with our intention, they are more powerful. My prayers are with you and I have faith that you will receive. Create a sacred space for yourself. You may want to start with soft music, but allow there to be silence during the final five-minute meditation. Perhaps dim the lights or light a candle, wear special jewelry or clothing, or smudge yourself with sage.

First, stand up and say aloud: "Holy Spirit come fill me. Allow the words I read in this book to fully absorb in my heart. I ask you to send me a word of wisdom, a vision, or heal me in whatever way I need."

Place your hands over your heart, pause for a moment, then breathe deeply three times. Pause again. Now sit or lie down. Don't have any expectations about how your healing will happen. You have full permission to express any emotion, such as crying or laughing. Trust the Spirit of Guidance in the form it chooses to manifest. It may be a vision; you may hear guidance as a soft voice or feel a shift in your body, heart, or soul.

Close your eyes and, if you can, have someone read the Guided Meditation slowly to you; otherwise read it slowly to yourself and follow the directions the best you can. If you want soft music, turn it on now, before you continue.

GUIDED MEDITATION:

Sit comfortably with your spine erect and your bare feet solidly on the floor. If you would be more comfortable, you may lie down and close your eyes, but remain awake. Now, take your time to slowly relax the muscles, starting at the top of your head, face, jaw, back of the neck, tongue, chest, shoulders, arms, each individual finger, the full length of your back from top to bottom, abdomen, hips, pelvis, thighs, hamstrings, knees, calves, ankles, bottoms of the feet, and each individual toe. Feel the surface under your body and feel your skin relax. Focus on your breath for a moment.

Now, when you are ready, slowly take three deep, slow breaths a few inches on each side of your heart center. It is three fingers above your sternum. Focus on the area, in this order: right and left, front and back, top and bottom. Afterwards take ten slow, deep breaths directly in your heart center. You may touch that point with your left index finger to help you stay focused.

After the ten breaths, lower your hands with palms down if you are sitting or palms up if you are lying down. Stay in your heart until you sense that you are being held. It's subtle; trust yourself. Stop doing anything. Just breath normally, in and out, through the nose if possible. Let go completely. Be held. Remain here with silence for five minutes. Allow yourself to receive. Trust any guidance given.

Let's finish by reading aloud the Healing Prayer called Nayaz, by Hazrat Inayat Khan:

Beloved Lord, Almighty God!
Through the rays of the sun,
Through the waves of the air,
Through the All-pervading Life in Space,
Purify and revivify me, and I pray,
Heal my body, heart, and soul.
Amen. [25]

Afterword
Acknowledgements

I would like to thank all my friends and the professional editors…Nick, Nicole, and Claire…who edited my book. Rebecca did an elegant job with her editing skills in the prologue and first few chapters. Natalie did a fabulous job resurrecting the Swan Song section. (She assisted by pulling out of me those emotionally crucial parts that I wanted to avoid.) Lost Son taught me about flow and non-judgmental writing and added his personal contributions. A special thanks to Chitra, Amber, and Janet, who all provided valuable editing assistance. Nancy's editing skills were worth far more than six pineapples. Mary did a tremendous job editing with the heart of a servant. Joan W. fearlessly told me which sections to cut. Rahan shared his perspective on silence. Sue gave Holy Spirit insights. Freedom reviewed my poems. Virginia ensured accuracy regarding SunDo. Sarada reviewed information about Baba Hari Dass. Rev. Prem Anjali, Ph.D., manager/editorial director at Integral Yoga Publications, reviewed all quotes by Swami Satchidananda. K'shatria reviewed the chapters on guided retreats. Vi Waln (who was an editor for the Lakota Country Times) and Swan Song reviewed parts of the Native American section. Pastor Tim and Bokton reviewed the sections on Jesus and scripture. Bob Pierce (www.BobsAwesomeBooks.com) did the graphic design.

I want to extend a special thanks to Pastor R.I.P. for his testimony. May Jesus receive glory from our testimonies! I also want to thank Wayne Scott of Swan Lake First Reserve of Manitoba, Canada for his poem: SunDancer. All the major characters (whom I could locate) were sent the sections about themselves to review. I appreciated the honest feedback from Swan Song, The Lion, The Lamb, Pandora, Helen Keller,

Cleopatra, Lost Son, my sister, Priceless, and my brother, Gadget. When they took the time to share their stories, I realized that the truth exists when all of our perspectives are combined. My view alone is tainted.

My mom, The Lamb, as always, went far above the call of duty. She was there to offer her support, editing skills, assisted with research, improved my grammar, and kept me honest. Lastly, to all my friends and family who read the book, I love you.

Just for laughs
Editors' murmurings and correspondence

"You need to write, knowing Swan Song will never speak to you again."   — Natalie

"I definitely cannot tell you how many beers I had on any given evening a decade ago, but I can tell you what I know about myself from living with myself for 54 years…assuming I was at my worst, my best guess would be that I may have had up to 7-9 beers that night, as I don't recall ever having more than 9 beers over a 3-4 hour period at any time in my life."   — Lost Son

"I read over Swan Song a few nights ago. Then I cried for all you have been through. I love you."   — Mom

"You're not in a position to speak on the scriptures with authority, "Thus saith the Lord," so don't try."   — Bokton

"Yoga is not Christian. It is evil"   — Pastor Tim

"Words like "unusual" or "unexpected" will draw the readers in. Words like "crazy" or "bizarre" could lead people to think you are a "nut" and not be as likely to be interested in the story."   — Rebecca (regarding The Guru)

"You have certainly lived an exciting life, and you do a good job of expressing your deepest feelings in this story. I was particularly interested in the section on The Guru; it was exciting to read and really made me question my own ideas

about spirits. I believe that by reading your story and relating it to their own experience, you will be able to help many readers."
— Nick

"Take it easy on me!" — The Lion

"Change my name, you are not going to call me Lolita."
— Pandora

RESOURCES:

The Author, Randolph C. Phelps
P.O. Box 255, Danville, VT 05828

Cristo Morpho Inc.,
E-mail: cristomorpho@gmail.com
Website: www.cristomorpho.com
Facebook: Cristo Morpho Community

HEALERS:

Don Candido Morales, Indigenous Plant Medicine, Costa Rica Email: candido.centroculturalindigena@gmail.com
Facebook: www.facebook.com/etnobotanicatururuwak
011 (506) 2756 8127

Althea (Elaine Koelmel), Meditation Teacher, Sarasota, FL
Email: illum.innate@verizon.net

Caring for the Heart Counseling Ministry,
Colorado Springs, CO
Email: caringfortheheart@msn.com (719) 572 5550
Website: www.Carefortheheart.com

Life Coach, Nora Queesting (Suzanne "Mileka" Damberg)
New Lebanon, NY
Email: youdeserveacoach@yahoo.com (917) 656 4637

SPIRITUAL RETREATS AND EDUCATIONAL LINKS:

SunDo Retreat Center, 45 South Main Street, Suite 90, West Hartford, CT 06107-2402 (860) 523-5260
Barnet, VT www.sundo.org (802) 748-3371

Omega Institute, 150 Lake Dr., Rhinebeck, NY 12572
www.eomega.org (845) 266-4444

Abode of the Message, 5 Abode Rd., New Lebanon, NY 12125 www.theabode.org (518) 794-8090
Saluk Academy www.sulukacademy.org

Himalayan Institute, 952 Bethany Turnpike, Honesdale, PA 18431 www.himalayaninstitute.org
(800) 822-4547 (570) 253-5551

Satchidananda Ashram (Yogaville), 108 Yogaville Way, Buckingham, VA 23921 www.yogaville.org (800) 858-9642

Mount Madonna, 445 Summit Rd., Watsonville, CA 95076
www.mountmadonna.org (408) 847-0406

World Harvest Outreach, Chambersburg, PA 17201
www.whocenterpa.com (717) 709-1129
Online Gatherings: youtube.com/whocenterpa

The Experiment in International Living,
PO Box 676. 1 Kipling Road Brattleboro, VT 05302
www.experiment.org   (800) 345-2929

Bibliography

(1) The Vermont Historical Society. (2010) *The Abenakis & the Europeans*. Permission granted by Vermont Historical Society, Barre, VT https://vermonthistory.org/explorer/vermont-stories/becoming-a-state/the-abenakis-the-europeans

(2) Marquardt, E. (2014) *Children deeply shaped by divorce*. Permission granted by Marriage Missions International, Oro Valley, AZ http://marriagemissions.com/children-deeply-shaped-by-divorce

(3) Ryan, T.C. (2013) *Where lust leads. Ashamed no more.* (2012) Downers Grove, IL: InterVarsity Press http://www.christianitytoday.com/le/2013/fall/where-lust-leads.html www.tc-ryan.com.

(4) Zychik, J. (2002-2012) *The Most Personal Addiction: How I overcame sex addiction and how anyone can*. Permission granted by Joe Zychik. Internet source: SexualControl.com p. 63.

(5) Got Questions Ministries (2002-2016) *What does the Bible say about an unhappy marriage?* Internet source: www.gotquestions.org Permission granted.

(6) Zychik, J. (2002-2012) *The Most Personal Addiction: How I overcame sex addiction and how anyone can*. Permission granted by Joe Zychik. Internet source: SexualControl.com pp. 41-43, 46-47.

(7) Didjshop.com. (1993-2014) *The Rainbow Serpent Story*. Internet source: www.didjshop.com/stories/rainbow.html.

Permission granted.

(8) Yogananda, P. (1946) *The Autobiography of a Yogi*, First edition, New York, N.Y.: The Philosophical Library, Inc. p. 5, 14 -15.

(9) Khan, H.I. (1978) *The Sufi Message of Hazrat Iniyat Khan, Vol IV, Mental Purification and Healing, Part I, Health*. Farnham Surrey, UK: Sevir p. 19.

(10) Bradley, D. (2009). Native Americans of San Diego County. Charleston, SC.: Arcadia Publishing. p. 35. Permission granted.

(11) Lame Deer, J., & Erdoes, R. (1972). *Lame Deer, seeker of visions; The life of a Sioux medicine man*. New York City, NY: Simon and Schuster Publishing. pp. 262–263.

(12) Reardon, J. (2013). *What Does It Mean to Fear God?* Carol Stream, IL: Christianity Today International. ChristianBibleStudies.com. Permission granted. http://www.christianitytoday.com/biblestudies/bible-answers/spirituallife/what-does-it-mean-to-fear-god.html

(13) Enroth, R. (1994) *Recovering From Churches That Abuse*. Grand Rapids, Michigan: Zondervan Publishing House, p 16. Permission granted by Zondervan. www.zondervan.com

(14) Got Questions Ministries (2002-2016) *What is the symbolism of water baptism?* Internet source: www.gotquestions.org Permission granted.

(15) Satchidananda, S. (1988) *To Know Your Self: The essential teaching of Swami Satchidananda*. Buckingham, VA:

Permission for all quotes by Swami Satchidananda granted by Integral Yoga Publications.

(16) Khan, H.I. (2007). *The Sufi Message of Hazrat Inayat Khan Vol. I, The Inner Life, Sufi Thoughts.* The Netherlands: Servire, Katwijk, and Zee. p. 16.

(17) Khan, P.V.I. (1999). *Awakening: A Sufi experience.* New York, NY: Jeremy P. Tarcher / Putnam, a member of Penguin Putnam Inc. Copyright held by Zenith Institute. p. 24.

(18) Khan, H.I. *The Sufi Invocation.* Internet source http://wahiduddin.net/dance/harmony.htm. Permission granted by Omega Press.

(19) Zychik, J. (2002-2012) *The Most Personal Addiction: How I overcame sex addiction and how anyone can.* Permission granted by Joe Zychik. Internet source: SexualControl.com p. 35.

(20) Ryan, T.C. (2013) *Where lust leads. Ashamed no more.* (2012) Downers Grove, IL: InterVarsity Presshttp://www.christianitytoday.com/le/2013/fall/where-lust-leads.html www.tc-ryan.com.

(21) Gems, E. (2010). *Native American medicine wheel: What is medicine.* Urbana, OH www.crystal-cure.com. Permission granted by Emily Gems. https://crystal-cure.com/article-medicine-wheel.html

(22) Lim, E. (2015) AkashicSecrets.com Akashic Records information shared by Evelyn Lim, Intuitive Consultant, Singapore. Permission granted. http://www.akashicsecrets.com/akashic-records/

(23) Gems, E. (2010). *Native American medicine wheel: What is the significance of the medicine wheel?* Urbana, OH www.crystal-cure.com Permission granted by Emily Gems. https://crystal-cure.com/article-medicine-wheel.html

(24) National Library of Medicine. (2008). *The medicine wheel and the four directions.* Bethesda, MD: U.S. National Library of Medicine. Open source: https://www.nlm.nih.gov/nativevoices/exhibition/healing-ways/medicine-ways/medicine-wheel.html

(25) Khan H.I. (2015) *The Prayer Nayaz: Gayan Vadan Nirtan* New Lebanon NY: Suluk Press/Omega Publications p.41. Permission granted.

About The Author

Randolph C. Phelps is a native Vermonter and a resident of Costa Rica. He is the founder of the Vermont non-profit, Cristo Morpho, which established a sustainable, spiritual community located on the Caribbean side of Costa Rica, called The Cristo Morpho Community. During winters, he hosts visitors and directs the Cristo Morpho Volunteer Program, which focuses on immersion into the community through individual service projects, and fostering spiritual growth.

Randolph was a wedding and stock photographer, traveling to Alaska and Australia to photograph the natives and wildlife. His photographs have been published in magazines such as Faces, Challenges, and vacation guides for Alaska Tourism Council and brochures for The Experiment in International Living. His poems have been published in the Green Mountain Trading Post and in the book *Nothing hardly ever happens in Colbyville, Vermont* by Peter Miller.

Randolph has a B.A. in Business Management and was enrolled for a Masters degree at Saint Michael's College in Colchester, VT. This included one semester abroad at Melbourne University to study Australian culture. He is certified by the American Sailing Association for Basic Coastal Cruising. He is a certified Integrative Yoga Therapist specializing in chronic conditions and restorative postures, an Integral Yoga Teacher, and a Thai-Yoga bodyworker. He is also trained as a "Caring for the Heart" counselor.

He has given his time to volunteer at Northeast Vermont Regional Hospital, The Hudson Valley Rapture Center, and the Nature Zone, an educational exotic animal park in Lynchburg, VA. For ten years he was a regular volunteer during the summer months at various spiritual communities. He served the wellness center at Omega Institute in Rhinebeck, NY and assisted with mountain retreats at The Abode of the Message in New Lebanon, NY. He has also been a volunteer at Satchidananda Ashram in Buckingham, Virginia.

I hope that my book touched you in some way. If it did, I am asking that you contact me and share the details. Nowadays, a book is usually a stepping stone to something more grandiose. I believe The Guru or Swan Song story has great potential to be made into a movie. I am seeking a spiritual-based organization to produce this movie. Contact me if you want to sponsor *The Movie* or would like to be updated about the progress.

My spiritual journey ultimately led to establishing the Cristo Morpho Volunteer Program and Cristo Morpho Community. If you are interested in being a volunteer or visiting our community in Costa Rica, please email me. I will gladly send you additional information about **Our History, The Cristo Morpho Volunteer Program and Cristo Morpho Community.** We are located on nearly one hundred acres of rain forest in the mountain village of Buena Vista on the Caribbean side of Costa Rica.

I wrote this book as an enjoyable way to invite people who resonate with my story, to become a part of our sustainable, spiritual community. Perhaps you have a dream of building your family a home or living seasonally in Costa Rica. Surrounding our property, there are approximately 200 hectares of land that can be purchased for a very reasonable price as part of our **Community Land Offer.** I offer my service to help you make connections to find the right community and location within Costa Rica.

May peace be with you,

Randolph C. Phelps
P.O. Box 255, Danville, VT 05828
cristomorpho@gmail.com
www.cristomorpho.com

Made in the USA
Middletown, DE
12 September 2016